CORPORATIONS AND MORALITY

THOMAS DONALDSON
Loyola University of Chicago

PRENTICE-HALL, INC., Englewood Cliffs, New Jersey   07632

HD
60
.D66 *Library of Congress Cataloging in Publication Data*

Donaldson, Thomas,   (date)
        Corporations and morality.

        Includes bibliographies and index.
        1. Industry—Soical aspects.   I. Title.
HD60.D66   658.4'08   81-12035
ISBN   0-13-177014-4   AACR2
ISBN   0-13-177006-3   (pbk.)

To Paul and Louisene Donaldson

© 1982 by Prentice-Hall, Inc., Englewood Cliffs, N.J. 07632

Printed in the United States of America

10   9   8   7   6   5   4   3   2   1

Editorial/production supervision
        and interior design by Barbara Alexander
Cover design by Tony Ferrara
Manufacturing buyer: Harry P. Baisley

PRENTICE-HALL International, Inc., *London*
PRENTICE-HALL of Australia Pty. Limited, *Sydney*
PRENTICE-HALL of Canada, Ltd., *Toronto*
PRENTICE-HALL of India Private Limited, *New Delhi*
PRENTICE-HALL of Japan, Inc., *Tokyo*
PRENTICE-HALL of Southeast Asia Pte. Ltd., *Singapore*
WHITEHALL BOOKS LIMITED, Wellington, *New Zealand*

Contents

Preface

Professional philosophers, among whom I count myself, are not expected to write about corporations. Books are available which describe the corporation, account for its success, and attempt to improve its efficiency; but few employ the methods which are philosophy's trademarks, such as conceptual analysis and systematic evaluation of moral arguments. Of traditional philosophers, Bentham, Mill, and Marx discuss the corporation, but they treat it as a tangential issue. Hegel gives it special attention, but unfortunately the corporation he addresses bears little resemblance to the complex institution it has become.

This neglect is fading. Philosophers have recently begun to discuss topics such as the moral status of corporations, theories of property appropriate to corporations, and the responsibilities of corporate managers. One reason for the increase in interest lies in the evolution of the corporation itself. It is to be expected that philosophers, with their attraction to ethics, should be drawn to explore an institution which has become so powerful that it daily touches the lives of hundreds of millions of people. To underscore the brute economic power of the modern corporation, one need only point out that Exxon, Inc. grosses more money than any single government in the world, excluding the United States and U.S.S.R. Can one doubt that such an organization is worthy of ethical inquiry, or that the concept which underlies the corporation's existence—that of an abstract individual possessing special rights and privileges—should undergo philosophical justification and analysis?

The book is not aimed exclusively at academic philosophers, nor academic business theorists, nor students, but at all of these. It struggles to avoid jargon, both philosophical and otherwise, while attempting to maintain the conceptual depth essential for good philosophy. This, I realize (much more now than when I began), is a risky path, since philosophers will wish for more technical philosophy, non-philosophers for less. I must beg the reader's patience and suggest that any discussion of morality and corporations involves the feat of talking, in the same breath, about moral philosophy and complex corporate fact. Surely attempting to do so, despite its hazards, promises a payoff for both the philosopher and the business-person.

Many issues deserving discussion have been omitted for want of space. One is that of the evaluation and implications of alternatives to capitalistic systems, including Marxism and contemporary movements such as "industrial democracy" or the "small is beautiful" campaign associated with E. F. Schumacher. Although these alternatives are discussed briefly in the book, most of the material assumes that the corporation, in some form or other, is a viable and acceptable social institution. Another neglected issue is that of the professional responsibilities of various personnel areas in the corporation, such as the responsibilities of corporate accountants, as distinct from corporate lawyers, engineers, and others. I regret omitting both issues, and recommend that the interested reader consult the bibliographies at the end of the chapters. Unfortunately, the line must be drawn somewhere, and some subjects must be neglected so that others can benefit.

Throughout history, the political state has demanded philosophical attention. Political philosophers have drawn up justifications for its existence, analyses of its rights and obligations, and descriptions of the relationship between it and its citizenry. It is not exaggerating to say that today issues relating to the corporation are frequently as significant as those concerned with government. Indeed, some theorists have suggested an analogy between corporate organizations and political ones, so that the historical evolution of political rights is seen as having a parallel in the ongoing, though slower, evolution of the concept of rights in large corporations. Recent examples lend weight to this view. Not that many years ago the right to be fired, promoted, or demoted on the basis of job qualifications—and not race or sex—was unrecognized. Today it is acknowledged both by government and popular consensus. Or, taking another example: a corporate employee who blows the whistle on serious safety problems with a product has traditionally lacked the right to keep his job if his boss decides to fire him for his trouble. But many now question such behavior. Increasing pressure is being exerted to introduce the right of due process into corporate systems in much the same way it is now integrated with our political and legal systems.

It is reasonable to ask what contributions, if any, a philosopher can hope to make in an area so well trampled by business theorists, social scientists, and economists. Why should the abstractions of philosophy be applied to an area so rife with practicalities? The answer, in part, is that corporations are highly complex entities which depend upon the acceptance of a series of abstractions for their very existence. The concept of the corporation itself is so unlike run-of-the-mill concepts as to be labeled an outright fiction by skeptics. It relies upon the notion of an invisible person, possessing rights in much the same fashion ordinary people do, who can suffer no pain or pleasure and who is granted limited financial liability and unlimited longevity. This concept is sufficiently abstract to flatter even the most idealistic of tastes.

This book, however, attempts to do more than apply existing philosophical concepts to issues confronting the corporation. It undertakes the more ambitious task of constructing and defending a philosophical view of the corporation, and it draws certain conclusions, including normative ones, about the corporation's character and its ultimate responsibility to society. At times this ambition has no doubt outstripped my capacities. Even so, I believe that attempting to develop a "neutral" perspective would have been virtually useless, and probably would have failed, since neutrality, like objectivity, is an elusive commodity. More important, such a perspective would hold little hope of catalyzing other philosophers into an ongoing dialogue of the kind which has characterized philosophy's contributions in the past.

ACKNOWLEDGMENTS

The present book would have been impossible without the help of numerous friends and colleagues. Among those who gave timely encouragement and insightful advice are Robert Ashmore, Norman Bowie, Robert Cooke, Richard De George, Noreen Dornenburg, Michael Hoffman, Elmer Johnson, Michael Keeley, Thomas McMahon, David Ozar, Mark Pastin, Michael Payne, David Schweickart, and Patricia Werhane. These people contributed more, both by pushing me to clarify problematic concepts and by making concrete suggestions, than the reader can know. For first-rate editorial and typing assistance, I want to thank Cindy Rudolph and Mary Ann Connelly, and for painstaking proofreading, my research assistant, Bill Kullman. For unstinting psychological, editorial, and theoretical support, I want to acknowledge the nonstop contributions of my wife, Jean. Loyola University of Chicago played a special role in facilitating the research opportunities to develop material for the book, especially through two Mellon Grants in 1978 and 1979, and a Summer Research Grant in 1980. Finally, a special word of thanks to Raymond O'Connell and Barbara Alexander for their excellent editorial assistance.

THOMAS DONALDSON

Chicago, Illinois

CHAPTER 1

Taking Stock of
Modern Corporations

Morally speaking, corporations are unusual entities. A judge once bemoaned that they have "no pants to kick or soul to damn," and concluded, "by God, they ought to have both."[1] Unlike a real person, the corporation has no conscience to keep it awake all night, no emotions for the psychiatrist to analyze, and no body to be thrown into jail. It is a *persona ficta,* and its fictional nature, coupled with remarkable down-to-earth power, makes it a thoroughly puzzling object of moral understanding. The purpose of this book is to construct and sharpen our moral vision of the corporation and to square that vision with certain dominant themes of moral philosophy. This is a formidable task.

It will help to begin by making a reasonably obvious point: namely, people perceive the corporation as a moral entity. Indeed, they credit it with the unmistakable mark of morality: a duty to acknowledge standards which transcend laws. Consider the much discussed case of Chisso, a Japanese industrial corporation. Following a lengthy series of trials, Japanese courts concluded that Chisso must compensate thousands of victims whom it had indirectly poisoned with mercury. The company had discharged mercury into the ocean, knowing it posed a danger to local residents. The mercury contaminated local fish and then accumulated in the bodies of local residents who ate the fish. Many years later the accumulation triggered an explosion of bizarre and crippling birth defects.[2]

But, remarkably, Chisso had broken no law. Throughout, it remained secure in the knowledge that its emission levels fell within Japanese government

---

[1] H. L. Mencken, *A New Dictionary of Quotations on Historical Principles from Ancient and Modern Sources* (New York: Knopf, 1942), p. 223.

[2] See *New York Times,* March 23, 1979, p. 5, sect. 4; and *New York Times,* March 29, 1979, p. 15.

1

guidelines, even though it suspected the guidelines were inadequate. Arguing on behalf of the victims, attorneys claimed that despite honoring legal niceties, Chisso had disregarded its moral responsibilities. The court agreed, and Chisso was forced to make massive payments.

Although uncommon from a legal perspective, the verdict expresses the common intuition that corporations have a *moral,* and not merely legal, character. The philosophical task is to confirm or deny that intuition, and, if it is confirmed, to articulate it in concrete terms. The first step must be backwards, to trace the logical and historical foundations of the *persona ficta* itself.

THE EVOLUTION OF THE CORPORATION

Corporations, like the aims they pursue, come in a generous assortment. We associate the word "corporation" with General Motors or Volkswagen, but since the corporation's beginning it has been flexible enough to accommodate such organizations as the Church, nonprofit trade guilds, and local governments. Ask a modern lawyer for his definition of "corporation" and he will say it is that thing which can endure beyond the natural lives of its members, and which has incorporators who may sue and be sued as a unit and who are able to consign part of their property to the corporation for ventures of limited liability.[3] These elementary characteristics, and especially the advantage of limited liability (whereby members are financially liable for corporate debts only up to the extent of their investment), are often taken as the *sine qua non* of corporate existence. Yet each of these characteristics was missing at one time or another in the corporation's history."

Both ancient and modern corporations can be sorted using a few simple distinctions. First, they may be profit-making or non-profit-making. For example, Wedgewood Pottery, Ltd., and Lockheed, Inc., are chartered for the express purpose of making a profit, while the University of Chicago and the Carnegie Foundation are chartered for educational or philanthropic purposes. Second, they may be privately owned or owned, to varying degrees, by the government. In the United States private corporations are virtually the only type, while in Europe public corporations, such as Renault of France, are common. Third, they may be privately held corporations in which a select group owns all the outstanding shares of stock, or publicly held ones in which stock is traded among the general public. Most good-sized U.S. corporations are publicly held.

Finally, corporations may be divided into "productive" and "nonproductive" organizations. A productive organization is any organization producing a good or service; this definition would include even noncorporations such as government agencies. Examples of corporations which qualify as productive organizations are numerous; in addition to the obvious—chemical, manufacturing, and assembly firms—there are law firms, counseling firms, and universities. Only habits of thought

---

[3] Clarence Walton, *Conceptual Foundations of Business* (Homewood, Ill.: Richard D. Irwin, 1969), p. 134.

obscure our understanding that virtually every corporation is a productive organization. Even law firms produce wills and contracts; counseling firms produce advice; and universities produce degrees, sporting events, and sometimes knowledge. Examples of nonproductive organizations are extremely rare. They would include organizations existing merely to hold a patent or copyright, or to provide a tax shelter for their members.

When most of us hear the word "corporation," we think of giants such as Exxon, Coca-Cola, and A.T.&T. These are profit-making, publicly held corporations which also qualify as productive organizations. Such giants affect the depth and breadth of society and for this reason have special ethical significance. They resemble each other sufficiently to constitute a natural locus of study; their size is a common denominator. General Motors shares little else with Bob's Market, Inc., the corner grocery store, than the name "corporation." Although this book will refer to small corporations and nonprofit corporations from time to time, its primary target will be medium-to-large-sized, profit-making, modern corporations.

In 1819 Chief Justice Marshall gave his often quoted interpretation of the corporation: "A corporation," he said, "is an artificial being, invisible, intangible, and existing only in the contemplation of law. Being the mere creation of law, it possesses only those properties which the charter of its creation confers upon it, either expressly, or as incidental to its very existence."[4] Marshall's definition postulates an abstract entity. It stresses the sense in which the corporation is a creation of the mind, existing only in the "contemplation of law," and this is unlike a rock, or a living person, since its very existence depends upon being recognized by human beings.

In the United States an organization attains the status of a "corporation" only through a formal act of government. With the passage of the Fourteenth Amendment to the Constitution, U.S. corporations acquired full status as abstract persons, complete with rights to life, liberty, and state citizenship. (Most U.S. corporations are citizens of the state of Delaware.) Although modern U.S. corporations do not possess certain features of personhood—i.e., they neither eat, require medical attention, nor vote—they are treated as persons in a multitude of ways: they must pay taxes, are liable for damages, can enter into legal agreements, and have the right to freedom of speech. Modern corporations are created by persons, but they are created in the image of their creators.

The roots of the corporation reach deep into the past, a past which is revealing about the modern corporation. Corporate theory has paralleled corporate reality, and both may be traced to early laws governing the conduct of groups which assigned responsibility not merely to individuals, but to collectives such as families and civic organizations. Even before these laws emerged, blood feuds were fought on the assumption that the clan, not the individual, was to blame; with the rise of group law, the prevailing assumptions about corporate wholeness could be formalized and legitimized.[5] Sometimes this resulted in unusual prohibitions; for

---

[4] Chief Justice Marshall, *Dartmouth College* v. *Woodward,* 4 Wheat 518.636 (1819).

[5] Henry Maine, *Ancient Law* (London: J. M. Dent and Sons, 1917), p. 143.

example Anglo-Saxon laws forbade the selling of certain group property on the grounds that it ultimately belonged to the immortal corporate collective. By the Middle Ages the group was regarded as having prime economic status. In Italy the "casa," or family business, not the individual, handled donations, taxes, fines, guild dues, entertainment, and the necessary bribes.[6]

Corporate evolution occurred in four stages. The first, encompassing the Medieval period, gave the Church, the guild, and the borough corporate status, but failed to do so for purely profit-making associations. In each of the former organizations, a common factor besides economic self-interest united members. For the Church, it was religion; for the guild, similarity of trade; and for the borough, geographical proximity and shared political interests.

The second stage witnessed the rise of corporations whose members shared nothing besides the desire to make money. This occurred in the early sixteenth century, when European entrepreneurs organized to launch trading voyages to the East. Such corporations, however, were a far cry from modern ones. Instead of pooling their capital, members financed their voyages individually and used the corporation only to act as bearer for special trading rights. For example, a company might hold a special trading right with Russia, a right bestowed by the Czar and available only to corporate members. Liability, however, was left to individual members, so that when an entrepreneur's vessel sank or was robbed by pirates, he alone was required to pay creditors.

The third stage of corporate evolution ushered in the prototypes of modern corporations. Beginning in 1612 with the reconstitution of the East India Trading Company, this stage saw capital being pooled, power being placed in the hands of a governor and his committees, and liability being distributed among the stockholders. The products of these changes were the "great trading companies" of the seventeenth and eighteenth centuries: in addition to the East India Company, there were the Hudson Bay Company, La Compagnie des Indes, the Company of Adventurers of London Trading into Africa, and counterparts in Spain, Italy, Russia, and Germany. The motives behind the creation of these companies lay predominantly in considerations of economy of scale: boats were becoming bigger and more expensive, so that merely buying and outfitting them exceeded the resources of wealthy individuals. Similarly, losing such boats through storms or pirates could be ruinous to an individual. The solution was pooled capital and shared liability: the trademarks of the modern corporation.

The final stage is characterized by the gradual shedding of government restrictions upon corporate chartering procedures. From the seventeenth century through the first half of the nineteenth, prospective English corporations were required to apply to the Crown for charters. In the United States following the Revolutionary War they were required to apply to state governments. In both instances, applications were scrutinized, accepted or rejected, and when accepted, sometimes burdened with special conditions. When the prospective Main Flour

[6] J. L. Reynolds, "Origins of Modern Business Enterprise: Medieval Italy," *Journal of Economic History,* 12 (Fall 1952), 350-65.

Company petitioned the State of Maine for its charter in 1818, Maine granted the charter only on the express condition that total corporate property be limited to $50,000, of which property the amount held in land was limited to $30,000, and all land had to be in Kennebec County.[7] This system was the target of vigorous criticism. Those unable to receive charters, or to receive them under favorable conditions, charged that winners in the system were granted monopoly powers by corrupt state officials. For a time, especially in the United States, losers adopted the strategy of circumventing the chartering process through clever legal maneuvers. Finally, as so often happened in the past, the law was forced to acknowledge the realities of existing practice. The old system of "special" incorporation with its uncertain review process was junked in favor of a "general" system which assured corporate status to any organization able to fill out forms and pay fees. This system, with minor modifications, is in effect today.

Lurking beneath the shift from "special" to "general" procedures of chartering lies a theoretical issue of profound importance. When nineteenth-century reformers attacked existing procedures, they talked not only about government favoritism, but about the principle of a corporation's right to exist. They asserted that *any* petitioning body with minimal qualifications has the right to receive a corporate charter. Since its beginning the corporation has been subject to two interpretations, at odds with each other, one of which stems from the early Crown-chartered corporations of Western Europe and the other from the doctrine of freedom of association. Not only were the early Crown-chartered corporations construed as creations of the state, but the privileges which made them possible were granted by the state. Thus the doctrine arose that all corporations are creations of the state. On the other hand, business organizations have existed since the dawn of history and appear to be creations not of the state, but of the habits of business people. Democratic societies recognize the right of people to assemble and form groups, i.e., the right of "freedom of association"; thus an alternative doctrine arose which saw corporations as the natural products of this right. In other words, the former doctrine holds that corporations are created by public act and not by mere agreement; the latter asserts that incorporation is simply a byproduct of people's exercising their right of association.[8]

Despite the modern emphasis on the latter doctrine, incorporation could never be fully reduced—without remainder—to the right of association. Granted, people are capable of organizing business organizations without the approval of government. Granted too, they can make agreements, conclude contracts, and draw up charters without government help. Indeed, many argue that they possess inalienable rights to do these things. But clearly also, modern corporations aspire to more than the status of mere organizations: they require the power to contract as a single agent under law and the status of an "invisible person" along with the rights this status entails. These characteristics, which are advantages for stockholders, must be

---

[7]Christopher D. Stone, *Where the Law Ends* (New York: Harper & Row, Pub., 1975), p. 20.

[8]Walton, *Conceptual Foundations,* pp. 136-38.

recognized and protected by the state. Because they belong to the concept of the modern corporation, it follows that the corporation itself continues to answer to Chief Justice Marshall's classic definition: it remains, at least in part, "an artificial being," existing "in the contemplation of law"—and not merely the product of free human association.

As corporations evolved, so did the moral problems they engendered. Society was prepared to cope morally with human persons, and to react to murder, fraud, and vice, but it was ill-prepared to cope with corporations. When, for example, an East India Company ship collided with another ship, who was liable? Was the company itself liable *only* for acts authorized in its charter, or for all acts undertaken by its agents? Were mental states relevant in the assessment of corporate punishment? Could the East India Company act with "malice" or "criminal intent"? The natural tendency was for corporate managers to pass liability off to the stockholders, but the tendency of stockholders was just the reverse. Both were able to come together through the policy of making the *corporation* liable, as distinct from managers or stockholders. Thus, the doctrine of the corporation as possessing its own moral and legal status, with limited financial liability for stockholders and managers, satisfied both camps.

If a corporation can be legally guilty, how should it be punished? This question acquired new overtones during the eighteenth and nineteenth centuries when European politicians inspired by the ideas of the Enlightenment moved to standardize policies of punishment. Instead of flogging one criminal and placing another in the stocks, they began to apply the same punishment to all, namely deprivation of liberty for varying time periods. But though corporations can lie, cheat, and steal just as individuals can, they cannot be thrown in jail. How, then, do they pay for their crimes?

Historically the form of punishment the courts hit upon was monetary. Instead of being deprived of liberty, corporations were deprived of money, in varying amounts depending on the severity of the crime. During the nineteenth and early twentieth centuries progressive steps were taken in the United States to expand the limits of corporate financial liability. By 1812, corporations were financially liable for acts instigated by documents bearing the corporate seal. By 1842 they were liable for any acts of corporate agents acting within the scope of their authority. And in 1862 they became liable for acts which contradicted company instructions in cases where the agent believed his act was in the interest of his employers.[9]

THE LARGE, MODERN CORPORATION

Every market-oriented system combines two forms of productive organization: the small, individual family-owned business, and the large, bureaucratized firm. In developed Western economies the latter accounts for the lion's share of production.

---

[9]Stone, *Where the Law Ends,* pp. 24-25.

In the United States over 60 percent of total production comes from this sector, and over 80 percent of employment is in organizations with twenty or more employees. Individual and family-owned businesses are numerous but have a lesser impact. (In the United States there are more than 4 million small manufacturing businesses, and in Japan, with a fraction of the U.S. population, there are almost 3 million.)[10]

Giant corporations employ vast numbers of people. The U.S. Department of Defense employs over a million civilians, but close behind are American Telephone and Telegraph, Inc., and General Motors, Inc., each with nearly one million employees. (No government agency besides the Defense Department employs over half a million people.) Corporations also receive enormous revenues. General Electric, Exxon, Ford Motor Company, General Motors, and A.T.&T. each gross more revenue than California or New York State. In the United States, sixteen of the twenty largest organizations in revenue, including state and city governments, are corporations. In addition to employment and revenue, giant corporations possess broad geographic reach. Of the largest 100 American corporations, over 60 produce in six or more countries, and one-third of their employees work in foreign countries.[11]

With size comes power. Large corporations are capable of influencing mainstream societal events and this power is not only economic, but social and political. A clear distinction exists between a corporation's formal power, its authority to act *intra vires,* which flows from its rights as defined by law or charter, and its practical power, which derives from its special role in society. From a legal perspective a corporation has nothing but the power conferred upon it either by its charter or from the legal statutes in the jurisdiction it inhabits. However, from a practical perspective corporations have considerable power, one aspect of which is simply the power of being organized. It is a dictum that organization itself breeds power, and corporations are organized social units. What is more, they participate in an environment with thousands of other organizations: the *Encyclopedia of Organizations in the United States* devotes over 250 pages to national business organizations while giving only 17 to labor organizations, 60 to public affairs organizations, and 71 to scientific and technical societies.[12] This vast matrix of business associations manifests power which, although largely uncoordinated, is sympathetic to corporate interests.

Top-level corporate executives have better than average access to government policymakers. If the owner of a small-town shoe store comes to Washington, D.C., politicians will be conveniently out to lunch. But when the president of General Electric arrives, politicians may well rearrange their schedules. There are obvious reasons for this. For one, the president of a major corporation is already known to voters; his name, if not his face, is familiar. For another, he may wield

---

[10] Charles E. Lindbloom, *Politics and Markets: The World's Political-Economic Systems* (New York, Basic Books, 1977), p. 94.

[11] Lindbloom, *Politics and Markets,* pp. 94-95.

[12] Lindbloom, *Politics and Markets,* p. 197.

some clout in campaign financing. Though direct campaign financing by corporations has been halted through legislation, corporations can contribute through personal donations of chief executives, or through Political Action Committees (PAC's) which serve to funnel money deducted from corporate paychecks to candidates. During the late 1970's PAC's became significant forces in U.S. politics.

The practical power of corporations is linked directly to the discretionary capacity of their chief executives. It is an exaggeration to say that corporate executives lack discretionary financial power because economic contingencies invariably force their hand. Economic forces restrict their choices, to be sure, and an executive saddled with a balance sheet in the red lacks the resources to make massive political contributions. But for the executive of a profitable corporation some room exists for discretionary projects. In this the executive is different from the politician. For the politician, canons of propriety distinguish his role in government his role as interest-group advocate and forbid him from using public funds for partisan objectives. But for the executive of a private corporation the distinction is weaker and nothing prevents her from using corporate funds, derived from corporate sales, to promote interests in line with her or the company's partisan objectives.

Executives have discretionary power in part because their salaries are more than mere reflections of corporate profits. In large corporations the connection between the two is indirect at best: higher profits will sometimes mean increased salary, but not always. The executive will be "instructed" to pursue profits, and to some extent these instructions will become embodied in his or her personal motives; but how completely the embodiment occurs is a function of many factors, including individual discretion. Other acceptable goals for executives include increased innovation, diversification, greater market share, and advancement of political ends friendly to business. Such goals are tolerated and, indeed, usually respected by the executive's peers.

Another difference between the power of a corporation on paper and the power it has as a "going concern" involves its role in society. As a going concern the corporation is a vital element in society, and an individual corporation may be the decisive factor in the life or death of a small community. In a small community a good-sized corporation plays much the same role as a vital organ in the human body. It is an integral part of the surrounding environment and its needs are met by a network of support systems: by roads, utilities, and most important, by a labor pool which must itself be housed and provided with schools, parks, and commercial facilities. In turn, the corporation provides jobs, tax revenues, and frequently civic leadership to the community. Neither town nor corporation can function well without the other. But while communities are locked into geographic locations, corporations are not, and for a variety of reasons—including wage scales, proximity to distribution points, and climate—corporations sometimes move. When they do, the results can be disastrous for the community.

The corporation is, in a sense, *imperium in imperio:* it is a state within a state, and it competes on some levels even with the government in the management of social and economic events. The corporation, like the government, has a citizenry from which it commands loyalty, and this citizenry includes shareholders, suppliers, and employees. Next to government, corporations constitute society's most prominent locus of ongoing control, and they hold this position in part through their capacity for efficiency and planning. As a political theorist once remarked, "In the use of . . . formal techniques of planning the most successful planners are not government agencies but corporations."[13] Three reasons help explain this. First, corporations are able, as government is not, to set clear goals for themselves, say for optimal product diversity, without fear that the entire program will be scuttled by the next election. Second, corporations can puruse goals without becoming entangled in the noble but regrettably messy mechanism of democratic decision-making. Finally, the demands of competition in the market-place create an absolute need for efficient planning in corporations in a way which is not true in government bureaucracies.

Despite similarities, the social atmosphere which corporations confront in the Western world varies from country to country. In West Germany, the United Kingdom, and Sweden over 30 percent of the labor force is unionized; Sweden leads with 55 percent, while in the United States, France, and Mexico the figure is only 20 to 25 percent.[14] In both France and Japan corporations have tended to work in close contact with government agencies, often jointly establishing economic goals. Americans, however, would find such bureaucratic cooperation suffocating. The characteristic tendency of U.S. business is to look for efficiency and autonomy by maintaining distinct spheres of influence for business and government. The merits of this policy are frequently debated, but its existence and impact are acknowledged by all.

Corporations in the West also differ in their attitudes toward employees. In most European countries as well as in Japan and Australia corporations tend to regard employees more as permanent members than in the United States. In such countries it is more difficult to fire a worker, even a lazy, nonproductive one, than in the United States. Sometimes, as in the case of Western Europe, this tendency is a product of legal pressure; elsewhere, as in Japan, it is a function of necessity and old habits.

The skepticism with which most U.S. corporate executives view government involvement in business is reflected in the society at large. It helps explain, for example, why critics of corporations in the United States have adopted unique strategies of attack. As David Vogel, a contemporary analyst, points out, "direct challenges to corporations are a distinctly American phenomenon."[15] Critics of U.S. corporations often attack their object directly: they lobby shareholders to vote against management; they organize consumer boycotts; and they yell at

---

[13] Lindbloom, *Politics and Markets,* p. 320.

[14] Lindbloom, *Politics and Markets,* p. 114.

[15] David Vogel, *Lobbying the Corporation: Citizen Challenges to Business Authority* (New York: Basic Books, 1978), pp. 11-18 and 211-20.

managers during shareholder meetings. If this fails, *then* they go to the government. Critics of Western European corporations tend to do the reverse: they go to
the government first and never stop moving in the direction of tougher government
regulation and stricter enforcement. The ordinary U.S. citizen shares with the business executive a skepticism toward government. He frequently refuses to trust
corporations; but similarly, he refuses to trust government.[16] As George Ball
remarked, "I see no greater virtue in corporate managements than government
bureaucracies—in fact, no inherent virtue in either."[17]

Some people assume that the moral attitudes and performances of all
corporations are roughly the same. This misrepresents the situation. Corporations,
like people, exhibit a variety of moral profiles. Some reject moral deliberation as
the sworn enemy of good business while others endorse it as a needed friend. Some
corporations make a point of denouncing "corporate responsibility" in speeches
and annual reports; they interpret it as a veiled attack upon the rights of managers
and stockholders. Other companies, taking the opposite line, go so far as to hire
specialists in ethics who serve as vice-presidents in charge of "social responsibility."
These companies frequently undertake annual "social audits" to evaluate their own
moral behavior.

The track records of corporations are equally diverse: in 1975 a survey was
released showing the relative performance of coal mining operations run by traditional coal companies on the one hand and by steel companies on the other. For
the same period and type of mining, the mines run by coal companies showed over
40 injuries and deaths per million man-hours worked, compared with less than 8 per
million for mines operated by the steel companies.[18] The same is true of tendencies
to experiment with the quality of work life. Some corporations use the same
assembly line routines and the same employee policies that were used 70 years
ago. Others, such as Volvo of Sweden, have experimented with "team-built"
automobiles, with work teams having responsibility for constructing cars from the
ground up. Corporations differ; each has a distinct "ethos," involving distinct
traditions, habits, and aspirations. From a moral point of view, those differences
are significant.

To underscore such differences, consider the following two examples:
The first is Cummins Engine Company, long respected for its pioneering efforts in
ethics, and specifically for its quality of work-life programs, integration of social
factors into corporate planning, and enlightened employee-management relations.
When Cummins considers a new product line or is confronted with a demand for a
"sensitive payment" (or bribe) abroad, it subjects the problem to moral as well as
financial scrutiny, and its decision-making apparatus is specifically designed to do
both. Cummins is profitable, but for decades it has sustained a reputation for also
being morally concerned. The second example is the Hooker Chemical Company. In

[16]Vogel, *Lobbying,* pp. 11-18 and 211-20.
[17]George Ball, *Global Companies: The Political Economy of World Business* (Englewood Cliffs,
N.J.: Prentice-Hall, 1975), p. 3.
[18]Stone, *Where the Law Ends,* p. 238.

1978 Hooker received notoriety for its history of dumping chemicals in the Niagara Falls "Love Canal" area. The chemicals eventually leached into the basements and back yards of residents, resulting in the evacuation of over 200 families.[19] As time passed, new information suggested that the Love Canal was not an isolated incident but only one event in an established pattern of Hooker's disregard for environmental issues. In the summer of 1979 *The New York Times* reported that Hooker's plant in White Springs, Florida, was convicted of polluting the air with fluoride. Even more damning were the copies of corporate memorandums, passed among Hooker executives, which revealed that Hooker's top echelon knew and approved of pollution violations. Finally, Hooker Company officials admitted to accidentally poisoning local water supplies not only at the Niagara Falls plant but at their Montague (Michigan) and Lathrop (California) plants.[20] One would be wrong to posit a single moral ethos for all corporations.

THE MULTINATIONAL CORPORATION

National boundaries are doorways to trade for multinationals. I.B.M. operates in 126 countries, communicates in 30 languages, has 23 overseas plants, and since 1970 has received more than one-half of its total net income from overseas business. Also called "transnationals," "extranationals," and "cosmocorps," these giants have advanced in tandem with striking technological changes: improved transportation, more efficient information processing, and rapid communications systems. In a sense, the term "multinational" is a misnomer, for although multinationals operate in a number of countries, they typically are chartered in a single, home country; thus, in terms of legal personality they are "uni-national." The biggest and most influential are based in the United States, Europe, and Japan.

Disagreement about the role and significance of such companies is marked: some observers see them as the last hope for world peace, as the only means to correct the blindness of nationalism, while others see them as engines of global injustice, allowing the rich nations to enslave the poor with wondrous, though regrettable, efficiency. From a moral point of view, the central issue is that of economic justice. In the confrontation between developed and undeveloped nations, do multinationals aggravate or help solve social and political problems?

One of the first and most controversial cases involving charges of injustice concerned the United Fruit Company. Organized in 1899, the company specialized in the growing, transportation, and sale of bananas, most of which were produced in Central America. Now called "United Brands," the company is well known for its "Chiquita" label. It first attracted notoriety in 1910 when it attempted to enter Honduras. There, it faced a rival bid by a firm controlled by J. Pierpont Morgan, a bid it overcame when a business associate organized an armed invasion of Honduras.

---

[19] *New York Times,* August 5, 1979, pp. 1 and 39.

[20] *New York Times,* August 5, 1979, p. 39.

According to reports, it took only a case of rifles, a few thousand rounds of ammunition, a yacht, and a mercenary named Machine Gun Malony.[21]

United Fruit improved over the years but continued to be implicated in a web of misadventure. Because it owned railroad and shipping lines in host countries, and because bananas are highly perishable, it could effectively block competition by delaying the shipments of rivals. One of its competitors, Atlantic Fruit, charged that the company drove it from Costa Rica by delaying shipments and by ordering employees to destroy its bananas with machetes. Later, in Guatemala, United Fruit was hurt by the land reform program enacted in 1952 by the reformist president, Jacobo Arbenz Guzmán. When in 1954 Guzmán was dumped by an armed coup, United Fruit was blamed. The company denied wrongdoing, but critics point out that the CIA was heavily involved in the coup and that Allen Dulles, head of the CIA, had strong connections with the United Fruit Company.

Today, there is less evidence that multinationals are meddling directly with the domestic politics of Third World countries, although their negative power, called "leverage," is said to remain considerable. When an aid-giving organization (such as the World Bank) considers a loan to a Third World country, the country's record of treatment of foreign multinationals can be a factor. For example, Peru's dispute with the International Petroleum Company is said to have led to a U.S. veto on an IADB housing loan granted in 1969.

Ronald Müller, coauthor of the influential book *Global Reach*,[22] condemns multinationals for clever tax schemes and oligopolistic power. When a national company becomes international, he says, the goal remains that of total profit maximization; but this translates into international tax "minimization." In practice, companies divert profits from high-tax to low-tax countries, with the result that nations are not reimbursed fairly for their share of tax burdens. Even worse, he says, the very size and complexity of multinationals spawn oligopolies, and thus decreased competition and inflated prices. Because most multinationals are conglomerates containing a number of subsidiaries, they can "cross-fertilize" their subsidiaries at crucial junctures. When competition flares between the subsidiary of a conglomerate and an independent company, the parent rushes to provide the subsidiary with needed capital, resources, and technology. The inevitable result is a market increasingly dominated by a select group of multinationals.[23]

The story of multinationals is by no means all bad. Given the sorry record of political programs in curing human misery, multinationals offer hope for international cooperation based not on unstable political emotions, but on the proven human propensity for trade and commerce. Internationalism is the trend of the times, and the Third World desperately needs information and skills from developed countries. The most efficient means of communicating these, say defenders, is the

[21] Louis Turner, *Multinational Companies and the Third World* (New York: Hill and Wang, 1973), p. 22.

[22] R. Barnet and R. Müller, *Global Reach: The Power of Multinational Corporations* (New York: Simon & Schuster, 1974).

[23] Ronald Müller, "A Qualifying and Dissenting View of the Multinational Corporation," in *Global Companies,* ed. George Ball (Englewood Cliffs, N.J.: Prentice-Hall, 1975), pp. 21-42.

multinational. The very product sold by a multinational can symbolize the spirit of internationalism: witness the tractor produced by Canada's Massey-Ferguson, Inc. The tractor is made in the United States, sold in Canada, and constructed using British-made engines, French transmissions, and Mexican axles. Could not multinationals, with their already proven international skills, become powerful forces in international political, economic, and social progress?

Rising nationalism and popular politics in the Third World are changing the balance of power between governments and multinationals. If multinationals have "leverage," then Third World countries may be said to be developing "counterleverage": a case in point is the powerful OPEC cartel. A group of small nations, almost David and Goliath style, successfully defeated a circle of the largest multinationals. Because the companies were bound to the host countries by immobile investments, the governments were able to extract major political concessions and to charge exorbitant prices. Some governments even stipulated with *whom* the multinationals could trade. Traditional economic logic failed to predict the rise in host nation power which, spurred by the Yom Kippur war and rising feelings of Moslem unity, would send oil prices skyrocketing—and the multinationals scrambling. The multinational companies themselves were the last to know.

Despite concessions, the multinationals will survive. Not only does the average Third World country lack the power of Moslem oil, but the relationship between multinational and host country is symbiotic: the multinational needs raw materials and markets, but the country needs know-how, technology, and transportation.

A central moral issue for multinationals operating in the Third World centers on the striking discrepancy between political and economic conditions in home and host countries. This is nowhere better illustrated than in South Africa, where about 4 million whites have maintained a tradition of blatant racism through apartheid. Multinationals in South Africa must deal with ongoing and institutionalized racism. In the 25 years following the Second World War, the ratio between white and non-white salaries widened from 4-1 to 6-1; and even these figures are misleading since they miss a large proportion of unemployed non-whites. During the 1970's there were over 2,000 arrests a day connected with the "passbooks" which every black was required to carry at all times.[24] And every year saw almost 100 court-ordered executions of blacks.

Polaroid, Inc., encountered special problems. Despite its having worked hard to develop its image in the United States as an "equal opportunity employer," South African blacks accused it of supporting apartheid. The nexus of contention was Polaroid's sale of an identification system, known as ID-2, which would take, develop, and enclose in unbreakable plastic a person's picture (along with other identification information), all in less than two minutes. Outraged blacks pointed out that ID-2 was used for the hated "passports" they were required to carry; they united to form the Polaroid Revolutionary Workers' Movement. At one rally they handed out leaflets saying "Polaroid imprisons blacks in just sixty seconds."[25]

[24] Turner, *Multinational Companies,* p. 232.
[25] Turner, *Multinational Companies,* pp. 232-33.

The Polaroid controversy raged throughout the 1970's. In response to demands, the company stopped helping with the passport program and formally condemned apartheid; but it refused to comply with demands to leave South Africa entirely. At least three black workers who pushed for more extreme demands were fired. The company, however, moved to introduce further reforms in the mid to late 1970's: it raised the wages of black workers nearly 33 percent and promoted several black workers to supervisory positions. At home, the company met increasing opposition from citizens and stockholders, with some stockholders encouraging others to force Polaroid out of South Africa. Conscientious Polaroid managers faced a moral dilemma: should the company abandon South Africa altogether and leave the country to its increasingly racist government, or stay to work for improved conditions? Polaroid is not the only multinational to confront such a dilemma.

CAN CORPORATIONS BE MORALLY EVALUATED?

The task of moral theory is largely one of evaluation. But *can* the large modern corporation be conveniently evaluated alongside human beings? Can one evaluate a multinational giant as one would a person? When asking such questions it is worth remembering that the corporation is an amalgam of artifice and nature. That is, it is composed of natural human beings and reflects the natural tendency of humans to form organizations; but at the same time it is an artifact in the sense that it is a product of human intention and has a humanly malleable character. Unlike purely natural objects, we *decide,* up to a point, what the corporation is. We can grant or deny it unlimited longevity, limited liability, state citizenship, and so on. However, this makes the ethical task all the harder. Philosophically, we cannot fix the character of this abstract hybrid as we would an item in nature, such as a rock or tree, for part of what a corporation *is* is the product of our moral and legal imagination.

To be sure, some age-old questions facing the corporation are the same questions that confront individuals. St. Thomas Aquinas retells the story, which Cicero presented in his *De Officiis,* of the merchant confronted with a moral puzzle. The merchant is en route to a town stricken by famine, carrying grain to the starving townspeople. He knows, however, that other merchants are following him with more grain. Is he bound to tell the townspeople of the additional grain, or may he remain silent and command a higher price?[26] Cicero concludes he must tell out of a sense of moral duty. Aquinas, however, reaches the opposite conclusion on the grounds that, although it would be commendable to tell, the merchant is not bound to predict a future event which, if it failed to occur, would rob him of a just price. The point is not whether one agrees with Cicero or Aquinas. The point is that regardless of the outcome, the moral issue is the same for corporations as it is for persons: namely, must corporations divulge information contrary to their interests

[26] St. Thomas Aquinas, *Summa Theologica,* II-KK, qv. 77.9.3, obj. 4.

when it would significantly benefit the consumer? And regardless of the correct answer, it should apply just as well to corporations as to individuals.

Other moral issues are less adaptable. Take the issue of the proper punishment for moral misbehavior. When an individual commits a crime, the punishment chosen applies to the entire person; we do not (except in barbaric systems) single out one part of the person, say his hand or eye. But when punishing a corporation, society frequently singles out a part of the corporation, say the board of directors, for special treatment.

Corporations thus present a fundamental ambiguity. For some purposes they may be treated as individuals; for others, not. The ambiguity is reflected in our psychological attitudes toward them. Leo Tolstoy writes that people's moral tolerance is greater for large organizations, especially legislatures, churches, and bureaucracies, than for individuals. Christopher Stone applies this idea to corporations. "If we are subjected to the noise of a motorcyclist driving up and down our street at night," Stone remarks, "I think a deeper and more complex level of anger is tapped in us than if we are subjected to the same disturbance (decibelly measured) from an airlines operation overhead."[27] Theoretical attitudes reflect a similar ambiguity. The philosopher John Rawls in his celebrated *A Theory of Justice* includes corporations (as well as states and churches) along with individuals when he lists the parties in the "original position."[28] But elsewhere he states there is a "certain logical priority" of human individuals.[29]

Apparent differences between corporations and persons cloud the application of traditional moral theories. These theories were designed with individuals in mind, not corporations. Consider two theories of morality well known among philosophers: Kantianism and utilitarianism. Advancing the former, the eighteenth-century German philosopher Immanuel Kant maintained that people should prefer "reason" to "inclination" and should act on rules or "maxims" which they would wish everyone to follow. Advancing the latter, the nineteenth-century philosopher John Stuart Mill maintained that people should promote the greatest amount of happiness for the greatest number. Now one could try adapting these theories to corporations by merely substituting "corporations" for "people." Thus, Kantianism would declare that a *corporation* should prefer reason to inclination and should act on rules it would wish every *corporation* to follow. Utilitarianism, in turn, would recommend that a *corporation* maximize overall happiness.

But notice the problems raised by the shift from individuals to corporations. Corporations have no human "inclinations," so what can it mean to say they should subordinate them to reason? Or how about utilitarianism's call to promote the greatest happiness for the greatest number? Should corporations consider the consequences for their *own* well-being (or the well-being of *other* corporations)

---

[27] Stone, *Where the Law Ends*, p. 248.

[28] John Rawls, *A Theory of Justice* (Cambridge, Mass.: Harvard University Press, 1971), p. 146.

[29] John Rawls, "Justice as Reciprocity," in *Utilitarianism*, ed. Samuel Gorovitz (Indianapolis: Bobbs-Merrill, 1971), pp. 244-45.

or merely the well-being of human individuals? Utilitarianism and Kantianism may be applicable to corporations but not without adjustments.

In stretching theories designed for individuals to cover corporations, one may also err by overlooking the economic mission of profit-making corporations. Whereas people exhibit a multitude of interests—friendship, money, love, and so on—corporations have exceedingly narrow personalities. They are chartered primarily for economic purposes and are designed for efficient economic production and little else. Where it may be a shortcoming for an individual to terminate his or her own existence or to be unmoved at the loss of an acquaintance, it is less clearly a flaw for a corporation. The corporation is an economic animal; although one may deny that its sole responsibility is to make a profit for its investors, one may nonetheless wish to define its responsibility differently than for individual humans.

This chapter has given no answers to the nagging problem of the moral status of corporations; that will be the job of the next chapter. Instead, it has provided a groundwork for the moral investigation of the corporation by describing, both in concept and fact, the rudiments of the corporate character. The corporation emerged from a confusing past in which society, especially through its legal systems, conferred increasing reality upon the notion of the "corporate whole." The Church, the guild, and later the great trading companies were all steps toward creating the complex nucleus of concepts which underpins the modern corporation. Today, the large corporation is a fact of everyday life, one becoming all the more important through the influence of multinational corporations. Today's giant corporations are construed as fictitious persons, but they are taller and richer than most of us. These characteristics enhance their capacity for effecting both human good and harm and, in turn, make their moral analysis a matter of direct and pressing concern.

SUGGESTED SUPPLEMENTARY READINGS

APTER, DAVID, *The Politics of Modernization.* Chicago: University of Chicago Press, 1965.

BARNET, R., and R. MULLER, *Global Reach: The Power of Multinational Corporations.* New York: Simon & Schuster, 1974.

BELL, DANIEL, *The Coming Post-Industrial Society.* New York: Basic Books, 1973.

BEST, MICHAEL, and WILLIAM E. CONNOLLY, *The Politicized Economy.* Lexington, Mass.: Heath, 1976.

BROWN, PETER and DOUGLAS MCLEAN, eds., *Human Rights and U.S. Foreign Policy.* Lexington, Mass.: Heath, 1979.

CHAMBERLAIN, N. W., *The Limits of Corporate Power.* New York: Basic Books, 1973.

COMMONER, BARRY, *The Closing Circle.* New York: Knopf, 1971.

DRUCKER, PETER, *Concept of the Corporation.* New York: John Day, 1972.

GALBRAITH, JOHN KENNETH, *The New Industrial State.* New York: New American Library, 1967.

GARRETT, T., and R. BAUMHART, and T. PURCELL, and P. ROETS, eds., *Cases in Business Ethics.* New York: Appleton-Century-Crofts, 1968.

HEILBRONER, ROBERT, *Business Civilization in Decline.* New York: W. W. Norton & Co., Inc., 1976.

———, *The Making of Economic Society.* Englewood Cliffs, N.J.: Prentice-Hall, 1962.

JACOBY, NEIL, *Bribery and Extortion: A Study of Corporate Political Payments Abroad.* New York: Macmillan, 1977.

KANT, IMMANUEL, *Critique of Practical Reason.* Indianapolis: Bobbs-Merrill, 1958.

LINDBLOOM, CHARLES E., *Politics and Markets.* New York: Basic Books, 1977.

LYONS, DAVID, *Forms and Limits of Utilitarianism.* Oxford: Oxford University Press, 1965.

MILL, J. S., *Utilitarianism.* Indianapolis: Bobbs-Merrill, 1976.

REYNOLDS, R. L., "Origins of Modern Business Enterprise: Medieval Italy," *Journal of Economic History,* 12 (Fall 1952): 350-65.

SAYRE, K. M., ed., *Values in the Electrical Power Industry.* Notre Dame, Ind.: University of Notre Dame Press, 1977.

SETHI, S. P., *Advocacy Advertising and Large Corporations.* Lexington, Mass.: Heath, 1977.

SILK, L. and D. VOGEL, *Ethics and Profits.* New York: Simon & Schuster, 1976.

SINGER, PETER, *Practical Ethics.* London: Cambridge University Press, 1979.

VERNON, R., *Storm Over the Multinationals: The Real Issues.* Cambridge, Mass.: Harvard University Press, 1977.

VOGEL, DAVID, *Lobbying the Corporation: Citizen Challenges to Business Authority.* New York: Basic Books, 1978.

WALTON, CLARENCE, and RICHARD EELLS, *Conceptual Foundations of Business.* Homewood, Ill.: Richard D. Irwin, 1969.

CHAPTER 2

The Moral Status of Corporations

What does "moral responsibility" mean when the entity to which it applies has no human feelings, feels no pleasures or pains, and enjoys unlimited longevity? Such is true of a corporation. When people mistreat us, we reason with them, exhort them to sympathize with us, and may even try to shame them into doing their duty. But the case is different for a corporation. We may yell at a corporate clerk, appeal to reasons, and try to promote a sense of shame; but typically the clerk is unmoved—for he or she is just following the rules. Our anger has missed its moral target, the corporation, which stands mysteriously apart from its employees.

THE PROBLEM OF MORAL AGENCY

What is the moral status of a corporation? Is it, as the legal metaphor suggests, an invisible "person"? Or does it more closely resemble an impersonal machine, geared to generate rules, procedures, and profits? If corporations are moral agents as are persons, then we must demand that they assume the burdens of morality just as people do, and that they develop something akin to consciences. If they are like persons, then they also should have the rights that people have: to own property, to conclude contracts, and to exercise freedom of speech, even when it means using their vast financial reserves to promote personal political views. But if they are not moral agents at all, but resemble complicated machines, they must be directly controlled to prevent injury to society. And this direct control will likely come from the only force sufficiently powerful to control corporations, the government.

Considered as an artifact, the corporation is remarkable in that it consists, at least in part, of the very people who create it. Stockholders and corporate employees (to name only the two most prevalent classes of participants) are essential for bringing the corporation into existence, and the end product, the corporation itself, in some sense "contains" its very producers. Yet a corporation must be viewed as more than the mere aggregate of individuals participating in it. When the Exxon Corporation buys another company, its action is not equivalent to the managers' buying the company, or the stockholders' buying the company. Exxon even may be said to continue to own the other company long after its present management has retired and after shareholders have died or sold their stock. Exxon is more than its collection of participants, but does "more" here imply *moral agency?*

The prima facie case for counting corporations as moral agents is remarkably strong. It may even appear odd to question corporate moral agency since both ordinary discourse and the legal tradition seem to grant such status already. We hear that Standard Oil "deceived the public by claiming that U.S. profits were foreign profits," or that "Hooker Chemical Company engaged in corrupt environmental practices." Less frequently, we hear praise of corporations, e.g., "Xerox is socially responsible for curtailing its sales in South Africa." These pedestrian remarks show that corporations are taken to be moral agents, at least in their capacity to be subjects of predicates such as "is responsible," "is to blame," "ought to have foreseen," and the like. When this fact is coupled with the acknowledgement that corporations often *do* the sorts of things humans do, such as conclude contracts, take precautions, apologize for actions, and make promises, there seems to be a strong prima facie case for granting them moral agency.

Corporations are considered to be moral agents in a variety of legal contexts: they are included as persons under statutes such as the Federal Food, Drug, and Cosmetic Act, and are subject to legal guilt, liability, and punishment.[1] In at least two instances they are regarded as bearers of natural rights: (1) they are included among the persons referred to in the Fourteenth Amendment to the U.S. Constitution who are not to be deprived of "life, liberty, or property, without due process of law"; and (2) in 1978 the Supreme Court of the United States upheld the right of corporations to free speech, including the right to promote political ideals through paid advertisements on television and in newspapers.

Yet the otherwise plausible assumption of moral agency is marred by puzzling irregularities. Although we commonly count corporations as moral agents, we sometimes excuse the behavior of corporations and of their employees in ways we would never excuse ordinary agents. A man who made the same exaggerated claims at a dinner party made by a paid actor in a television soap commercial would be the object of moral ridicule.[2] We tend to excuse the Proctor and Gamble

---

[1] Act of Congress of June 25, 1938, c. 675, 52 Stat. 1040, 21 U.S.C. 301-302.

[2] John Ladd makes this point in his article, "Morality and the Ideal of Rationality in Formal Organizations," *The Monist,* 54 (1970), 488-516.

Company, as well as actors in its commercials, for exaggerations we would not excuse in ordinary human affairs.

The suspicion that corporate agency differs from ordinary agency finds additional support in the history of law. Although legal decisions from the twentieth century concur in treating corporations as moral agents, there has been, and still is, significant disagreement about the sort of moral agency at stake. Corporations are considered to be the bearers of certain rights, but they are not assigned, say, the right to vote or the obligation to register for the draft. Historically they have received different treatment from that of individuals: as long ago as 1279 the Statute of Mortmain prohibited giving land to corporations on the basis that, since they never die and consequently never divest themselves of property, this practice might have the undesirable effect of taking property out of commerce.[3] Although present U.S. law treats corporations as artificial persons, English law never has, nor did U.S. law prior to the mid-nineteenth century.[4] Differences between corporate moral agency and human moral agency also continue to be recognized through the doctrine of strict liability, which is applied in practice almost exclusively to corporations and not to human persons.[5]

Corporations often are said to "take precautions," "apologize for actions," and "conclude contracts"; and also like people, they may behave reasonably or stupidly, advance arguments, and own property. However, corporations do not feel pain, remorse, or pleasure; they are not descended from human parents, and they enjoy both limited financial liability (they may be dissolved when their debts reach the limit of their invested capital), and unlimited longevity. Thus, the mere fact that corporations share characteristics with human persons is inadequate to establish moral agency, since they also fail in this regard. Some additional argument is required which will identify the characteristic or set of characteristics which corporations possess that is sufficient to establish moral agency.

THE MORAL PERSON VIEW

One familiar attempt at such an argument is embodied in what might be called the Moral Person view. The Moral Person view employs the following line of reasoning: if corporations are agents, then they also are *moral* agents, because anything which is an agent is also a moral agent. The problem then becomes one of proving that corporations are agents. However, this is easy to prove, it is claimed, so long as one uses the proper definition of an "agent"—namely, anything which behaves *inten-*

---

[3] F. H. Lawson, *Introduction to the Law of Property* (Oxford: Clarendon Press, 1958), p. 143.

[4] Walter Goedecke, "Corporatons and the Philosophy of Law," *The Journal of Value Inquiry,* 5 (Summer 1976).

[5] See R. McKeon, "Products Liability: Trends and Implications," *The University of Chicago Law Review* (1970-71), 3-63; and Richard A. Wasserstrom, "Strict Liability in the Criminal Law," *Stanford Law Review,* 12 (1960).

tionally. Since corporations do behave intentionally, they are therefore moral agents. As one Moral Person theorist puts it, "In short, corporations can be full-fledged moral persons and have whatever privileges, rights, and duties as are, in the normal course of affairs, accorded to moral persons."[6]

But why does the Moral Person view insist that corporations are moral agents just as people are? Why does it not simply hold, as the law seems to imply, that corporations are artificial legal persons, or "juristic" persons, who are merely creations of the law? The view of juristic personhood has evolved from Roman law and seems well entrenched in legal practice. Why take the additional step of referring to moral persons? The answer is that juristic personhood fails to establish full-fledged moral agency. To say that something is a juristic person is in some instances inadequate for attributing moral responsibility. For example, the deceased in a probate case is a juristic person with certain legal rights (to have his will executed properly, for instance), but this fact is inadequate for establishing that the deceased is a moral agent, because, except for his or her past deeds, a deceased person cannot be held *morally* responsible for anything.

In order for corporations to be agents, the Moral Person view holds that they must satisfy the definition of agency, or in other words, be capable of performing intentional actions. But can corporations really perform such actions? Flesh and blood people clearly perform them when they act on the basis of their beliefs and desires, yet corporations do not appear to have beliefs, desires, thoughts, or reasons.

The Moral Person view needs somehow to demonstrate that corporations act intentionally. Typically, it attempts to do so by referring to a corporation's decision-making structure. When Exxon "decides" to acquire a smaller corporation, its decision can be traced to a variety of corporate mechanisms, among which are a board of directors, a management hierarchy, and procedures about, for example, making loans and maintaining a certain level of product diversity. Every corporation has an organizational or responsibility flow chart delineating stations and levels in the power structure, and every corporation has procedures for recognizing genuine corporate decisions. The procedures for recognizing decisions are of two principal kinds: (1) rules for decision-making (such as a rule specifying that a majority vote of the board of directors under normal circumstances can bind the corporation to specific courses of action), and (2) basic beliefs or policies of the corporation (such as a policy of profit maximization). This kind of intentionality involves the use of deliberation (undertaken by members in the corporate structure) and the use of reasons (contained in corporate policy).[7]

So if we add the premise that all agents are moral agents, then it follows that corporations are *moral* agents.

But the matter is not so simple. To begin with, the Moral Person view assumes that the activities of Exxon Corporation manifest intentions which belong

[6]P. French, "The Corporation as a Moral Person," *American Philosophical Quarterly,* 16 (1979), 207.

[7]French, "Moral Person," p. 207.

to *Exxon itself* and not merely Exxon's stockholders or employees. But what does this mean? Consider the analogy of a game. In games, the rules determine which actions count as legitimate moves, and in corporations certain rules determine what counts as, say, a decision by the board of directors. But the rules of a game fail to tell us what the game *itself* intends—in fact, it makes little sense to say that the game intends anything—and one can argue that the same is true for corporations. If corporations are made up of rules, policies, and power structures, then we can tell what counts in the context of those rules, policies, and structures; but we cannot tell clearly from these what the combined rules, policies, and structures themselves intend.[8]

It seems plainly wrong to say that whatever corporations *do,* they also intend, since presumably corporations, like people, may have different opinions about what a given corporate act is intended to accomplish. Some people, such as managers and stockholders, may see a manufacturing operation as a means to make a profit. Other people, such as employees, may see the same operation as a means to provide a salary. It seems we cannot appeal to the corporation to tell us which interpretation is correct, for corporate intentions are just what are at issue. One well-known organizational theorist was driven to remark that "If one cannot point out the collective analogue to individual intent, organizations are strange looking persons. They don't look much like metaphysical persons, and they don't look much like moral persons."[9]

More is wrong with the Moral Person view, however, than merely the difficulty in establishing the locus of intentions. The view assumes that anything which can behave intentionally is an agent, and that anything which is an agent is a moral agent. But some entities appear to behave intentionally which do not qualify as moral agents. A cat may behave intentionally when it crouches for a mouse. We know that it intends to catch the mouse, but we do not credit it with moral agency (though we may object on moral grounds to its mistreatment). A computer behaves intentionally when it sorts through a list of names and rearranges them in alphabetical order, but we do not consider the computer to be a moral agent. Perhaps corporations resemble complicated computers; perhaps they, according to a complicated inner logic, function in an intentional manner but fail altogether to qualify as moral agents. One seemingly needs more than the presence of intentions to deduce moral agency.

The final problem with the Moral Person view lies in one of its implications. If, morally speaking, corporations are analogous to persons, then they should have the rights which ordinary persons have. But although it may be plausible to say corporations should have many of the rights ascribed to humans, such as the right to own property, enter into agreements, and make profits, it seems implausible they should have the right to vote or to draw Social Security benefits. In fact,

[8]This point is made by Michael Keeley in a forthcoming paper, "Organizations as Non-Persons," *Journal of Value Inquiry.* I am indebted to Professor Keeley for this observation.

[9]Keeley, "Non-Persons."

many rights seem logically impossible to attribute to corporations: Can corporations have a right to worship as they please? To pursue happiness?

The combined weight of such arguments suggests that corporations fail to qualify as moral persons. They may be juristic persons, granted legal rights by courts and legislators; they may even be moral agents of some other kind; but they do not appear to be "moral persons" in any literal sense of that term.

THE STRUCTURAL RESTRAINT VIEW

The failure of the Moral Person view can tempt one to consider an opposite approach, namely, the view that corporations are never moral agents of any kind. Let us call this the Structural Restraint view. Endorsed by such contemporary philosophers as John Ladd and Patricia Werhane, the Structural Restraint view emphasizes the fact that corporations are controlled by their very structures and are thus frequently incapable of exercising moral freedom. In its extreme version the view denies moral agency of any kind to all corporate organizations; the corporation cannot be blamed for its actions, since its actions are merely outputs of its structure.

The Structural Restraint view is more sophisticated than it appears. It claims that corporations fail to qualify as moral agents because they are members of the class of "formal organizations," all of which are structurally incapable of accommodating moral motives. Ladd's influential paper, "Morality and the Ideal of Rationality in Formal Organizations," argues that the corporation can act only in accordance with a means-end formula. It argues that corporations are formal organizations, which, by definition, are "planned units, deliberately structured for the purpose of attaining specific goals."[10] (The corporation is only one instance of a formal organization; another would be a government bureaucracy.)

As a formal organization, the corporation is analogous to a player in a game; acting *rationally* as a player means acting in accordance with the formal rules under which it is considered a participant. It fails to qualify as a moral agent, for it fails to utilize moral considerations as fundamental factors in decision-making. Only information about how to achieve its formal ends can be relevant to the corporation's calculations. This means that corporations are designed to pay attention *only* to information about how to achieve goals such as profit maximization. Thus, a television broadcasting company might consider the viewers' moral condemnation of pornography but it would consider such condemnation only in terms of the effect on long-range corporate profits.

If we were to reduce the Structural Restraint view to a series of steps, it would read as follows:

1. A corporation is a member of the class of formal organizations.

2. Formal organizations must, by definition, act exclusively to maximize the achievement of a specified set of goals, e.g., profit.

[10] Ladd, "Morality and Rationality," p. 498.

3. Maximizing the achievement of a specified set of goals rules out the possibility of acting on the basis of moral norms.

4. The capacity to act on the basis of moral norms is a necessary condition for moral agency.

5. Corporations cannot be moral agents.

Step 3 is crucial. The argument assumes that *because* corporations must act primarily to achieve a specified set of goals, they cannot act on the basis of moral norms. But an obvious question arises. Might not a corporation have as one of its goals the goal of adhering to moral norms? Defenders of the view appear trapped. Presumably they must acknowledge that people, in contrast to corporations, *can* act on the basis of moral norms; so why can't corporations?[11]

In order to save the third premise, the argument requires a modified premise, or set of reasons, to indicate why corporations are unable to build the goal of acting morally into their formal structure. Suppose 2 were altered to read:

2. Formal organizations must, by definition, act exclusively to maximize the achievement of a set of *empirical* goals. ("Empirical goals" here would refer to goals that can be defined in terms of measurable facts, e.g., rate of profit, increased productivity, or decreased employee turnover.)

In turn, the expression, "empirical goals," would be substituted in 3 for "goals." This reformulation may have problems of its own, but it appears necessary to patch up the problem in the Structural Restraint view described above.

Ladd himself suggests such a reformulation when he speaks of the manner in which formal organizations pursue goals. The only time moral considerations can influence decision-making in a formal organization, he claims, is when the considerations are *factual* ones. Facts about the moral attitudes of customers or about the moral attitudes of the general public might influence corporate decision-making, because they might be relevant to the corporation's pursuit of its specific goals. (Offending the moral sensibilities of a television audience might drop ratings and profits for broadcasting corporations.) But moral matters per se could never influence corporate decision-making, Ladd adds, because morality is "not even a matter of empirical knowledge."[12]

To evaluate the argument, let us consider two basic challenges to the Structural Restraint position. One such challenge agrees that corporations are formal organizations, but it questions the conclusion that corporations cannot undertake genuine moral deliberation.[13] It criticizes the Structural Restraint view

[11]See David Ozar, "The Moral Responsibility of Corporations," in *Ethical Issues in Business,* ed. T. Donaldson and P. Werhane (Englewood Cliffs, N.J.: Prentice-Hall, 1979).

[12]Ladd, "Morality and Rationality," p. 498.

[13]This point is made by Kenneth Goodpaster in "Morality and Organizations," in *Ethical Issues in Business,* ed. T. Donaldson and P. Werhane (Englewood Cliffs, N.J.: Prentice-Hall, 1979).

for comparing corporate structure to the rules of a game. Game rules are static, but corporate structure can change. Whereas the rules of chess are presumed fixed and cannot be altered by players, the players in the corporation, i.e., the executives, stockholders, and employees, can change its structure and organization. The rules of chess remain virtually unchanged over the span of, say, 50 years, but during the same span we might expect a change in the goals of companies such as Lockheed or General Motors. The view is mistaken in claiming that corporations are forced to act "rationally," where acting rationally means nothing but doggedly pursuing formal goals. It may be rational for people to abdicate control over rule changes in the game of chess but it would not be rational for corporations to abdicate control over the definition of their own goals.

Although this criticism weakens the original version of the Structural Restraint argument, it cannot do the same for the revised version. This is because 2, when combined with the dictum that "ought implies can," will rule out the kind of rationality which would prompt corporations to alter their own goals in the light of moral norms. In other words, because no entity should be held responsible for behavior unless it can control its behavior (ought implies can), the fact that corporations are restrained by their structure means that they cannot be morally "rational" about changing their own structures. The problem turns on the double-edged sense of the term "rationality." It is one thing to consider the issue of whether a corporation is rational in terms of how efficiently it achieves its pre-determined goals. The Structural Restraint view uses the word "rational" in this sense. But it is another to consider the issue of whether a corporation is rational in terms of whether it can morally improve and redefine its own goals. This is a much broader sense of rationality. The Structural Restraint argument concludes that corporations cannot be rational in this broader sense. It claims that they cannot be moral agents because they are analogous to goal-pursuing machines which are *not* machines built to evaluate and change their own goals.[14]

A second criticism of the restraint view draws an analogy between corporations and other organizations. It argues that some organizations are considered moral agents by virtue of the fact that they can perform actions which, according to convention, qualify them as moral agents. For example, nations or governments are considered moral agents (and held responsible for bombing civilians in wartime) because they are able to perform acts such as declaring war and concluding treaties.[15] Now corporations, just like nations or governments, are said to perform actions which confer moral agency. For example, corporations are acknowledged to have power, in accordance with their charters, to own property and conclude contracts.

But, though this argument helps to provide one independent reason for regarding corporations as moral agents, it cannot dispense with the Structural Restraint view insofar as that view is intended to stand independently of general

---

[14] This fact follows from the definition of a formal organization. Professor Patricia Werhane, in her paper, "Formal Organizations, Economic Freedom and Moral Agency," forthcoming in *The Journal of Value Inquiry,* develops the sense in which, for Ladd, corporations must be analogous to goal-pursuing machines.

[15] Ozar, "Moral Responsibility of Corporations."

social conventions and practices. The restraint view can deny that social practices which confer moral agency on organizations such as nations and governments also confer moral agency on corporations. Social practices can also be wrong: pagans could follow practices which confer moral agency on pieces of wood—but that does not make the pieces of wood moral agents.

Neither of the two criticisms we have examined is fully successful in dispensing with the restraint argument. Both, however, tend to advance our understanding of the underlying problem; we should now be aware that (a) the case against moral agency rests largely upon the doctrine of "ought implies can"; and (b) the case must be supported by reasons which are independent of mere convention. For if either (a) or (b) were false, then the Structural Restraint view would be overturned.

Before proceeding, the Restraint view's striking implications should be considered. If corporations are restrained in a manner which precludes moral agency, then like any nonmoral agents—like any powerful, complicated machine—they must be watched and regulated. Without some automatic economic mechanism which ensures moral behavior (an unlikely possibility), and without the capacity to assume moral responsibility, corporations threaten to exercise their enormous power as would a giant machine. With no automatic controls or internal moral controls, some external agent must take control—and there is no theoretical limit to the justified level of such control.

The spectre of unlimited government regulation will prod some to question the Structural Restraint view. "Have we been wrong all these years," they might ask, "to regard corporations as moral agents, and to blame them, praise them, and look for responsible behavior?" Despite its persuasive logic, the Structural Restraint view seems not to account for the fact that people speak about corporations *as if* they were moral agents—except to say, of course, that such talk is mistaken.

Closer inspection does reveal two chinks in the armour of the Structural Restraint view. Both those problems involve tendencies toward oversimplification. The first involves an oversimplification of what corporations *are,* the second an oversimplification of how corporations *behave.*

The Structural Restraint view assumes that corporations *are* formal organizations. This much was assumed in premises 1 and 2: However, notice that although 1 and 2 may purport to define the corporation, the resulting definition cannot be a stipulative one (designed just to stipulate word meanings), since it makes a factual claim (that corporations are the sorts of things which pursue empirical goals); and moreover, it directly contributes to a factual conclusion (that corporations are not moral agents). Premises 1 and 2, then, have factual significance. But, granting this much, it is noteworthy that so far their factual accuracy has merely been taken for granted.

This is not taken for granted by many whose business it is to understand the workings of organizations. The concept of a formal organization is drawn from organizational theorist Herbert Simon; but Simon's model is only one of many competing models in circulation, and no consensus exists about which model is most accurate. Indeed, if there is a consensus, it holds that more than one model may be needed to characterize corporate organizations.[16]

In order to demonstrate how the truth status of 1 and 2 really is crucial for the Structural Restraint view, and to show further how this affects the overall problem of moral agency, let us examine briefly three other models of organizations. Each of the following models has gained acceptance by some organizational theorists,[17] and each model suggests a fundamentally different way of construing corporations.

The Rational Agent Model

The Rational Agent Model assumes that corporate actions are outcomes of a unified process in which an act is chosen when it appears to maximize the corporation's values. In this way the model suggests that decision-making is rational; corporations self-consciously attempt to pursue values just as human agents do.[18] Such a model need not be interpreted as goal-directed: the maximization of organizational values could refer to either the pursuit of concrete future states of affairs, in which case the decision-making would be goal-directed, or to the attempt to adhere to a specific set of rules or principles, in which case it would not be. According to the model, the "mind" of the corporation would consist of its top executives and members of the board of directors, and it is assumed that the executives and board members are able to confer with one another in order to arrive at decisions.

The Organizational Process Model

The Organizational Process Model denies that corporate decisions are the results of a unitary decision-making process. Instead, a corporation is seen as a loosely allied combination of decision-making units, e.g., a marketing group, a manufacturing group, and a lobbying group; and although some coordination exists among the various groups, no unitary and self-conscious decision-making occurs. The model sees corporate activities against a backdrop of organizational rules and tacit norms. When decisions must be made, a search is instituted for the appropriate rule which covers the case at hand. The rule need not be a formalized principle; it may instead be a tacit norm or general expectation. The rules themselves are, on

---

[16]See Simeon M. Kriesberg, "Decision-making Models and the Control of Corporate Crime," *The Yale Law Journal,* 85 (July 1976).

[17]See Michael Keeley, "A Social Justice Approach to Organizational Evaluation," *Administrative Science Quarterly* (June 1978).

[18]For an historical account of how the corporation came to be regarded as analogous to a human agent, see Frederick Pollock and F.W. Maitland, "Corporation and Person," in *Anthropology and Early Law,* ed. Lawrence Krader (New York: New York University Press, 1965), pp. 300-336.

this model, the results of organizational habits and so-called "standard operating procedures," some of which are, and some of which are not, articulated in written corporate documents, such as stockholders' reports, memos, and managerial directives.[19]

The Political Egoism Model

The Political Egoism Model views corporate decision-making in terms of decisions of individual employees and the interests they pursue. The struggle which results from the pursuit of individual interests in a corporation may be compared to the struggle of participants in a political contest. The participants are assumed to have specific interests, such as economic advancement, social status, and ongoing friendships; and it is assumed that the pursuit of these egoistic interests inevitably generates conflicts between participants. The rules of the political game are defined by such things as corporate charters, expectations of consumers and the investment community, traditions within the organization, and the atmosphere of the general industry within which the company participates. Important players in the game would be, for example, the plant manager, the marketing specialist, and the lobbying agent. The political game can yield actions which do not bear the obvious stamp of the participants who generated the action. For example, it might be difficult to tell from the fact that Lockheed bribed a Japanese official, which particular political interests prompted the bribe.

We cannot discuss all these models in detail or even assess the evidence supporting each; but the mere presence of an array of empirical models is significant, for it indicates the striking variety of models used to describe what corporations *are*. Most important, it indicates that merely assuming, as the Structural Restraint view does, that corporations are examples of a single model, namely, of formal organizations, is a mistake. Perhaps corporations are not formal organizations as premise 1 suggests, but instead fit the Rational Agent Model. If so, then moral agency might, after all, be ascribed to corporations. Or perhaps corporations adhere to no single model, but display characteristics of many models so that many models are necessary to understand a single corporation. Or perhaps corporations differ among themselves so that one corporation fits the Formal Organizational Model, another the Political Process Model, and so on. Thus the Structural Restraint view oversimplifies matters through its assumption that all corporations are formal organizations.

The second oversimplification of the restraint view is closely connected to the first; indeed, it may be seen as an aspect of the same problem. It concerns not what the corporation is, but how the corporation behaves. The Structural Restraint view assumes that corporations must pursue empirically specifiable goals and that

---

[19] An account of a broad range of such corporate procedures may be found in Peter Drucker, *Concept of the Corporation* (New York: John Day, 1946).

this is *all* they can do. But although some corporations may be restricted in this fashion, there are some striking counter-examples. Consider the diversity in corporate decision-making procedures. The following are hypothetical cases:

1. Smith and Jones are partners in the advertising business. They work daily in the same office, exchange information regularly, and decide all issues by mutual consultation. Together, they own 98 percent of the company's stock.

2. General Motors, Inc. manufactures everything from refrigerators to automobiles and grosses more revenue than do most world governments. Owned by literally millions of stockholders, G.M. is divided into thousands of subunits (both line and staff) which sometimes decide issues autonomously and sometimes submit to central authority. These organizational subunits frequently embody their own decision-making structures.

3. Acme Marketing, Inc. specializes in door-to-door sales and employs thousands of salespeople, all of whom are paid by commission and most of whom work for Acme for a short time. Most decisions are made by employees in the field, with little central coordination. The assets of the company are minimal, and stock is owned almost exclusively by managers.

These examples exhibit the diversity of decision-making procedures occurring in profit-making corporations. Each organization functions according to a different logic. One cannot identify the same decision-making procedures at work in Smith and Jones' corporation as in General Motors, especially since the decision-making procedure of Smith and Jones, who are in constant contact and communication, will be similar to the decision-making process of a single individual. Here we see that the Structural Restraint argument misses the mark when it concludes Smith and Jones cannot act on the basis of moral norms, since presumably *individuals* can act on such a basis and the decision-making of Smith and Jones *resembles* that of an individual.

Both oversimplifications of the Structural Restraint view imply that we have been asking the wrong questions. Instead of simply asking whether *all* corporations are moral agents, or *all* corporations are not (thus assuming that all corporations are one way or the other), it would have been better to ask whether *some* corporations are moral agents and *some* are not. Clearly, if the conclusion reached about Smith and Jones is correct, then some corporations can be moral agents. And if there are some corporations that fit perfectly the model of the Structural Restraint view, then they might fail to qualify as moral agents. Let us proceed, then, by specifying the conditions that any corporation would need to satisfy in order to qualify as a moral agent. Once having done this, it will be possible to ask whether or not a given corporation satisfies the conditions.

CONDITIONS OF MORAL AGENCY

In order to qualify as a moral agent, a corporation would need to embody a *process of moral decision-making*. On the basis of our previous discussion, this process seems to require, at a minimum:

1. The capacity to use moral reasons in decision-making.
2. The capacity of the decision-making process to control not only overt corporate acts, but also the structure of policies and rules.

1 is necessary to raise the corporation above the level of a mere machine. To be a moral agent, something must have *reasons* for what it does, not simply *causes* for what it does, and for something to be a moral agent, some of those reasons must be moral ones. Obviously, corporations are unable to think as humans, but they can employ reasons of a sort, and this is shown by the fact that they can be *morally accountable*. That is, with the proper internal structure, corporations, like humans, can be liable to give an account of their behavior where the account stipulates which moral *reasons* prompted their behavior.

For a corporation to be a moral agent, not only must it be able to use moral reasons in its decision-making, but it must be capable of controlling the structure of its policies and rules (condition 2). We remember that human beings are morally responsible not only for their actions, but also for maintaining their moral capabilities (as Aristotle notes, we are responsible not only if we injure another person, but if we alter our faculties through alcohol or drugs in a way which makes us liable to injure another). In an analogous manner corporate moral agency implies responsibility for maintaining corporate moral faculties, such as certain corporate policies, rules, and procedures. Condition 2 is actually a further specification of condition 1. Condition 1 specifies that moral agency requires moral control over overt corporate acts; condition 2 further specifies that the moral control must extend to the maintenance of the corporation's decision-making machinery.

Corporations fulfilling these conditions would qualify as moral agents, but not "moral persons." It would be a mistake to assume that because a corporation can use moral reasons in decision-making, it automatically possesses other moral properties identified with persons, such as intentions, pleasures, human obligations, and human rights. The mere capacity to use moral reasons in decision-making would certainly not entitle a corporation to the right to vote, nor thrust upon it the obligation to register for the draft. Thus the moral agency of a corporation is of a special kind. In Chapter 6 more will be said about the special differences separating the concept of *corporate* moral agency from the concept of *personal* moral agency.

There is no reason, in principle, why most corporations cannot fulfill the two conditions. Indeed, some observers will argue that nearly every corporation already fulfills them. The conditions are not so strict as to require a perfectly functioning, moral decision-making process. Few humans would qualify by such standards. Corporations need not have perfect moral control; a reasonable amount will do. A corporation which, despite having the requisite amount of control, failed to correct faulty procedures in its product safety division and procrastinated until a consumer was injured ought not be let off the moral hook by disclaiming moral agency. Only if the decision-making process of a corporation were thoroughly mechanistic and fit perfectly the Structural Restraint model, or if the corporation were thoroughly fragmented and lacked any significant decision-making mechanisms, would the organization be analogous to the sick or insane person who could not tell right from wrong. Then it would not be expected to improve and maintain its moral capabilities, for it would have none; it would fail even to qualify as a moral agent. Society should, however, be protected from such corporate moral sickness. One method of doing so would be to require, as a condition for qualifying as a "corporation," that an organization meet the conditions of moral agency.

Since small organizations can more closely approximate the decision-making of individual persons, the real challenge is for the large ones, especially ones with massive bureaucratic structures. to develop and maintain genuine accountability. Organizations that gross billions of dollars, employ hundreds of thousands of workers, and operate in scores of foreign countries, must utilize complex, specialized systems of accountability.

The possibility is open that conditions 1 and 2 will be realized differently by different organizations. Just as corporations differ in terms of the means they choose to achieve economic ends, so they might differ in terms of how they achieve moral ones. G.M. may develop a process of moral decision-making through, among other things, a systematic deliberation of moral issues by a restructured board of directors. The Donnelly Mirror Company, on the other hand, may ensure moral decision-making by allowing many corporate interest groups, such as shareholders, employees, and consumers, to participate in corporate decision-making. (In Chapters 8 and 9, strategies to improve corporate responsibility will be considered in detail.)

The door should also be left open to different *types* of corporate moral agency. Thus, in one corporation it may be decided that each participant in the corporation is partially responsible for what the entire corporation does, whereas in another it may be decided that only some participants (say, the managers and the board of directors) are responsible for what the corporation does. Talking about this issue from a legal perspective, Richard De George remarks: "There is no one correct way of legally assigning responsibility with respect to corporate activity. . . . The question of how many of the freedoms of natural persons corporations should enjoy is a question that many recent court decisions have been concerned with. But the answer is in part one that must be decided—decided for good reasons, to be sure—but decided." "It is not a matter," he concludes, "of somehow seeing, in some arcane sense of seeing, which freedoms the corporation really has."[20]

---

[20] Richard De George, "Moral Responsibility and the Corporation," a paper presented at the 1978 meeting of the Society for Value Inquiry, in conjunction with the American Philosophical Association, December 27, 1978, pp. 19-20.

As De George's remark implies, the capacity of corporations to qualify as moral agents, along with the kind of moral agency they embody, are crucial issues for deciding how outsiders, including the courts and the government, should regard corporations. Any corporation which fails to qualify as a moral agent, i.e., which fails to embody conditions 1 and 2, also fails to qualify as a holder of *rights or responsibilities*. Since certain rights and responsibilities automatically accompany corporate status, society may wish, again, to make the conditions of moral agency also be conditions of corporate status.

The Moral Person view of the corporation was shown to exaggerate the similarity between corporations and people. Corporations are not, morally speaking, "persons." Neither the fact that they behave intentionally, nor the fact that they are granted certain legal rights by the courts implies that they are persons. Corporate "intentions" differ from individual human intentions, and the mere existence of intentions fails by itself to guarantee moral agency (witness lower animals and computers). However, the opposite of the Moral Person view, the Structural Restraint view, was also found wanting. The view is misleading because it oversimplifies both the nature of corporations and how they behave. As we have seen, even giant corporations can qualify as moral agents so long as they meet the two necessary conditions.

A PRELIMINARY SCHEME FOR UNDERSTANDING CORPORATE RESPONSIBILITIES

If corporations can be moral agents, what does their agency amount to? Consider the class of all corporations that meet the minimum qualifications for moral agency: how are their duties and obligations to be defined? One should avoid the trap of thinking that corporations have the same duties as people; corporations have a duty to consider the wishes of stockholders, whereas people do not, and corporations have a duty to abide by their charters, whereas people do not, and so on. But if corporate obligations are not mirror images of personal ones, what are they?

As a first approximation, let us separate all corporate moral obligations into two classes: *direct* and *indirect*.[21] Direct obligations are those that are specified explicitly and formally and that as a rule are owed to people who conduct business directly with corporations, such as stockholders, employees, suppliers, and customers. For example, corporations can have direct obligations to stockholders where the obligations are specified by law and corporate charter, or to employees as specified by union contracts. Legal statutes (say, requiring corporations to compensate victims of faulty products), or contracts with suppliers, or pension agreements with employees all create direct obligations for corporations.

Indirect obligations have opposite characteristics. They are not specified formally and sometimes are owed to people who conduct no direct business with

---

[21] Clarence Walton, *Conceptual Foundations of Business* (Homewood, Ill.: Richard D. Irwin, 1969), pp. 162-87. Dr. Walton introduces the distinction between "direct" and "indirect" corporate obligations. The distinction I use, although inspired by his, is somewhat different.

the corporation, e.g., competitors, local communities, and the general public. Despite the absence of formal agreements, corporations may be said to have obligations to treat competitors fairly, to avoid destroying small communities, and to prevent injury to members of the general public. Classes of people to whom corporations have direct obligations may also be beneficiaries of indirect ones. That is, corporations may have not only obligations to honor union contracts and pension agreements, but obligations to honor certain rights of employees. It is a matter of dispute how many indirect obligations a corporation has, but it is indisputable that corporations have some: even without formal restraints, few would deny that a corporation is obliged to avoid blatant deception of the consumer and to refrain from racist advertising.

Direct Obligations

From a moral perspective, direct obligations are easily handled. They are easily identified and they carry their specifications on their face: a contract or a legal statute is itself an attempt to formalize an obligation. Except in unusual cases, the mere existence of a direct obligation is a decisive moral reason for fulfilling it. The only exceptions would be cases where specified obligations conflicted with more fundamental moral duties, as when a contract itself might bind the signing parties to commit fraud. With direct obligations the vexing moral problems lie not with discovering what they are, but with discovering how corporations can best honor them.

Celebrated moral disasters have often involved the violation of direct obligations. When Hooker Chemical Company violated pollution regulations, for example, it violated the direct obligations which the regulations established. Another case, occurring in 1978 at a General Motors truck plant in Flint, Michigan, involved direct obligations to employees. Three plant managers installed in a supervisor's office a secret control box which was used to speed up the assembly line. This act constituted a serious violation of General Motors Corporation's contract with the United Auto Workers. The only explanation offered by the managers for the device was that production targets were being missed and that "the bosses were putting pressure on us to do something about it."[22] Here the moral issue is relatively straightforward: G.M. violated its direct obligation created by the union contract.

Indirect Obligations

Less straightforward are issues involving indirect obligations. Let us consider two cases where indirect obligations appear to be involved. The first concerns a handful of large U.S. companies, including Nestle and Bristol-Myers, and their sales of infant formula to mothers in developing countries. Through policies of aggressive advertising, including the use of free samples, these companies have persuaded some mothers in Third World countries to switch from breastfeeding to

[22] *Wall Street Journal,* November 8, 1979, p. 1.

infant formula. Critics challenge this practice on moral grounds, citing a swarm of possible health problems. In underdeveloped countries, they argue, water supplies which must be mixed with the formula are laden with bacteria; mothers frequently lack money to continue formula feeding; and, once having switched to formula, they cannot return to breastfeeding. The result, they say, is a higher than normal rate of infant mortality and malnutrition. Whether such claims are true or not, they point to the existence of possible moral obligations corporations have which are indirect in character. (U.S. companies are not subject to any legal sanctions that would prevent such sales.)

Consider also the situation of a large company in a small community where the company wants to close or move. As mentioned earlier, such actions can spell disaster for small communities. In one well-known case the Lykes-Youngstown Sheet and Tube Company terminated 5,000 employees in the Youngstown, Pennsylvania, area without warning. Its action eventually resulted in the loss of over 11,000 associated jobs in the community. Few people would deny that corporations sometimes have a right to move or close, but most would agree that they have indirect obligations regarding the manner in which they do so—say, to warn the community in advance, if possible. Here, too, the obligations at stake are indirect.

Indirect obligations, in contrast to direct ones, are difficult to bring into ethical focus. Which specific indirect obligations do corporations have? What is their ethical justification?

This chapter has revealed that the corporation has a moral dimension, but has not spelled out the character of that dimension. It has shown that corporations that meet certain minimum conditions—of employing moral reasons in decision-making, and of having the capacity to control fundamental policies and procedures —qualify as moral agents, but it has not shown what their corporate agency amounts to. It has demonstrated that the corporation resists being lumped naively with humans in the context of traditional moral theories, but it has failed to detail a better method of treatment. In short, the chapter has depicted the issue of moral agency in broad strokes, indicating a variety of moral issues but offering few of the solutions.

The concluding paragraphs separated corporate obligations into direct and indirect. Direct obligations appear relatively straightforward, while indirect ones are stubbornly elusive. The aim of the next chapter will be to begin clarifying the content of a corporation's indirect obligations.

SUGGESTED SUPPLEMENTARY READINGS

BEAUCHAMP, T., and N. BOWIE, eds., *Ethical Theory and Business.* Englewood Cliffs, N.J.: Prentice-Hall, 1979.

CAREY, TONI VOGEL, "Institutional Versus Moral Obligations," *Journal of Philosophy,* 74 (1977): 587-89.

COHEN, J., *The Conscience of Corporations,* Baltimore: John Hopkins Press, 1971.

DE GEORGE, R.T., and J. A. PICHLER, eds., *Ethics, Free Enterprise and Public Policy.* New York: Oxford University Press, 1978.

DENNISON, HENRY S., *Ethics and Modern Business.* Boston: Houghton Mifflin, 1932.

DONALDSON, THOMAS, and PATRICIA WERHANE, eds., *Ethical Issues in Business: A Philosophical Approach.* Englewood Cliffs, N.J.: Prentice-Hall, 1979.

FRENCH, PETER A., "The Corporation as a Moral Person," *American Philosophical Quarterly,* 16 (July 1979): 207-15.

———, "Institutional and Moral Obligations," *Journal of Philosophy,* 74 (1977): 575-87.

GEWIRTH, ALAN, *Reason and Morality.* Chicago: University of Chicago Press, 1978.

GOEDECKE, WALTER, "Corporations and the Philosophy of Law," *The Journal of Value Inquiry,* 10 (Summer 1976).

KEELEY, MICHAEL, "A Social Justice Approach to Organization Evaluation," *Administrative Science Quarterly,* June 1978.

KRIESBERG, SIMEON M., "Decision-making Models and the Control of Corporate Crime," *The Yale Law Journal,* 85 (July 1976).

McKEON, R., "Products Liability: Trends and Implications," *The University of Chicago Law Review* (1970-1971): 3-63.

NADER, RALPH, *The Consumer and Corporate Accountability.* New York: Harcourt Brace Jovanovich, Inc., 1973.

OLSON, MANCUR, JR., *The Logic of Collective Action.* Cambridge, Mass.: Harvard University Press, 1965.

VON WRIGHT, GEORG HENRIK, *Norm and Action.* London: Routledge & Kegan Paul, 1963.

CHAPTER 3

Constructing a Social Contract for Business

In a speech to the Harvard Business School in 1969, Henry Ford II stated:

> The terms of the contract between industry and society are changing
> . . . Now we are being asked to serve a wider range of human values and to
> accept an obligation to members of the public with whom we have no
> commercial transactions.

The "contract" to which Henry Ford referred concerns a corporation's *indirect* obligations. It represents not a set of formally specified obligations, but a set of binding, abstract ones. A social contract for business, if one exists, is not a typewritten contract in the real world, but a metaphysical abstraction not unlike the "social contract" between citizens and government that philosophers have traditionally discussed. Such a contract would have concrete significance, for it would help to interpret the nature of a corporation's indirect obligations, which are notoriously slippery.

The aim of this chapter is to discover a corporation's indirect obligations by attempting to clarify the meaning of business's so-called "social contract." The task is challenging. Although people speak frequently of such a contract, few have attempted to specify its meaning. Although businesspeople, legislators, and academics offer examples of supposed infractions of the "contract," few can explain what justifies the contract itself. Consider the assertion that Chisso Corporation violated its "contract" with society when it knowingly dumped toxic mercury into the ocean, or that the Nestle Corporation violated its "contract" when it promoted sales of infant formula in Third World countries. What serves as the ultimate basis for such claims? No contract can be pulled from a drawer and pointed to; no signatures can be checked for authenticity. Just what, then, *is* the social contract?

A good starting point is the so-called "social contract" that philosophers have spoken of between society and the state. This political contract has usually been viewed as a theoretical means for justifying the existence of the state. Philosophers have asked, "Why should people let a government exist at all?" in other words, "Why should people prefer to have a government control much of their actions—to impose taxes, raise armies, and punish criminals—instead of having no government at all?" They never doubted for a moment the need for a state, but they believed raising such questions would clarify not only the justification for the state's existence, but also the reciprocal obligations between the state and its citizens. If a government began to abuse its citizenry, to trample on its rights or to diminish social welfare, then according to such philosophers it had broken the tenets of the social contract and could be overthrown. Such a theory in the hands of the seventeenth-century English philosopher John Locke, provided much of the theoretical support for the American Revolution and design of the Declaration of Independence and the U.S. Constitution.

The political social contract provides a clue for understanding the contract for business. If the political contract serves as a justification for the existence of the state, then the business contract by parity of reasoning should serve as the justification for the existence of the corporation.

Thus, crucial questions are: Why should corporations exist at all? What is the fundamental justification of their activities? How can we measure their performance and say when they have achieved their fundamental purpose? Consider a case involving General Motors and the production of automobiles. The automobiles that General Motors produced during the 1950s and 1960s all had noncollapsible steering wheels (called by Ralph Nader "ram-rodding" steering wheels), and evidence indicated that they contributed to hundreds of thousands of highway deaths. But General Motors and other auto manufacturers kept them on the cars anyway, claiming the added expense of collapsible steering wheels would reduce car sales and profits. Their claim may well have been true. However, by refusing to install safer steering wheels, had they failed to achieve a fundamental corporate mission? Had they violated a tenet of an implied social contract between them and society? Or had they just attended to business—although in a way which had unfortunate consequences for society? To answer these questions, we must first know what justifies General Motors' existence.

It is reasonable to look for a fundamental purpose, or set of purposes, that justifies corporate existence. Doing so makes conceptual sense, despite the fact one would never look for what justifies, say, human existence. As we learned in the last chapter, corporations, unlike humans, are artifacts, which is to say *we* create them. We *choose* to create corporations and we might choose either not to create them or to create different entities. Corporations thus are like political states in their need for justification.

THE METHOD OF JUSTIFICATION

But, one might ask, aren't corporations justified already? Do they not already contribute to society by supplying it with goods and services? And do they not possess an inherent *right* to exist? These questions suggest that one might explain corporate existence without struggling to articulate the tenets of a "social contract."

One might attempt to justify corporate existence by appealing simply to corporate productivity: to the automobiles, irons, tools, clothing, and medical equipment corporations create. Because society demands such items, it seemingly also requires the corporations that produce them. Adam Smith, the eighteenth-century Scottish philosopher, emphasizes productivity when he justifies a set of economic practices through their contribution to the wealth of nations. But although productivity is surely a crucial piece in the puzzle of corporate justification, it fails to provide a full solution. To say that an organization produces wealth for society is not sufficient to justify it from a moral perspective, since morality encompasses the entire range of human welfare. To say something produces wealth is to say something morally good about it—assuming that wealth is counted as a human good—but it fails to tell us what else the thing does, or how its process of creation affects society. Consider the example of a nuclear power reactor. To say that a nuclear reactor generates electricity is to say something good about it, but it fails to consider the reactor in the context of the possibility of melt-downs, the storage of nuclear waste, the costs of alternative production, and so forth. And this is true even if we suppose that ultimately nuclear reactors are fully justified. The logic of the problem of corporate justification is similar. To achieve a complete moral picture of a corporation's existence, we must consider not just its capacity to produce wealth, but rather the full range of its effects upon society: its tendencies to pollute or to harm workers, or, alternatively, its tendencies to help employees by providing jobs and other benefits for society.

Suppose, on the other hand, that one tried to justify corporate existence simply through the inherent "right" of corporations to exist. We remember that one of the two rival interpretations of the corporation sees it as a product of free human association: people freely come together for the purpose of conducting business, and they constitute the corporation. And we remember that in the United States since the mid-nineteenth century corporate status has been regarded as a right, not a privilege. Why, then, is there even a need to justify corporate existence?

Again, this line of reasoning falls short of providing a complete justification. Granted the act of incorporation does not happen in a vacuum; at a minimum there must be a petitioning group of persons. But even granting that individuals, by virtue of their freedom, are allowed to create these superpersonal entities, and even granting that the entities themselves should possess unlimited longevity and limited liability, these facts by themselves say nothing about *why* people ought to do such a thing. An analogy reveals the distinction: people may, by virtue of their freedom, be allowed to become drunk nightly; but it is abundantly clear that their *right* to

do so fails to justify their nightly drunkenness. Similarly, even if there were a right
to incorporate, it would fail to justify corporate existence in the sense of showing
why corporations *ought* to exist. Doing so requires more than merely showing that
people have a right to incorporate.

THE HISTORY OF THE SOCIAL CONTRACT

Because neither method of justification appears satisfactory, let us return
to the idea of a social contract. Other methods, such as traditional utilitarianism,
are available and promising, and should not be ruled out. But the focus of this
chapter's efforts will be upon the method of social contract. The aim will be to
determine what a social contract for business might look like. Since none has been
constructed, the best strategy will be to look again at its counterpart, the *political*
social contract. Perhaps if we discover the inner workings of the contract between
citizens and the state, a blueprint will emerge for constructing the contract between
society and corporations.

In the hands of political philosophers the term "social contract" has referred not to an item, but to a method for justifying and explaining the state. The
most renowned classical philosophers adopting it were the English philosophers,
Thomas Hobbes (1588-1679) and John Locke (1632-1704), and the French philosopher Jean-Jacques Rousseau (1712-1778). Each first imagined society *without* a
civil state (without, that is, any government), and then society with it. The strategy
was to highlight the benefits that society should expect to receive from the state.
Yet, despite similarity of method, each reached different conclusions. Hobbes
argued that people must obey the king, or sovereign, because the social contract
itself is a contract between sovereign and people. Without such a contract, i.e., in
the state without government which Hobbes called a "state of nature," only a
condition of "war" could exist, with each person being pitted against his or her
fellow human, and no power or authority to make peace among them.

John Locke, writing after Hobbes, repudiated such pessimism. The state
of nature preceding the contract, Locke contended, was not one of war, but rather
a tolerable, though mildly unruly situation in which people possessed natural rights,
such as the right to property and freedom. Indeed they lacked only an efficient
means to arbitrate their disputes and protect their rights. To remedy these drawbacks, society must construct the social contract. However, the agreement is not, as
Hobbes thought, between the people and a sovereign. Instead, people first establish
"civil society," and afterwards civil society negotiates an agreement (a fiduciary
trust) to establish a legislative power, or government, that will protect society's
rights.[1] If the government fails to protect society's rights, then the trust is broken
and revolution is justified. Locke is more wary of government abuses than Hobbes.
For Locke, the relationship between people and legislative power is not one of

[1] J. W. Gough, *The Social Contract* (Oxford: Clarendon Press, 1936), p. 143.

contract; rather it is the same kind that exists between employer and employee, that is, a "trust" between principal and agent. "This conception," J. W. Gough remarks, "fitted Locke's intention admirably, for unlike the contract of government, in which rights and duties were reciprocal, it left the duties on the side of the government, and the rights on the side of the people."[2]

Rousseau's version of the social contract differs from the earlier two. According to him, the contract is created when rights are surrendered *in toto* by individuals to the whole community. As he puts it paradoxically, "Each, giving himself to all, gives himself to nobody." With this, the state is born. The state's desire for its own welfare, dubbed by Rousseau the "general will," thus becomes the yardstick by which all government actions are to be measured. This complex version of the contract has struck many as odd, but it has a special aim: to place the moral underpinnings of the state squarely with the desires and well-being of its people. Ernest Barker sums it up:

> [Rousseau] was hardly concerned with practical necessities; he was hot in pursuit of the logical symmetry of an ideal scheme of popular sovereignty.[3]

This chapter cannot do full justice to the arguments of the social contract philosophers; instead, a few general observations about their methods must suffice. *First,* the tradition of social contract theory is a tradition of social change and reform. This holds not only for the arguments of Hobbes, Locke, and Rousseau, but for ones less well known. The Huguenots, a persecuted Protestant group in France, used a social contract argument in the sixteenth century to defend religious tolerance; and the English Whigs, a political group, used it in the seventeenth century to bolster the cause of civil liberty. Consider Robert Ferguson's remark in his *Brief Justification of the Prince of Orange's Descent into England:* "No government is lawful," Ferguson writes, "but what is founded upon compact and agreement between those chosen to govern and those who condescend to be governed."[4] Social contract arguments have unsettled the clergy, shaken monarchies, and brought on revolution. There may never have been a pen and ink contract, but remarkably enough, thousands of people have acted *as if* there were.

The contract has been used as a moral ideal, as a law higher even than the state, against which the state must be evaluated. It is not unlike the "higher law" invoked by the Greeks and Romans. We are reminded of Sophocles' play, *Antigone,* in which a grief-stricken woman learns that her brother's body has been condemned to rot outside the city's walls, stripped even of the honor of a burial. She defies the orders of the king and risks her own life to bury her brother. When asked why she disobeys, she tells the king that his laws have less authority than the ones she obeys: the eternal, unwritten laws of the gods.

[2] Gough, *The Social Contract,* p. 143.
[3] Ernest Barker, *Social Contract* (London: Oxford University Press, 1947), p. xxxvi.
[4] Gough, *The Social Contract,* p. 130.

Second, two basic forms of the contract can be distinguished. The first postulates people as being in a "state of nature," and agreeing to create an organized society. By "state of nature" is meant a situation prior to the emergence of government, prior, that is, to legislatures, courts of law, police, and public officials. The government is seen as a creation of the people; it emerges from the people and owes its very existence to them. The second approach does not imagine people *creating* government, but rather defining the terms of an implied contract between them and an existing government. This implied contract imposes obligations upon both parties: upon the government and the people. In the seventeenth century, for example, the people of England who wished to overthrow James II claimed that he had violated an implied contract: although this contract was not understood to explain the structure and formation of James' government, it was viewed as setting down certain conditions which he and the people were bound to follow.[5]

Third, amid the various versions of the social contract theory a common strand exists: an emphasis on the *consent* of the parties. Most versions invite one to imagine the situation in which rational people, outside ordinary society, must consent to a proposal about the structure of social institutions. The characteristics of the situation—for example, what information people are presumed to have, what interests they bring to the decision, or what issues they are to decide—vary from theory to theory. Yet each version relies upon the consent of the parties: force cannot be a factor, nor can techniques of persuasion.

Critics have repeatedly attacked the social contract for its failure to represent historical fact. No one, the critics charge, could seriously believe that people once gathered in the woods to establish a contract for the world's first governments. Marx and other theorists (such as Paley, Maine, and Blackstone) have made this very point. What is more, modern anthropology appears to confirm their suspicions.

But perhaps such criticism misses the mark, since, as was noticed already, social contract theories have typically been used to analyze *existing* institutions rather than to create new ones. Locke wanted to discover the moral foundation for English government, not dig up the historical causes of the Sumerian or Egyptian kingdoms. Even if no pen and ink contracts ever existed, many would argue that an abstract contract exists, not unlike the invisible laws of the gods, which obliges governments to serve the social welfare. Even if no pen and ink contract ever existed, they would argue that the point of the social contract is to clarify the *logical* presuppositions, not the historical antecedents, of political power.

APPLYING THE CONTRACT TO BUSINESS

The social contract has typically (though not always) been applied to governments. Is there any reason to suppose it is applicable to economic institutions? To productive organizations such as General Motors? One reason for doing so

[5] Gough, *The Social Contract,* p. 213.

is that companies like General Motors are social giants. They affect the lives of millions of people, influence foreign policy, and employ more people than live in many countries of the world. Equally important is the fact that General Motors exists only through the cooperation and commitment of society. It draws its employees from society, sells its goods to society, and is given its status by society. All of this may suggest the existence of an implied agreement between it and society. If General Motors holds society responsible for providing the condition of its existence, then for what does society hold General Motors responsible? What are the terms of the social contract?

Before we attempt to spell out the terms of the social contract, a prior issue must be settled; namely, *who* are the parties to the contract? So far we have spoken of a contract between society and business, but the concepts of both "business" and "society" are vague. "Business" might include, for example, independent businesspeople such as professional entertainers or craftsmen, as well as large corporations; or it might include *all* corporations, including nonproductive ones. For clarity, let us stipulate, then, that "business" refers to productive organizations: ones where people cooperate to produce at least one specific product or service. Productive organizations would include corporations (of the productive sort), manufacturing partnerships, and service organizations. Later this definition will need to be restricted further, but it will suffice for now.

By attempting to find the moral underpinnings of all productive organizations, we will indirectly be searching for the moral underpinnings of corporations. This happens because virtually all corporations, as we saw earlier, are productive organizations. Once the moral underpinnings of productive organizations are known, it will be possible to answer from a moral perspective questions such as why does General Motors exist and what is General Motors' fundamental purpose? Or, speaking more precisely, it will be possible to answer such questions about General Motors when General Motors is considered *as a member of the class of productive organizations.*

The term "society" is similarly vague. It might refer to the aggregate of individuals who make up society, or to something over and above the sum of those individuals. On the second interpretation, "society" might be construed as having interests (like Rousseau's "general will") which are not the direct products of its members' interests. For clarity, let us stipulate that the contract is between productive organizations and *individual members of society,* not between productive organizations and some supra-individual, social entity.

CONSTRUCTING A CONTRACT

The simplest way of understanding the social contract is in the form: "We (the members of society) agree to do X, and you (the productive organizations) agree to do Y." Applying this form to General Motors (or any productive organization) means that the task of a social contract argument is to specify X, where X

refers to the obligations of society to productive organizations, and to specify Y, where Y refers to the obligations of productive organizations to society.

It is relatively easy in this context to specify X, because what productive organizations need from society is:

1. Recognition as a single agent, especially in the eyes of the law.
2. The authority: (a) to own or use land and natural resources, and (b) to hire employees.

It may appear presumptuous to assume that productive organizations must be warranted by society. Can one not argue that any organization has a *right* to exist and operate? That they have this right *apart* from the wishes of society? When asking such questions, one must distinguish, as we did in Chapter 1, between claims about rights of mere organizations and claims about rights of organizations with special powers, such as productive organizations. A case can be made for the unbridled right of the Elks Club, whose members unite in fraternal activities, to exist and operate (assuming it does not discriminate against minorities or women); but the same cannot be said for Du Pont Corporation, which not only must draw on existing stores of mineral resources, but must find dumping sites to store toxic chemical by-products. Even granted that people have an inalienable right to form and operate organizations, and even granted that this right exists apart from the discretion of society, the productive organization requires special status under the law and the opportunity to use society's resources: two issues in which every member of society may be said to have a vested interest.

Conditions 1 and 2 are obviously linked to each other. In order for a productive organization to use land and hire employees (conditions of 2), it must have the authority to perform those acts as if it were an individual agent (the condition of 1). The philosophical impact of 1 should not be exaggerated. To say that productive organizations must have the authority to act as individual agents is not necessarily to affirm that they are abstract, invisible persons. Rather it is a means of stating the everyday fact that productive organizations must, for a variety of purposes, be treated as individual entities. For example, a corporation must be able to hire new employees, to sign contracts, and to negotiate purchases without getting the O.K. from *all* its employees and stockholders. The corporation *itself*, not its stockholders or managers, must be considered to be the controller of its equipment and land; for its stockholders or managers may leave, sell their shares, or die. If they do, the organization still controls its resources; it still employs its work force, and it still is obliged to honor its previous contracts and commitments.

Defining the Y side of the contract is as difficult as defining the X side is easy. It is obvious that productive organizations must be allowed to exist and act. But it is not obvious precisely why societies should allow them to exist, that is, what specific benefits society should hope to gain from the bargain. What specific functions should society expect from productive organizations? What obligations should it impose? Only one assumption can be made readily: that the members of society should demand at a minimum that the benefits from authorizing the existence of productive organizations outweigh the detriments of doing so. This is nothing other than the expectation of all voluntary agreements: that no party should be asked to conclude a contract which places him or her in a position worse than before.

The task of specifying society's terms for the social contract is a challenging one. To do so, let us return to a traditional device in social contract theory, the device of imagining society *without* the institution that is being analyzed. In short, let us consider society without productive organizations, in a "state of nature." Instead of the traditional state of nature where people live without government, we shall consider a state where people live without *productive organizations.* To avoid confusing this state with the traditional ones, let us call it the "state of individual production." Thus, the strategy involves:

1. Characterizing conditions in a state of individual production (without productive organizations).
2. Indicating how certain problems are remedied by the introduction of productive organizations.
3. Using the reasons generated in the second step as a basis for specifying a social contract between society and its productive organizations.

Such a strategy has obvious advantages. If step 2 indicates the specific benefits which society should expect from productive organizations, it should help specify the terms of the social contract.

The details must be spelled out. How are we to imagine the state of individual production? What people occupy it? Are they selfish? Charitable? How do they labor?

At a minimum the people in the state of individual production should be imagined as having "economic interests," i.e., as being people for whom it is desirable to have some things or services produced by human labor. Under such a definition almost any human would qualify, except perhaps ascetics or persons who prefer death to life. Thus, the people envisioned by the present strategy are ordinary, economically interested persons who have not yet organized themselves, or been organized, into productive organizations.

Should they be imagined as purely egoistic, wanting only to satisfy their own selfish interests, or as purely benevolent, wanting only to satisfy the interests of others? In the real world both characterizations are extreme—ordinary people are neither devils nor saints—and thus is suggested the strategy of assuming the same about people in the state of individual production. Let us adopt this strategy; if the contract has application to ordinary people, it will help to keep ordinary people in mind.[6]

---

[6]Some social contract theorists, e.g., Thomas Hobbes and John Rawls, have adopted a different approach, preferring to emphasize people's self-interested tendencies in the state of nature. This view has some definite advantages, since one can say "Even self-interested people will

To imagine a state of individual production, i.e., without productive organizations, is to imagine a society in which individuals produce and work alone. It is to imagine society without factories, banks, hospitals, restaurants, or railroads, since all these organizations, as well as many others, count as productive organizations, that is, they are organizations in which people cooperate to produce at least one specific product or service. (For our purposes, noneconomic factors such as family structure, religious attitudes, and educational interests shall be disregarded.) Now in such a state we may imagine any level of technology we wish. The only crucial fact is that people produce *individually*.

THE TERMS OF THE CONTRACT

Two principal classes of people stand to benefit or be harmed by the introduction of productive organizations: (1) people who consume the organizations' products, i.e., consumers; and (2) people who work in such organizations, i.e., employees. The two classes are broadly defined and not mutually exclusive. "Consumer" refers to anyone who is economically interested; hence virtually anyone qualifies as a consumer. "Employee" refers to anyone who contributes labor to the productive process of a productive organization, including managers, laborers, part-time support personnel, and (in corporations) members of the board of directors.

Benefits for Consumers

From the standpoint of our hypothetical consumers, productive organizations promise to *enhance the satisfaction of economic interests*. That is to say, people could hope for the introduction of productive organizations to better satisfy their interests for shelter, food, entertainment, transportation, health care, and clothing. The prima facie benefits for consumers include:

1. *Improving efficiency* through:
   a. Maximizing advantages of specialization.
   b. Improving decision-making resources.
   c. Increasing the capacity to use or acquire expensive technology and resources.
2. *Stabilizing levels of output and channels of distribution.*
3. *Increasing liability resources.*

Each benefit, of course, needs explanation.

---

agree to such and such a principle," and, in turn, one's argument gains a persuasive edge. Rawls does not literally assume that people are egoists, but he does assume that they wish to maximize their possession of primary goods. But in the present instance, no compelling reasons exist for representing people worse than they are, and one good reason does exist for representing them as they are: the presence of even ordinary (i.e., non-self-interested) motives can help clarify the conditions of the social contract.

The first benefit, improving efficiency, is the special excellence of productive organizations. Productive organizations tend to generate products that are equal or better in quality and price, with lower expenditures of human labor, than is possible in the state of individual production. Let us examine a few of the reasons for this remarkable capacity.

1A. Maximizing the advantages of specialization. Adam Smith's well-known thought-experiment in the *Wealth of Nations* provides ready evidence for the truth that two can often be more efficient than one. He showed that in the production of pins, one person working alone could account for a mere handful of pins, whereas in a system of first-order specialization—where one cuts the wire, another points the wire, and so on—the proportionate share of pins per worker increases dramatically. The same is true today. To produce clocks, erasers, and antibiotics efficiently, an enormous degree of cooperative specialization is required: the mere existence of products like the space shuttle owes itself to such specialization. Economists agree that many products are further subject to *economies of scale;* that is, their efficient production is dependent not only upon cooperative specialization, but on a certain level of it. Because of this factor, a company like American Motors may be too small to compete successfully with General Motors in the production of automobiles.

The greater efficiency which derives from productive organizations is partially dependent upon the level of technology. At minimal levels it may be less efficient to have such systems. One person working alone with stone implements may be able to clean and prepare vegetables as efficiently as three working in concert. At higher levels of technology this would not be true. The reverse is also possible: advanced technology may allow one person to be efficient in a situation where, minus the technology, he or she would not be. Equipped with a mechanical combine, one individual may be efficient at harvesting wheat, whereas without it six or more would be required. But no matter what the level of technology, some tasks benefit from cooperative specialization. Even in a futuristic, thoroughly technological society, a group of scientists who cooperate to perfect an additional piece of technology should, all other things being equal, be more efficient than an aggregate of individual scientists working without contact among themselves.

1B. Improving decision-making resources. Productive organizations share with individual persons the tendency to err in decision-making. Despite this, such organizations have decision-making advantages. First, they can utilize the ongoing talents of people with different backgrounds. Thus, a decision by Westinghouse, Inc., to manufacture a new appliance may call on the knowledge of chemists, accountants, engineers, and marketing specialists. One person could never possess such knowledge.

Second, they can increase information storage. In the same way a person can collect and remember information on a small scale, organizations do so on a large scale. Productive organizations can have superhuman memories: some corporations have libraries larger than those in universities, where all their information bears either directly or indirectly upon productive success.

1C. Increasing the capacity to use and acquire expensive technology and resources. This advantage is nearly self-evident. All other things being equal, two or more people will have greater financial resources than one; hence productive organizations can make capital expenditures on a larger scale than single individuals. Often the use of large, expensive equipment is important not only for increasing production, but for generating higher quality production, since expensive equipment is frequently necessary to improve productive efficiency. An individual who intends to produce bread cannot compete in today's world without mechanical ovens, assembly lines, and mechanical bread-slicers. Yet few individuals can afford such items, much less attempt to operate them single-handedly. By combining their energies and resources in a productive organization, people can increase the cost effectiveness of production.

2. Stabilizing levels of output and channels of distribution. The imaginary inhabitants of our state of individual production stand to benefit by the merging of individual craftsmen into organizations which are relatively stable, and whose level of output and pattern of distribution are relatively constant. Individual craftsmen are subject to illness, psychological problems, and the need for rest. For example, to rely on an individual mail carrier for the delivery of one's mail is riskier than depending on a large postal organization. Individuals must sleep, eat, and rest, but a large postal organization never sleeps, never eats—it even grows larger at Christmas. In general, then, productive organizations promise to stabilize the market for the benefit of the consumer.

3. Increasing liability resources. Under this heading are grouped the benefits that consumers reap because organizations, in contrast to individuals, have "deep pockets." In short, they are better able to compensate injured consumers. In the late 1970's Ford Motor Company was forced by the courts to compensate victims of the Ford Pinto's exploding gas tank. Because of design defects, the Pinto's tank was prone to ignite when hit from behind. The money paid by Ford to victims (and relatives of victims) was astounding; it ran into the millions of dollars. Although few productive organizations are as large as Ford, it remains true that organizations are better able to back their products with financial resources than individuals. Contrast the capacity of any automobile company in this regard with the capacity of the individual person who builds an auto in his or her backyard.

Benefits for Employees

These, then, are the prima facie benefits from introducing productive organizations for consumers. But productive organizations should also be viewed from the standpoint of their effects on people as workers, that is, from the standpoint of their effects upon individual laborers and craftsmen in the state of individual production who opt to work for productive organizations.

It is not difficult to discover certain prima facie benefits, such as the following:

1. Increasing income potential (and the capacity for social contributions).
2. Diffusing personal liability.
3. Adjusting personal income allocation.

1. Increasing income potential and capacity for social contributions. This benefit follows immediately from the earlier fact that cooperative specialization increases productive efficiency. The person, like Smith's hypothetical pin maker, who joins others in the production of pins is able to make many times more pins than he would alone. This increase also represents an increase in his chance to receive a higher income.

It also increases, if he is so inclined, his overall capacity to contribute to society. For if he feels some personal obligation to contribute productively to society, or if he merely wishes to be benevolent, his increased productivity increases his power of doing so. Two options are available: he can either accept lower than normal personal remuneration, thus increasing his net contribution; or he can accept normal remuneration and give some of it away. An example of the former would be those who work in voluntary organizations, e.g., the Women's Service League or the Peace Corps. An example of the latter is the person who works for a major company, but who donates some of his salary to charity. In any case, the person who increases his productivity by joining a productive organization thereby increases, all other things being equal, *both* his income potential and his capacity for contribution. Of course ambitious owners or unjust economic arrangements may deprive workers of the additional income which they (the workers) have generated. But this is a by-product of the particular owners or of particular economic systems, and not a feature of productive organizations per se.

2. Diffusing personal liability. A second prima facie benefit from the standpoint of workers lies in the capacity of an organization to diffuse liability, or in short, to insure the individual against the risk of massive compensation demands. A worker in the state of individual production who sells faulty, dangerous products is morally liable for the damages her product causes. If she negligently drops poison in the medicine she manufactures, then she is ethically bound to compensate the victim. But the extent of this liability can exceed her capacity to pay. Therefore she stands to gain by working with others in a productive organization, for it then becomes the productive organization, not she, who assumes ultimate liability.

3. Adjusting personal income allocation. The increased resources of the productive organization allow the worker to participate in an income-allocation scheme which is detached from the vicissitudes of his capacity to produce, and which is more closely tied to his actual needs. The vicissitudes of the worker's capacity include occasional illness, disabling accidents, and a tendency to lose speed and strength as he ages. Yet his needs persist and sometimes even increase in the face of these vicissitudes. The employee can work harder when he is healthy; but he needs as much money, and sometimes more, when he is ill. The worker may not be able to produce more when he is 50 than when he was 20, but if he marries and has a family his need for income may be greater at 50. When the worker joins a productive organization, the organization can allocate personal income according to a scheme more equitable for him and everyone else. Income may, for example, be raised in accordance with length of service, even in a proportion greater than the individual's productivity, and it can continue to be distributed to workers even when they are ill and disabled.

These prima facie benefits to the worker may be added to the prima facie consumer benefits discussed earlier. Together they constitute a set of reasons which rational people living in a state of individual production might use to justify the introduction of productive organizations. Indeed, if some such set of prima facie benefits did *not* exist, then people would be foolish to introduce such organizations; there would be nothing to gain.

It now becomes possible in light of this analysis to begin the task of specifying the general character of a hypothetical social contract. From the standpoint of society, the goal of a productive organization may be said to be *to enhance the welfare of society through a satisfaction of consumer and worker interests.* In turn, each of the prima facie benefits that we have discussed can be construed as specific terms of the social contract. Productive organizations should attempt to satisfy consumer interests through enhancing efficiency, stabilizing output, and augmenting liability, and they should attempt to satisfy employee interests through increasing income potential, diffusing personal liability, and adjusting income allocation. These terms of the contract thus constitute fundamental positive goals of productive organizations.

It is not in society's interest to settle for less instead of more. As mentioned earlier, it can choose either not to create productive organizations, or to create ones with different standards. A rational group of people in the state of individual production will *a fortiori* choose to create organizations that observe the highest standards—to maximize welfare—and will build such standards into the bargain.

Drawbacks for Consumers and Employees

An obvious question arises. If people in the state of individual production must agree upon the terms of the social contract, and if these terms directly relate to the task of enhancing society's welfare, then why stop with maximizing prima facie benefits? Why not also minimize prima facie drawbacks? John Locke employed a similar strategy in structuring his political social contract; he not only specified the positive goals of government, but, recognizing government's tendency to abuse privilege, also saw fit to specify certain pitfalls that government must avoid. Are there prima facie drawbacks to introducing productive organizations as well? Are there drawbacks from the standpoint of consumers? Of workers?

Our imaginary consumer stands to benefit because productive organizations, along with the technology they encourage, improve productivity and put more shoes, clothing, electricity, and automobiles on the market. But there is an unwanted consequence of which twentieth-century consumers are painfully aware: increased production tends to deplete natural resources while increasing pollution. More shoes, clothing, electricity, and automobiles require more leather, cotton, coal, and iron. The world has a finite supply. Moreover, the amazing machines so well adapted to productive organizations—the gas engines, the coal furnaces, and the nuclear reactors—all generate by-products which render the environment less fit for human life.

The problem of the increased pollution and depletion of natural resources is more obvious than a second problem, which is the diffusion of individual moral responsibility which sometimes occurs in productive organizations. In the state of individual production, the consumers buy their goods from the individual craftsman who stands behind his product, or at least if he does not, the consumers know where to go. When the cobbler sells a pair of shoes to John Doe and the shoes fall apart, he must confront Doe face to face. Contrast this situation with that of productive organizations, in which workers never see the consumer. To the employee, the consumer is faceless, and the employee's level of psychic accountability tends to lower along with a rise in consumer anonymity. The employee is responsible for his behavior, but to his superior, not to the customer; and his superior sometimes is more apathetic than he. In extreme instances the employee may participate in a form of rebellion unknown to the independent craftsman: "industrial sabotage," where workers retaliate against management by intentionally damaging products.

While speaking of potential drawbacks of productive organizations, one must also acknowledge that the political power of productive organizations is sometimes used to enhance individual interests. Such power sometimes is used to secure favors from government which damage both consumer interests and the interests of the general public. Organizations can receive favors which bolster monopoly power and aggravate inefficiency, as when the railroads in the United States in the late nineteenth century used government grants and privileges to develop a stranglehold on public transportation. Organizations can also use power to divert government expenditures from consumer items to items that actually harm the consumers' interests. In Germany prior to World Wars I and II, for example, large munitions manufacturers used their political influence to increase taxation, and thus decrease consumers' buying power, for massive purchases of cannons, tanks, fighter planes, and warships. Undeniably, from the overall standpoint of the German public, these purchases were disastrous.

From the perspective of consumers these problems represent potential drawbacks often associated with the introduction of productive organizations. But drawbacks also exist for employees.

Workers in the state of individual production possess a few obvious advantages. For one, they are close to the product and able to take pride in their own creations and the fact that their hands were responsible for the lamp, the soap, or the shirt being sold. But workers in productive organizations are typically removed from the product. They are, in the words of Marx, "alienated" in a way that may block their very capacity for self-expression. During World War II the U.S. aircraft manufacturers discovered that alienation was hampering production. Production was shown to increase when the draftsmen, riveters, and sheetmetal workers were taken to *see* the finished product they had worked on—the airplane itself.

In addition to possible alienation and loss of pride, the worker may also suffer from losing control over the design of the product and of his or her work structure. Whereas the individual craftsman can structure her hours and conditions to suit herself, the organizational worker must suit the needs of the overall organization. A man or woman working on an assembly line is powerless to improve the design of the product, and equally powerless to change the design of the work process. The look of the product, the speed of the conveyor belt, and even the number of steps to perform the task all have been determined by others, who are frequently strangers to the worker. Seldom even does the worker have control over safety arrangements or levels of in-plant pollutants.

The increased capacity of productive organizations (over individuals) to use large, expensive technology and massive resources reveals on the other side a decreased capacity of the workers to control their lives. They must adapt to the machines. If a machine operates most efficiently at a certain pace, then the worker must, like the spool boys of the nineteenth-century cotton industry, hurry to meet that pace. In such cases it is as if the machine were controlling the person instead of the person controlling the machine. Similarly, the increased efficiency which results from specialization reveals, on its reverse, the monotony of the simple task repeated thousands of times. The man who knocked the struts into place on the wheels of Henry Ford's Model T was far more efficient than the old craftsman who built a carriage from the bottom up. But the Ford worker knocked struts in place on wheels every minute of every working day.

These prima facie *drawbacks* may be seen as reasons for *not* introducing productive organizations. Unless the prima facie benefits discussed earlier outweigh these prima facie drawbacks, no contract will be concluded because rational people will not choose a lesser over a greater good. And if the benefits outweigh the drawbacks, it follows that in order maximally to enhance welfare, productive organizations should both pursue positive goals and minimize negative ones. Thus, using our discussion as a basis for this list of negative goals, we have:

From the standpoint of *consumers,* productive organizations should minimize:

1. Pollution and the depletion of natural resources.
2. The destruction of personal accountability.
3. The misuse of political power.

From the standpoint of *workers,* productive organizations should minimize:

1. Worker alienation.
2. Lack of worker control over work conditions.
3. Monotony and dehumanization of the worker.

Thus the social contract will specify that these negative consequences be minimized.

Trade-Offs

The social contract sketched out requires, then, that productive organizations maximize goods and minimize evils relative to consumer and worker welfare. But how will an organization know how to make the inevitable trade-offs between maximizing and minimizing, and between consumer interests and worker interests? For example, a corporate decision may impair worker interests while at the same time enhancing consumer interests. Consider the age-old trade-off between higher salaries and lower consumer prices. If coffee workers are paid higher salaries, then coffee drinkers pay higher prices. Conversely, if doctors are paid lower salaries, then patients pay lower prices. These trade-offs are common not only in the area of salaries, but in many others as well. Where does one draw the line?

How would the rational inhabitants of our state of individual production answer this question? Because the contract specifies that the function of productive organizations is to enhance the welfare of society, our inhabitants might choose a utilitarian standard for making trade-offs, that is, a standard that would specify that organizational policies or action should aim for *the greatest good for the greatest number.* On the other hand, they might prefer a nonutilitarian, or deontological standard, which would specify that *organizational action should accord with general policies or rules which could be universalized for all productive organizations* (i.e., which society would want all productive organizations to adopt).

Whatever the standard—and it must be acknowledged that determining the standard is difficult—two things seem certain. First, society does acknowledge that trade-offs often must be made. Society could not reasonably expect productive organizations to maximize worker interests come what may, say by adopting the policy of paying workers the absolute maximum possible at a given time, for to do so would grossly neglect consumers. If General Motors expended every bit of its resources on employees, the result for society would be catastrophic. Similarly, the consumer must not receive all the attention. Such a policy would result in poor working conditions, low salaries, and frustrated workers (no matter how satisfied employees might be in their life as consumers).

Because trade-offs must be made, it remains logically possible that people in the state of individual production would choose to introduce productive organizations and to establish the social contract, even when they expected either worker interests or consumer interests to be less satisfied than in the state of nature—so long as *overall* welfare were enhanced. In other words, the inhabitants might believe that, on balance, people as workers stand to lose from the introduction of productive organizations, and that potential alienation, loss of control, and other drawbacks make the overall condition of the worker worse than before. But if the benefits to people as consumers fully *overshadowed* these drawbacks, we should still expect the contract to be enacted.

Justice

There is a caveat which has application to the overall contract. People would make a trade-off of the kind just discussed only on the condition that it did not violate certain minimum standards of justice, however these are specified. For example, they would refuse to enact the contract if they knew that the existence of productive organizations would systematically reduce a given class of people to an inhuman existence, subsistence poverty, or enslavement.

This point, in turn, provides a clue to one of the specific tenets of the contract. Although the contract might allow productive organizations to undertake actions requiring welfare trade-offs, it would prohibit organizational acts of injustice. It might allow a corporation to lay off, or reduce the salaries of, thousands of workers in order to block skyrocketing production costs; here, worker welfare would be diminished while consumer welfare would be enhanced. But it is another matter when the company commits gross injustices in the process—for example, if it lies to workers, telling them that no layoffs are planned merely to keep them on the job until the last minute. Similarly, it is another matter when the organization follows discriminatory hiring policies, refusing to hire blacks or women, in the name of "consumer advantage." These are clear injustices of the kind that society would want to prohibit as a condition of the social contract. We may infer, then, that a tenet of the social contract will be that productive organizations are to remain within the bounds of the general canons of justice.

Determining what justice requires is a notoriously difficult task. The writings of Plato, Aristotle, and more recently, John Rawls, have shed considerable light on this subject, but unfortunately we must forego a general discussion of justice here. At a minimum, however, the application of the concept of justice to productive organizations appears to imply *that productive organizations avoid deception or fraud, that they show respect for their workers as human beings, and that they avoid any practice that systematically worsens the situation of a given group in society.* Despite the loud controversy over what justice means, most theorists would agree that justice means at least this much for productive organizations.

An Overview of the Contract

Our sketch of a hypothetical social contract is now complete. By utilizing the concept of rational people existing in a state of individual production, we have indicated the terms of a contract which they would require for the introduction of productive organizations. The questions asked in the beginning were: Why should corporations exist at all? What is the fundamental justification for their activities? How can we measure their performance, to say when they have performed poorly or well? A social contract helps to answer these questions. Corporations considered as productive organizations exist to enhance the welfare of society through the satisfaction of consumer and worker interests, in a way which relies on exploiting corporations' special advantages and minimizing disadvantages. This is the *moral foundation* of the corporation when considered as a productive organization. The social contract also serves as a tool to measure the performance of productive organizations. That is, when such organizations fulfill the terms of the contract, they have done well. When they do not, then society is morally justified in condemning them.

Productive organizations (whether corporations or not) that produce quality goods at low prices, that reject government favoritism, and that enhance the well-being of workers receive high marks by the standards of the social contract. Those that allow inefficiency, charge high prices, sell low-quality products, and fail to enhance the well-being of workers receive low marks. The latter organizations have violated the terms of the social contract. They must reform themselves, or lose their moral right to exist.

It is well to notice that such a social contract does not specify additional obligations or rights which *corporations* have in contrast to *productive organizations* in general. The social contract justifies corporations as *productive organizations*, not as *corporations*. Presumably, then, further reasons remain to be discovered for society's establishing a certain type of productive organization, such as the corporation—with limited liability, stockholder ownership, and its other characteristics. The important task of discovering those reasons, however, must wait for another occasion. Our development of the social contract has fallen short of a full moral comprehension of corporations, but it has secured a solid footing in an equally important area: comprehending the moral underpinnings of productive organizations.

THE SOCIAL RESPONSIBILITY OF BUSINESS

Assuming that such a contract exists, it clashes with the argument of the controversial economist Milton Friedman, in his article entitled "The Social Responsibility of Business Is to Increase Its Profits."[7] There Friedman condemns "social responsibility" by appealing to the "fiduciary" duties of managers. He argues that when stockholders bring a company into existence through buying stock, they do so on the condition that corporate managers will follow their wishes —usually, to make a profit. A moral obligation is thus generated for managers, namely, to serve as fiduciaries for profit-seeking investors; and it follows that using

[7]"The Social Responsibility of Business Is to Increase Its Profits," *The New York Times Magazine,* September 13, 1970.

e managerial activity. This is because even the right to make voluntary
ts has been shown to have exceptions; and, as also demonstrated, there
overriding moral considerations (such as the social contract). Friedman's
t is incomplete, on the other hand, if it is meant to imply that the exist-
a voluntary agreement generates a prima facie obligation for the manager
e profit. That implication is correct as far as it goes, but it neglects to
that there may be other responsibilities which are incumbent on the
r stemming from different sources—in this case, from a moral obligation
ed through a social contract.

In fairness both to Friedman and others who take similar positions, it must
itted that considerations other than the right to undertake voluntary agree-
can be invoked to defend the propriety of profit maximizing. For example,
an argues elsewhere that a system in which productive organizations attempt
ximize profit yields *maximum consumer satisfaction.*[10] It might even be
ed that the social contract is *best* satisfied when business managers pursue
sive profit maximization. If this were true, the social responsibility of business
d remain with satisfying the social contract, but the way to satisfy it would be
gh profit maximization. It would be a bit like telling a golfer *not* to aim at his
t but to aim left of it to counteract his slice. The possibility that the social
ract is served by profit maximization will be investigated in detail in the next
ter.

PLICATIONS OF THE SOCIAL CONTRACT

It might be imagined that the social contract implies that consumers and
orkers should participate in the management of productive organizations since
e interests of these groups are the basis of the contract itself. Many corporate
eformers recommend co-determination of the corporation by all affected parties.
ome endorse experiments with worker-controlled factories similar to those in
Yugoslavia, and others recommend placing public and employee representatives
on boards of directors in accordance with the West German model (West Germany
has incorporated co-determination into the governing mechanism of many of her
corporations). It might be argued that such proposals are directly supported by
the social contract.

Caution, however, is in order. As noted above, even arguments for profit
maximization can be launched in the name of the social contract. An attempt also
could be made to prove that the contract is best fulfilled when organizations are
controlled by professional managers. Whether the empirical evidence justifies such
a view is the crucial issue. From the perspective of the social contract, the questions of organizational structure must be decided in terms of how well various
structures satisfy the contract. What the preceding analysis has shown is that any

[10]Milton Friedman, *Capitalism and Freedom* (Chicago: University of Chicago Press, 1962).

the stockholders' money otherwise, say, to conforn
tantamount to stealing.[8]

This argument owes its credibility to the san
agreements. We champion voluntary agreements and be
make them, good or bad. When a person has freely oblig
presumably does to the stockholder who contributes cap
with the agreement, at inserting additional conditions.

It is obvious, however, that the social contract
voluntary agreements and contracts, but only those who
commit managers to act contrary to the terms of the soc
commitments by managers to pursue profits are excluded, l
to pursue profits in a way that conflicts with the contract. I
commitments that violate the contract should be made *illegal*.
ses a *moral* force in the sense of providing the moral founds
organizations, yet its legal implications have not yet been clarifi

The significant question, then, is whether the moral f
is in conflict with the right of managers to make voluntary agre
holders. The answer is that it is not. To begin with, almost no
rights understands rights as exceptionless principles: rights can cc
to own the fruits of one's labor does not permit one to *own* one'
one is a woman who bore the children, because children have a
which *outweighs* the earlier right.[9] Similarly, if managers have rig
agreements with stockholders, then workers and consumers also ha
may take priority. For example, if managers voluntarily agree to
even at the expense of workers' lives, then the workers' right to lif
precedence.

But although one right can sometimes outweigh another, c
contract ever outweigh a right? Can something other than a right outw
Frequently nonrights considerations do outweigh certain rights. For ex
ple are said to have the right to control their property, yet an excepti
when governments condemn property for public purposes, say, to build i
act is justified by an overriding public interest. Thus, the fact that the soci
is not itself a right does not preclude its overriding rights under certai
stances. To take an obvious example: the social contract's requirement
ductive organizations serve consumer interests would *outweigh* the rig
stockholder and manager to agree to market an inherently dangerous produc

Thus Friedman's claim that the social responsibility of business is
to increase its profits is either in error or incomplete. It is in error if it is me
imply that the force of a hypothetical fiduciary agreement between manage
stockholder prevents managers from using the social contract as the yardstic

[8] As will be shown later, however, the U.S. courts have disagreed with this principle, allo
corporations to give up to 5 percent of profit to charity.

[9] Lawrence C. Becker, "The Labor Theory of Property Acquisition," *Journal of Philosop*
73 (1976), 657.

organizational structure *must take into account* the interests of consumers and rank-and-file workers. Functional myopia must be avoided: the productive organization exists to satisfy more than one privileged group in society.

To conclude, it must be said that the most important application of the social contract sketched out in this chapter is evaluation of the performance of productive organizations from a moral perspective. We have seen that the productive organization cannot be viewed as an isolated moral entity unconstrained by the demands of society, for its very reason for existing lies with its capacity to satisfy certain social interests. Productive organizations, whether U.S. corporations or not, are subject to moral evaluations which transcend the boundaries of the political systems that contain them. The underlying function of all such organizations from the standpoint of society is to enhance social welfare through satisfying consumer and worker interests, while at the same time remaining within the bounds of justice. When they fail to live up to these expectations, they are deserving of moral criticism. When an organization, in the United States or elsewhere, manufactures a product that is inherently dangerous, or when it pushes its employees beyond reasonable limits, it deserves moral condemnation: the organization has failed to live up to a hypothetical contract—a contract between itself and society.

When Henry Ford II referred to the social contract, he left the term "social contract" undefined. This chapter has attempted to sharpen the focus of what such a contract might mean, and thereby clarify the content of a corporation's indirect obligations. Clearly, other methods of specifying the contract are possible, and the version presented in this chapter should not be regarded as the last word. Whatever form it takes, however, the social contract expresses an underlying conviction that corporations exist to serve more than themselves. This conviction emerges in the speeches of businesspeople as well as in the writings of philosophers. It is the conviction expressed by the inventor of the Model T, the grandfather of Henry Ford II, when he said: "For a long time people believed that the only purpose of industry is to make a profit. They were wrong. Its purpose is to serve the general welfare."[11]

SUGGESTED SUPPLEMENTARY READINGS

AACKER, D., and G. DAY, *Consumerism: Search for the Consumer Interest.* New York: Free Press, 1974.

BARKER, SIR ERNEST, *Social Contract.* London: Oxford University Press, 1947.

BARRY, BRIAN, *Political Argument.* London: Routledge & Kegan Paul, 1965.

BENN, S. I., and R. S. PETERS, *The Principles of Political Thought.* New York: Free Press, 1959.

[11] Quoted in David Ewing, *Freedom Inside the Organization* (New York: McGraw-Hill, 1977), p. 65.

BOWIE, NORMAN E., and ROBERT SIMON, *The Individual and the Political Order*. Englewood Cliffs, N.J.: Prentice-Hall, 1977.

HOBBES, THOMAS, *Leviathan*. Oxford: Oxford University Press, 1948.

KANT, IMMANUEL, *The Metaphysical Elements of Justice*, tr. John Ladd. Indianapolis: Bobbs-Merrill, 1965.

LESSNOFF, M. H., "Justice, Social Contract, and Universal Prescriptivism," *The Philosophical Quarterly*, 28 (January 1978): 65-73.

PAUL, ELLEN, "On the Theory of the Social Contract Within the Natural Rights Traditions," *The Personalist*, 59 (January 1978): 9-28.

RAWLS, JOHN, *A Theory of Justice*. Cambridge, Mass.: Harvard University Press, 1971.

STEINER, HILLEL, "The Natural Right to the Means of Production," *The Philosophical Quarterly*, 27 (January 1977).

STERBA, JAMES, "Justice as Dessert," *Social Theory and Practice*, 3 (Spring 1974): 101-116.

CHAPTER 4

Challenging
Corporate Responsibility

C ritics insist that doctrines of corporate responsibility can be economically dangerous. They charge that corporate deliberation about moral issues may cut sales, promote moral arrogance, and breed inefficiency. Since the business of business is business, they ask, what are corporations doing wasting time on abstract issues of ethics? Consider the following case: Years ago, a small metal fabricating company named Multifab opened in Tulsa, Oklahoma. Organized by public-spirited businessmen, the company operated on the assumption that good business and social responsibility go hand in hand, and it planned to train and employ minimally skilled workers who would share in the profits of the company. The promotional literature boasted that the "free enterprise system of earning a profit" would be used to "demonstrate the concept of self-help through mutual assistance."[1]

Multifab was a complete flop. Despite massive aid from the Tulsa business community, it fell quickly into the red, lost its customers one by one, and was eventually chalked off as a failure even by its founders. Cases such as Multifab are common enough to warrant attention: many businesses begin with the noble intention of mixing social responsibility with profit only to founder on the rocks of economic realities.

Or consider the case of General Motors, which in the late 1960's was confronted with a list of demands from a handful of stockholders organized by Ralph Nader. The stockholders demanded that General Motors design a car to be crash-testable at 60 m.p.h., devote as much money to pollution control as to

---

[1] Lyle Trueblood, "Multifab Manufacturing Company," in *Business and Society: Cases and Text,* ed. Robert Hay and Edmund Gray (Cincinnati: South-Western, 1976), p. 250.

advertising, and provide 50,000-mile, five-year warranties on all cars.[2] G.M.'s management was probably correct when it said that the demands would price the company out of the market. Consumers were unwilling to accept the larger price tags that social responsibility brought, and prior to mandatory seat belts few paid even the small amount necessary to install them as options.

J. M. Roche, chairman of the board of General Motors, replied to the Nader campaign by emphasizing General Motors' *economic* contribution to society. General Motors, he pointed out, provided quality cars to society at reasonable prices. "The Board of Directors sincerely believes" he said, "that General Motors could not have achieved its record of growth and progress unless it had well served the interests of the public and the stockholders."[3] Implicit in his remark is the suggestion that profitability is a litmus test for corporate responsibility.

By themselves, cases like Multifab and General Motors prove little; but they raise the troublesome issue of the extent to which, if at all, corporate moral deliberation might foster undesirable consequences. We live in a competitive world, and corporations must compete not only with domestic industry but with increasingly efficient foreign industries. The Japanese regularly embarrass U.S. firms by undercutting prices for transistors, video machines, and autos. The game of business is tough. Does not the bulk of a company's moral responsibility lie, some ask, in efficiently satisfying consumer interests? Was this not part of the social contract sketched out in the last chapter? And might not embracing *non*economic responsibilities—valorous though it may be—reduce efficiency in satisfying consumer interests? With this in mind, some economists and businesspeople have concluded that corporations should adopt policies of "moral disinterest."

Let us note that corporate moral disinterest is not necessarily in conflict with the doctrine that corporations have moral responsibilities. If it could be shown that the best way to satisfy responsibilities is (ironically) to forget about them and focus on profits, then disinterest might be the optimal policy. This possibility was not ruled out in the last chapter. Perhaps I.B.M., General Electric, and Pepsi-Cola will best satisfy the social contract, *not* when they try to calculate what they "ought" to do, but when they maximize profits by producing the computers, refrigerators, and soft drinks people want.

The seeming virtues of moral disinterest are dramatized in a classical article by Theodore Levitt entitled "The Dangers of Social Responsibility."[4] Levitt asserts that executives should abandon talk about social responsibility because although it seems benign enough when heard at public banquets and board meetings, it obscures the fact that corporations are not designed to promote, nor are they efficient at handling, social issues. Doing that is the business of gov-

---

[2] John W. Collins, "Campaign to Make General Motors Responsible," in *Business and Society,* ed. Hay and Gray (Cincinnati: South-Western, 1976), pp. 51-69.

[3] Collins, "Campaign," p. 59.

[4] Theodore Levitt, "The Dangers of Social Responsibility," *Harvard Business Review* (September-October, 1958).

ernment, of publicly elected officials. According to Levitt, the best guide to business success is and always has been the profit motive. Talk of social responsibility is dangerous precisely because it creates misplaced guilt that might prompt regressive social actions by business. Were business to become a protector of the welfare of society, the result could be disastrous. Corporate officials are not democratically elected, Levitt reminds us, and "Nothing is more corrupting than self-righteousness." Some people regard his remarks as foreshadowing the problems of the 1960's and 1970's, in Chili and elsewhere, when U.S. corporations acting presumably for the national welfare helped support corrupt military regimes. For Levitt, business should stick to business; it has no "holy mission," and it ought not become a new "Church."

And so we are brought to an impasse. How is it possible on the one hand to take seriously the demands of the social contract as outlined in Chapter 3, while on the other accounting for the economic realities that confront modern business? One thing seems clear: we must assess in greater detail the validity of the arguments in favor of policies of corporate moral disinterest.

The origins of these arguments lie squarely in the history of economic and philosophical thought, and so the first step is to sketch—using broad strokes—some of those classical arguments.

THE HISTORICAL ROOTS OF THE CHALLENGE

History is full of two kinds of treatise on this subject: one attempts to glorify money-making, the other to condemn it. The earlier the treatise was written, the better the chances of its being a condemnation. In the Medieval Christian Church, the love of riches was labeled "avarice" and elevated to be one of the Seven Deadly Sins. Still earlier, Plato was openly critical of the mercantile spirit, believing that it corrupted individual virtue. In his ideal state, the Republic, he denies all private property to the Guardians who must rule the state. If pursuing money is evil—if not the root of evil—why is it given the place of honor in modern capitalism?

The philosophical roots of the defense of money-making reach far beyond Adam Smith's invisible hand, back to the simple idea that one passion can block another passion. By the time of the Renaissance, the view of St. Augustine and others that all passions are bad and should be eliminated had given way to the more modern view, that although all passions may be bad, some are better than others, and in any case the better ones should counter the worse ones. It is in this spirit that the seventeenth-century philosopher Benedict Spinoza wrote, "the only thing that can counter one emotion is another emotion."

When philosophers began turning their attention to the questions of social engineering, or of how best to structure society for the common good, Spinoza's view found ready application. The social philosopher Montesquieu applied it not to money, but to honor. The result was an "invisible hand" of a different sort: "The pursuit of honor in a monarchy," he wrote, "brings life to all the parts of the body politic"; as a result, "it turns out that everyone contributes to the general welfare while thinking that he works for his own interests."[5]

When the idea was applied to the world of commerce, it was hoped that money-making would be able to restrain the more dangerous passions for war, glory, and power. The historian A. O. Hirschman writes that the reaction to money-making in the eighteenth century by the intellectual and administrative elite was "favorable, not because the money-making activities were approved in themselves, but because they were thought to have a most beneficial side effect: they kept the men who were engaged in them 'out of mischief,' as it were, and had more specifically, the virtue of imposing restraints on princely caprice, arbitrary government, and adventurous foreign policies."[6] One of the eighteenth-century thinkers who subscribed to this view, William Robertson, declared that "Commerce tends to wear off those prejudices which maintain distinctions and animosity between nations. It *softens and polishes* the manners of men."[7]

Adam Smith's Defense of the Profit Motive

The eighteenth-century moral philosopher Adam Smith shared the brighter view of money-making. Best known for his theory of the "invisible hand," Smith argued that the pursuit of self-interest in the marketplace can result in tangible benefits for society. A free market, he said, exhibits a spontaneous order so remarkable that it suggests the existence of an external natural force which directs self-interest toward the common good; this is the famous "invisible hand." It is not from the benevolence of the butcher, the brewer, or the baker that we receive our dinner, Smith said, but from their regard of their own self-interest. We speak to them not in terms of *our* own necessities, but of *their* advantage.

Each merchant pursues his own self-interest, but to do so he must minister to the interests of others. If the consumer wants yams, he must supply yams; if silk stockings, then silk stockings; and if the consumer wants improved eyesight, then—if the merchant is sufficiently clever—he will invent and supply eyeglasses. Because the market is free, excess profits are impossible; a profit-oriented merchant is barred from selling his yams or stockings for a penny more than they are worth, for if he tries, another merchant will sell his for a penny less. Better quality, better availability, better prices—these are what the merchant must contribute to his fellow humans if he is to maximize his own self-interest.

Prior to Smith, self-interest was often identified with vice, and benevolence with virtue. But for Smith virtue is not the absence of self-interest; rather it is the restraint and moderation of it into proper channels. For this reason it is not correct to characterize his defense of self-interest, as some have done, through the catch phrase, "Private vices can be turned into public virtues." That was the maxim

---

[5] Albert O. Hirschman, *The Passions and the Interests* (Princeton, N.J.: Princeton University Press, 1977), p. 130.

[6] *Esprit des lois,* Book III, Chapter VII (trans. A. O. Hirschman).

[7] William Robertson, *View of the Progress of Society in Europe* (1769).

of an earlier economist named Mandeville, who equated virtue with the absence of self-interest. If virtue were synonymous with the absence of self-interest, or with asceticism, Smith pointed out, then civilization could advance only at the expense of virtue. The only level of economic success morally justifiable would be a minimal one which merely satisfied basic human needs. It is not morally evil to seek satisfaction of one's nonbasic desires, and in Smith's famous book, *The Wealth of Nations,* he instructs society in the best means of doing so.[8]

According to Smith, however, society must pay a price for the invisible hand: it must allow it sufficient freedom to operate. In particular, he believed that society must struggle to prevent the suffocation of the free market by monopolies or government intervention. Businessmen, Smith thought, were continually drifting toward monopolies, and governments continually toward destructive intervention. He had little faith in the tendencies of businessmen, but even less in government, which he regarded as fundamentally stupid and inept. Freeing the natural mechanism of the market from the intrusions of government ranked high on Smith's list of economic priorities. The pursuit of profit could enliven and advance society, but only in the context of a free market.

Smith's arguments against government intervention should be placed in the context of one of his principal ambitions in *The Wealth of Nations:* the refutation of mercantilism. Mercantilism, the leading economic theory of Europe for hundreds of years, presupposed the existence of a fixed amount of wealth, so that the task of the economist became that of devising strategies for nations to secure bigger pieces of the fixed economic pie. Nations hoarded gold, regulated commerce, and imposed heavy tariffs, embargoes, and quotas. Smith discovered mercantilism's flaw, however, when he realized it had no way of explaining the sources of wealth. Smith himself was able to provide the explanation: Wealth, he said, derives from (1) capital and (2) the division of labor (specialization). The game of economics was forever changed. The new challenge became that of devising strategies for more efficiently employing capital and labor and, in turn, reevaluating the bankrupt policies of mercantilism. Instead of the intervention championed by mercantilism, economists came to advertise the benefits of free trade, free market entry, and free pricing.

Despite his emphasis on the role of self-interest in generating economic growth, Smith regarded the pursuit of wealth as problematic from a moral standpoint. He disagreed sharply with his old teacher of philosophy, Hucheson, who claimed that self-interest could never be good, but he agreed that the chief human virtue is not self-interest, but benevolence. Wealth, for Smith, was fraught with illusory pleasures, and he wrote that it is the "deception of the pleasures of wealth which rouses and keeps in continual motion the industry of mankind." A scholar once gave the following nutshell account of Smith's invisible hand: Imagine, he

---

[8] Adam Smith, *An Inquiry into the Nature and Causes of the Wealth of Nations,* 1776; reprinted in the *Glasgow Edition of the Works and Correspondence of Adam Smith,* ed. R. H. Campbell (London: Oxford University Press, 1976); also reprinted (London: Cannon Press, 1930).

said, someone who lies in bed every night, unable to sleep because he is furiously calculating how to achieve a higher salary, a larger estate, or a new yacht. Now Smith's message is only this: that the free market, because it requires that people satisfy the needs of others, provides a social structure in which even such a selfish person will contribute to overall welfare.

Smith's championing of self-interest must be held in perspective. So far was he from offering a blanket endorsement of the pursuit of profit that he viewed the motives of businessmen as regularly at odds with laissez-faire. "People of the same trade seldom meet together," he reports, "but the conversation ends in a conspiracy against the public, or in some contrivance to raise prices."

His suspicion of commercial motives is accompanied by an acknowledgement that even the invisible hand requires a solid foundation of moral and civic virtues.[9] Unless moral concepts are generally accepted throughout society, unless honesty, fairness, trust, and goodwill are the norm rather than the exception, Smith asked, then how can business affairs be successfully transacted? For example, *The Wealth of Nations* divides industrial society into laborers, landlords, and capitalists, all for the express purpose of determining how, if at all, the interest of each class is compatible with the interests of society at large.

The picture sketched of Smith indicates that his thinking has a clearly moral flavor. At every turn he justifies economic practices by reference to their contribution to social welfare. His attitude toward the inevitable gap between rich and poor in capitalistic society bears this out. Though acknowledging that the poor suffer in comparison with the rich, Smith believed they are better off than they would be otherwise. Wealth in civilized society extends down to the humblest classes; it trickles down to benefit even the worst off, and "The English peasant," Smith remarks, "is better accommodated than the African King."[10]

Consider his attitude toward the tedium brought on by specialization. He grants that people will be stifled by the monotonous, repetitive tasks the division of labor creates; but having granted it, he allows that the government has a moral obligation to help alleviate the problem by offering educational opportunities to the poor. Thus, although people may be bored at work, they will be more able to exercise their intellectual talents off the job. Again, Smith's concern for morality is obvious, even when it means, as it does here, espousing government intervention.

Can Smith's moral defense of the profit motive be applied to *corporations*? The answer to this question may depend on which part of Smith's philosophy one emphasizes. Most of his discussion is cast in terms of individuals, or at most classes of individuals, and he seldom speaks of the "corporation" per se. Surprisingly, he was skeptical about the possibility of corporations' becoming major economic forces. Few corporations existed in his day and he believed that unless corporations could develop monopoly privileges, they held little promise except in a few isolated fields where all the operations could be reduced to "routine." (He gave as examples: banking, operating canals, and insurance.)

[9]For an analysis of how Smith's system requires a moral underpinning, see Warren J. Samuels, "The Political Economy of Adam Smith," *Ethics,* 87 (April 1977), 189-207.

[10]Smith, *Wealth of Nations* (London: Cannon Press, 1930), p. 6.

Thus, the conclusions one draws concerning Smith's prescriptions for corporations must be extrapolated largely from his remarks about individuals. With this in mind, if one stresses his endorsement of individual virtue and his belief that benevolence, not self-interest, should guide the individual, then it follows that moral motives are as crucial for corporations as for individuals. But if one stresses the other side of Smith—the side championing the role of self-interest—then one may conclude that corporate self-interest deserves vindication.

Perhaps it is wrong even to squeeze Smith's theory of individual self-interest to fit the more modern mold of corporate self-interest. Individual self-interest still wears a human face and is understood in terms of human characteristics: of desires, passions, hopes, and fears. The corporation has no passions or fears; it is not restricted by a natural life span, and it maintains power and influence which dwarfs that of individuals.

In any event Smith's view cannot be that the exclusive pursuit of profit by corporations is compatible with society's maximum overall welfare. This would clash with his belief that, at a minimum, a viable economic system demands that its participants generally adhere to the common moral norms of society. Were a trade-off to occur between maximizing profit and adhering to standards of morality, then Smith is bound to advise in favor of the latter and against the former. We are reminded of his remark that:

> In the race for wealth . . . he may run as hard as he can, and strain every nerve and every muscle, in order to outstrip all his competitors. But if he should jostle, or throw down any of them, the indulgence of the spectators is at an end. It is a violation of fair play, which they cannot admit of.[11]

Thus the consequences of Smith's philosophy for the doctrine of corporate profit maximization are mixed. He offers a moral defense of the pursuit of profit by individuals and, perhaps by analogy, corporations. But he does not offer a vindication of social irresponsibility or of an "anything goes" philosophy, as some have contended. For Smith, economics and ethics are a natural unity: separating them is as impossible as separating the concept of "number" from mathematics. For stronger criticisms of moral responsibility in corporate affairs, and for philosophies that do endorse a sharp separation between economics and ethics, we must look not to the eighteenth century but to the nineteenth and twentieth, to the writings of the Social Darwinists, and later Milton Friedman.

Social Darwinism

The revolution in thinking which transformed a deadly sin into a savior for humankind failed to persuade everyone. It failed especially to persuade many of the nineteenth-century intellectuals living in the wake of the Industrial Revolution who discovered that the supposedly benign effects of money-making apparently included poverty-level wages, dangerous working conditions, and children in the

---

[11] Adam Smith, *The Glasgow Edition of the Works and Correspondence of Adam Smith* (London: Oxford University Press, 1977), p. 83.

factories. By the middle of the nineteenth century it was obvious that capitalism had its ugly side, but the revolution it had nurtured largely remained. In particular, it was impossible that society should return to the old and Medieval view of money-making. The pursuit of wealth had its faults, and it was not a guarantee of perpetual international peace, but it was an acceptable human activity and not a sin. It was an "interest," not a "passion."

Meanwhile, the obvious shortcomings of the Industrial Revolution required justification. With the same zeal for unobstructed markets as Smith, but with little of his underlying rationale, the Social Darwinists rose to the challenge. They diagnosed the ills of the Industrial Revolution not as the result of self-interest but as the inevitable price of evolutionary "advancement." Drawing on Darwin's theory of biological evolution, the Social Darwinists argued that just as plants and animals struggle in life-death competition, so people and corporations struggle for economic survival. And just as some species of plant and animal win in the process of natural selection, so some people and corporations win in the pursuit of profit. The greater the profits, the greater their proof of economic superiority. And the more society allows the struggle to proceed unrestrained, the more society benefits; for the weak, inefficient players will fall away and leave only the best to control society.

The remarkable popularity of Social Darwinism faded quickly. Critics pointed out that the theory allows severe inequalities in wealth; while one man might own half the country's railroads and leave hundred-dollar bills for his dinner guests to light their cigarettes, another might live in poverty and go hungry at dinner. Such inequities made little difference to Social Darwinism: economically destitute people were seen as the unfortunate by-products of a natural process in which there are winners and losers. Soon onlookers began to realize that Social Darwinism's analogy between evolution in nature and success in the marketplace was strained to the breaking point. Because Darwin's original theory decreed that a species' success in the evolutionary drama is measured ultimately by the abundance and permanence of its offspring, the theory holds no implications for how species *ought,* morally speaking, to evolve. One criterion for success in Darwin's theory is abundance of progeny, so that the cockroach is an evolutionary winner and the saber tooth tiger a loser; but the theory says nothing about the cockroach's increased capacity over the tiger to contribute to the world. Similarly, there are by analogy no implications for how the survival of a particular business firm will enhance social welfare, even *if* we could construe business on the model of natural selection—a possibility which Darwin himself explicitly denied. Darwin described the world as it is, not as it ought to be. It is little surprise that near the end of the nineteenth century the doctrine of Social Darwinism died a timely death.

Joseph Schumpeter and the Role of the Entrepreneur

Classical economists such as Adam Smith, J. S. Mill, and David Ricardo construed economics as a "moral science" the business of which was not only to describe reality as it "is" but to make normative judgments about how it "ought" to be. Most, for example, believed in free markets. But Neoclassical economists in the later nineteenth century, such as Jevons, Walras, and Marshall, broke step with this tradition by declaring economics to be "value neutral." Although their hearts remained with free enterprise, they renounced attempts to make economic theories speak directly to political and moral issues, including even the issue of laissez-faire. Using a method of analysis known as "marginal utility theory," they postponed value issues while attempting to purify and professionalize economics—a major consequence of which was to mathematize it.

Even as proclamations of theoretical "neutrality" were made, faith in the profit motive remained strong. One of the most respected Neoclassical defenders of profit was Joseph Schumpeter (1883-1950), who launched a theoretical campaign on behalf of profit-seeking entrepreneurs which is staggering in its complexity and comprehensiveness. His theory is outlined in two major works, *The Theory of Economic Development* and *Capitalism, Socialism and Democracy*.[12]

Schumpeter begins with a concept of pure competition called "market equilibrium." Capitalism, he says, tends to settle naturally into equilibrium, which is defined as a hypothetical state in which all production is the result of land and labor, or, in other words, the result of nature's gifts *plus* people's work. In this hypothetical state there can be no profits because, just as in the earlier instance of the merchant with inflated prices, the demands of the market will force down the selling price of any commodity, and in *pure* competition it is forced to rock bottom. I cannot sell oranges for a penny more than it costs me to produce them, because if I do you will undercut my price and dominate the market. Naturally enough, equilibrium presents a dismal, frustrating prospect to the person eager to make money, for he cannot build his fortune with nonexistent profits.

But this ambitious person, as it turns out, is the crucial factor which overthrows the state of equilibrium and plants the seed for the evolution of capitalism. Because this person, the "entrepreneur," recognizes that equilibrium allows no profits, he knows he must discover a means to provide the market with something *in addition to* labor and land. He must therefore introduce new products, new methods, new sources of supply, or find new markets. These innovations combine to create a force which Schumpeter calls "development." In the state of equilibrium the entrepreneur was forced to sell oranges at the same rock-bottom price as others. So, to sell at a higher price he must produce a "better" orange, or invent a system to produce *more* oranges while still using the same amount of labor. He must, as it were, invent a better mousetrap. Schumpeter respects the entrepreneur; he makes him the pivotal point in his theory. Sometimes the entrepreneur is described in language almost embarrassingly heroic: The entrepreneur, says Schumpeter, has a "dream and the will to found a private kingdom," "the will to conquer; the impulse to fight, to prove oneself superior to others; to succeed for the sake, not of the fruits of success, but of success itself."[13]

---

[12] Joseph Schumpeter, *The Theory of Economic Development* (Cambridge, Mass.: Harvard University Press, 1934); and *Capitalism, Socialism and Democracy* (New York: Harper Brothers, 1942).

[13] Quoted in "Memorial: Joseph Alois Schumpeter," in *Schumpeter* (Cambridge, Mass.: Harvard University Press, 1951), pp. 11-25.

The aims of the entrepreneur may lack moral refinement, they may even approach blind ambition, but they constitute the force, says Schumpeter, that powers capitalism. Without the desire for profit, capitalism would lack the source of its own advancement and would spiral quickly into a state of equilibrium, i.e., no advance, no profits. The tendency toward equilibrium is always present. It opposes the power of entrepreneurial development and has its roots in society's traditional resistance to change and in the businessperson's penchant for relying on old habits and proven strategies. To break from this economic inertia, the entrepreneur is needed to invent light bulbs, telephones, synthetic rubber, televisions, computers, and wonder drugs. When the entrepreneur gives society what it wants *more* than existing products, then—and only then—does it give him a *profit*. Schumpeter's model explains, then, what a static classical model of pure competition could not: how the absence of profit in the theoretical state of "pure competition" is compatible with the claim that capitalism's driving force is the lure of profits. Moreover, it advances beyond the static, classical view by appealing to a panoramic vision encompassing patterns of historical development. (Ironically, Schumpeter, the ardent advocate of laissez-faire, acknowledged Marx as a major influence.) But it has a classical ring to it: when reading Schumpeter's portrayal of the heroic entrepreneur who advances society, one can almost hear the voice of Adam Smith.

Milton Friedman: Modernizing the Invisible Hand

As we saw in Chapter 3, Milton Friedman resembles Smith in defending the profit motive against its critics; but there are two important differences. First, Friedman applies his theory explicitly to corporations; second, he advocates that corporations pursue policies of profit maximization in which they reject so-called "social responsibilities." In his best-known book, *Capitalism and Freedom*, Friedman acknowledges that there is increasing acceptance of the view that corporate officers have moral responsibilities, but he declares the view "bankrupt," saying:

> It shows a fundamental misconception of the character and nature of a free economy. In such an economy, there is one and only one social responsibility of business—to use its resources and engage in activities designed to increase its profits so long as it stays within the rules of the game, which is to say, engages in open and free competition, without deception or fraud.[14]

Here we find the same insistence upon fair play as in Smith, but without his concern for other moral norms. Friedman even specifies the moral rules he believes corporations should follow: they must compete openly, they must not deceive, and they must not engage in fraudulent activity. Beyond this, presumably, anything goes.

[14]Milton Friedman, *Capitalism and Freedom* (Chicago: University of Chicago Press, 1962), p. 133.

Despite Friedman's stronger and more unambiguous conclusions, many of his arguments are tied to a thoroughly Smithian assumption, namely, that specialization maximizes overall welfare. This assumption applies to the activities of the corporation as well as the individual, so that corporations should specialize in efficient production for the sake of maximizing profits, and *not* attempt what they are ill-equipped to do: assume social responsibilities. Are corporate officials, Friedman asks, good judges of what the social interest is? They are not, and they *should* not be. Understanding social welfare lies beyond their specialized area of competence and should be left to those whose specialty it is: government officials. Friedman asks us to imagine a situation in which corporations take on moral responsibilities to keep prices and wages in line in order to reduce inflation. The consequences, he says, could be disastrous. If they do so when there is an upward pressure on prices (a fair assumption in a period of inflation) and consequently an increased money supply, then the results will be product shortages, labor shortages, and black markets.[15] Corporations are designed for business, not moral deliberation. Social welfare will be maximized if corporations realize this, that is, if they reject the temptation to be socially "responsible" and, instead, merely maximize profits— or so Friedman argues.

Friedman asserts not only that the sole responsibility of business is to maximize profits, but that doing so is an expression of an inalienable *right* in a free society. He argues that the *economic* freedom to pursue profit (i.e., to buy and sell freely) is essential for maintaining *political* freedoms such as the right to free speech and assembly. Without the right to buy and sell *what* one wants *when* one wants, he asks, how could even a Marxist exercise free speech by buying and selling radical pamphlets? And without economic freedom, a political radical would be barred from devoting full time to his or her mission.

Friedman's arguments have immediate application to corporate behavior, for if corporations are not allowed the freedom to maximize profits, then according to him a crucial economic freedom will be denied. To be sure, corporations are different from individuals, but their freedoms and restraints should be compatible with the rights of their owners and managers, who are individuals. If stockholders agree to pool their money to form a corporation and to establish the policy of profit maximization, can society deny them the right to do so? Is this not their right as *property owners*?

F. A. Hayek's Defense of a Catallaxy

The final figure in our historical tour is the contemporary political thinker F. A. Hayek. Hayek also defends a free market, which he labels a "catallaxy," but his defense is most important not for what it says, but for what it *fails* to say. It appears to be, just like Friedman's defense, a criticism of corporate social responsi-

---

[15] Friedman, *Capitalism and Freedom,* pp. 133-34.

bility, but it turns out to be something different—an endorsement of a "hands-off" government policy. The difference is worth noting.

Hayek is well known in business circles as a staunch defender of the free market, and he identifies himself with the eighteenth- and nineteenth-century "liberal" tradition which includes figures such as A. Tocqueville, David Hume, and Adam Smith. A key to his view is the concept of a "catallaxy," or spontaneous social order which arises among humans when they are more or less left to their own devices, that is, when they are left free to make market choices, contracts, and other agreements. Hayek's central claim is that this spontaneous social order will generate a more complex society, with a higher average personal income, than a society organized to pursue the welfare of its members. Put simply, people will do better if left free to trade and exchange than if controlled by government.[16] In this argument Hayek, like Smith, defends a natural order, but there is no re-course to the metaphysical concept of an "invisible hand." The argument does not attempt to provide, as the theory of the invisible hand does, a *moral* justifica-tion for self-interest.

Hayek's defense of a catallaxy is difficult to apply to moral issues such as corporate responsibility—though the temptation is strong—because its principal conclusion affects the issue not of responsibility but of government control. The spirit of his argument is in step with Thoreau's dictum that "The government is best that governs least." If correct, corporations should be left to pursue their own ends unfettered by government. But the argument says nothing per se about *which* ends, morally speaking, corporations should have. Thus, it would not be logically inconsistent to advocate that society adopt the form of a catallaxy *and* to advocate that corporations take issues of social responsibility with great seriousness. Indeed, Hayek himself asserts that a catallaxy can exist only under "universal rules of just conduct,"[17] and insofar as he means by this more than rules preventing fraud and monopoly,[18] the responsibilities of corporations for Hayek are broader than they are for Friedman.

The lesson to be gained is that arguments against government control must be separated from arguments against corporate moral responsibility. The two are only related contingently, and many theorists who endorse the idea of corpora-tions' assuming moral responsibilities are the same theorists who reject govern-ment interference with business. In fact, a good argument can be made that cor-porate moral responsibility is possible only insofar as government refuses to regulate completely. For, just as a person who is thoroughly controlled by another cannot exercise genuine moral responsibility, so a corporation dominated by government is precluded from genuine moral responsibility; that is, it cannot *decide* to act morally if it is constantly *forced* to do so.

[16]F. A. Hayek, "The Principles of a Liberal Social Order," in *Ethical Issues in Business: A Philosophical Approach,* ed. T. Donaldson and P. Werhane (Englewood Cliffs, N.J.: Prentice-Hall, 1979).

[17]Hayek, "Liberal Social Order," p. 215.

[18]Hayek, "Liberal Social Order," p. 222.

ANALYZING THE ARGUMENTS
AGAINST CORPORATE RESPONSIBILITY

Now that we have traced the historical roots of the challenge to corporate responsibility, what are the conclusions? We should first recognize that the list is not only incomplete, but lopsided in the sense that only free market defenders, and not critics, are included. No mention has been made of Marx, Thomas More, Proudhon, Saint-Simon, Veblen, C. B. Macpherson, or Michael Harrington, to name a few. The purpose of looking at Smith, Friedman, and the others has been only to clarify the underlying perspective typically taken by those who, like Levitt earlier, find corporate responsibility dangerous. The next step will be to untangle specific arguments against corporate responsibility, and then determine whether or not they succeed.

Note that of the four figures examined, Smith, Schumpeter, Friedman, and Hayek, only Friedman *explicitly* endorses corporate moral disinterest. The arguments of the other three may be used, in varying degrees, to challenge corporate responsibility, but only Friedman aims his remarks directly at the issue. The arguments from Smith provide a moral justification for the pursuit of profit but stop short of endorsing a policy of moral disinterest. And Hayek's defense of a catallaxy argues for the autonomy of corporate activity free from government control but holds no specific implications for the issue of corporate social responsibility.

A look through the various historical viewpoints, however, turns up two basic forms of argument which encompass most of those offered by today's corporate responsibility critics. These are:

1. Corporate policies of profit maximization and moral disinterest are justified insofar as they reflect the exercise of basic rights and liberties, especially those relating to the ownership of private property.

2. If corporations adopt policies of profit maximization and moral disinterest, the consequences will be more favorable for society than if they concern themselves with "social responsibility."

Here, the phrase "profit maximization and moral disinterest" does not refer to a policy in which fraud, deception, or lawbreaking are tolerated. Even Milton Friedman, as we saw, thinks corporations should avoid these evils. Rather it implies a "bare minimum" moral policy which carefully sidesteps these specific evils but then disregards other moral issues.

Philosophers will recognize that arguments 1 and 2 manifest separate and distinctive logical structures: argument 1 possesses a "deontological" form, and 2 a "teleological" one. "Deontological" and "teleological" are technical terms in ethics; roughly defined, "deontological" refers to a *principle*-oriented mode of ethical justification, whereas "teleological" refers to a *consequence*-oriented mode. Argument 1 attempts to justify a morally disinterested corporate policy by referring to basic *principles,* in particular to rights and liberties. Argument 2, on the other hand, attempts to justify a morally disinterested corporate attitude, not through principles, but through the *consequences* of such behavior. In particular, it argues that the consequences are better than for any alternative attitudes the corporation might adopt. Because these two arguments represent basic categories of moral argument, it is possible for each to contain a number of specific claims. Let us examine such specific claims individually.

Deontological Attempts to Justify Profit Maximization and Moral Disinterest (Argument 1)

Instead of defending profit maximization and corporate moral disinterest by referring to the desirable *consequences* of moral disinterest as teleological arguments do, most deontological arguments refer to the *rights* possessed by stockholders, consumers, or members of society at large. Here are three examples of such arguments:

1. **Limitation of consumer freedom.** Critics argue that the kind of market freedom endorsed by Friedman, Schumpeter, and others is jeopardized when corporations adopt so-called "moral responsibilities." The function of the market is to provide a smorgasbord of goods so that consumers determine the shape of distribution. This is the meaning of "consumer sovereignty." Only then can the invisible hand perform its magic. When self-righteous, moralistic producers decree that some products ought not be produced, they are in effect making the consumer's choice for him. For example, when a movie maker refuses to market a "blue" film because it might corrupt the morals of the viewer, he has limited market freedom by depriving the consumer of her *right* to choose. What is worse, the film maker represents a minority restricting the rights of a majority.

2. **Violation of rights of association.** A similar argument surfaced in Chapter 1 in the discussion of interpretations of the corporation. One of the competing interpretations argued for the corporation's right to exist by connecting it to the rights of the individual members to associate freely. Carrying this a step further, it can be argued that the right to free association allows stockholders of a corporation to adopt freely overall corporate policies including, if they wish, policies of profit maximization and moral disinterest. Like the members of a private club, stockholders are seen as possessing the right to structure their organization as they wish. They have a right to pursue noble, ignoble, or even silly goals: to pursue international peace, maximization of profits, or even nothing at all. The fact that their cause is not morally uplifting precludes neither their right to associate nor their right to control their association.

3. **Violation of property rights.** Not only rights of association, but property rights can be appealed to in a criticism of corporate responsibility. Granting that people have property rights, and also assuming that the corporation is the

property of the stockholders, one can argue that stockholders should be free to handle their property as they wish. If I tell my neighbor to stop using her car for business and to start using it to transport senior citizens to church, she will tell me to mind my own business—it is *her* car. Similarly, if society tells General Motors to stop using its factories to maximize profits and start using them to enrich society, are the stockholders not justified in telling society to mind its business? After all, it is *their* corporation. This argument is similar to but subtly different from the rights of association argument: this one relies on the right of property and the right to do with it as one pleases; the other relies on the right of free association and the right of people in an association to control it.

Teleological Attempts to Justify Profit Maximization and Moral Disinterest (Argument 2)

Virtually every teleological argument used to justify corporate moral disinterest is cast in terms of the enormous gains to consumer satisfaction promised through a system of competition and free enterprise. That is, they are cast in terms of the good effects which, however ironically, follow from one's forgetting about social responsibility and concentrating on profit. Thus, just as the theories of Schumpeter, Friedman, and Hayek did, these arguments are seen to incorporate versions of Smith's invisible hand. They are, in effect, arguments that weigh the policy of profit maximization and moral disinterest on a scale of social good and show that the good outweighs the bad; since the same cannot be said for alternative policies, profit maximization is presumably justified.

The final burden of the teleological argument is to demonstrate that profit maximization is, in fact, translated into the public interest. Here are some common strategies:

The role of competition. Competition is said to have beneficial consequences because, at least in part, it represents the driving force behind the invisible hand. There is a diminished need for self-conscious moralizing in the marketplace because, as Adam Smith observed, the desire for wealth "rouses and keeps in continual motion the industry of mankind." The virtues of competition are subtle yet powerful, and a modern theorist, John Clark, confirms Smith's vindication. "Only from a strife with the right kind of rules," he argues, "can the right kind of fitness emerge. . . . [Competition] is not the mere play of unrestrained self-interest; it is a method of harnessing the wild beast of self-interest to serve the common good—a thing of ideals and not of sordidness."[19] We remember that Schumpeter's entrepreneur, who finally gives society its lightbulbs, steam engines, and pocket calculators, is driven by the lure of profits and the desire to compete.

Equally important, a corporation's success in the competitive marketplace, as indicated by the level of its profitability, is said to be the crucial yardstick for measuring its overall efficiency. A company that squanders natural resources, capital, and labor, and that turns out an overpriced product, might persist unless falling

[19] John Clark, *The Control of Trusts* (New York: Macmillan, 1901), p. 201.

profits forced it to change. A company that manufactures shoes may have overpaid lazy workers and managers, but unless it is forced to compete with other shoe manufacturers, its inefficiency will remain hidden. In the United States the advantages of corporate competition were recognized by nineteenth-century judges who deliberately transformed the corporation from a "grant of monopoly for a public purpose" to an invisible person who would qualify as a player in the game of economic competition. In some socialist countries, including the Soviet Union, competition is traditionally deemphasized. However, recently even these countries have experimented with "profit-oriented" accounting and interfactory schemes of competition.

Finally, the very concept of pure competition considered as an ideal is claimed to have practical uses. Just as no one has ever encountered a perfect triangle, so no economist has encountered an ideal market structure with perfect competition. But such concepts may help correct existing economic systems in the same way that the concept of a perfect triangle helps straighten out existing ones. A concept of the ideal market, for example, may help reveal and avoid monopolistic and oligopolistic tendencies. Monopoly and oligopoly may be defined as competition where the market is dominated by a single producer or a small set of producers. Like it or not, cornering the market is profitable for those with power to accomplish it, and history reveals that plenty of people are willing to try. The Arab oil producers were not above forming the notorious OPEC cartel, and in doing so they participated in a long tradition of attempts, beginning at least in 600 B.C. with merchants who strove to corner the Grecian olive market. Every day brings fresh news of some corporation's being charged with violating the Sherman or Clayton Anti-Trust Acts. We remember that Adam Smith, perhaps the most vigorous champion of the free market, believed businessmen were sufficiently lax to let their conversations wander toward schemes to restrain trade. By serving as a standard against which to identify the evils of monopoly or oligopoly, the ideal of competition is meant to serve the down-to-earth purpose of helping to enhance consumer interests.

In each of the arguments stressing the beneficial consequences of competition, the notions of "free market" and "competition" are crucial. Presumably, it is the fact that corporations are able to compete in a free market which translates their pursuit of profits into the public good and obviates the need for moral deliberation. More will be said about these key notions later. For now, we should note simply that the argument from competition relies upon a traditional interpretation of competition and the free market, namely an interpretation which assumes that actors are pursuing maximal profits with single-minded diligence. Concern for social responsibility is not a part of this ideal.

Long-term vs. short-term profit maximization. By emphasizing "long-term" rather than "short-term" policies of profit maximization, critics of corporate responsibility are able to strengthen their case for the social benefits of the market, and, in turn, for corporate moral disinterest. Granting that shortsighted profit seekers may harm society by pursuing their self-interest, the next move is to show that the market punishes short-term seekers and rewards long-term ones. For example, it may maximize profits in the short run for Johnson Products, Inc., to claim in television commercials that its Ultra Sheen Permanent Creme Relaxer is "gentle" and "cool" when it straightens hair. In fact, this tactic sold thousands of bottles. But if (as also actually happened) word gets out that the active ingredient is sodium hydroxide—i.e., lye—and that, as the FTC found, it straightens "by breaking down the wall of the hair shaft" and in some instances causes "partial or total hair loss," then sales will plummet.[20] *Long-term* profit maximizing, as opposed to *short-term,* often requires ongoing consumer trust and a solid reputation and in the case of Johnson Products, using lye in Ultra Sheen was both immoral *and* unprofitable. Had it been a better profit maximizer in this instance, it would have been more moral.

Specialization of function. The final teleological argument relies on the age-old division of labor principle, advanced by Adam Smith and others, which asserts that people, or corporations, should do what they know best. Theodore Levitt's view, examined earlier, adopted a version of this principle. Productive corporations specialize in production: they have no business becoming entangled in moral, social, or political issues. These are the business either of government, of publicly elected officials, or of the Church. Corporations should concentrate on profits and leave morality to others, just as carpenters should concentrate on carpentry and leave teaching to others.

This chapter has attempted to articulate the elements of the challenge to corporate responsibility. The inspiration for the challenge, as we have seen, is largely historical and derives from the theories of writers such as Smith, Schumpeter, and Friedman. Yet until the middle of the twentieth century the issue of corporate responsibility remained vaguely defined and escaped explicit attention from such conservative theorists. Giving it that attention remained largely the task of those who, like Friedman and Levitt, drew heavily on the spirit of traditional thinkers while aiming their theoretical arsenal directly at the growing movement of corporate "social responsibility"—at a movement they believed to be ultimately self-defeating.

We saw that arguments challenging corporate responsibility may be divided into two principal categories: deontological arguments stress *rights* in the defense of profit maximization and moral disinterest, while teleological arguments stress *consequences*. The former defend special rights of stockholders and consumers, including rights that either require or allow the most mercenary of market motives. The latter, on the other hand, point to the remarkable benefits the ingenious mechanism of the market presumably produces—a mechanism fueled not by the motive of benevolence, but of self-interest. If these arguments are successful, then all the highsounding talk of public responsibility, no matter how sincere, will ultimately create only diminished social welfare.

[20]FTC in the Matter of Johnson Products Company, Inc., and Bozell and Jacobs, Inc., Docket no. C-2788 (February 10, 1976).

Yet, like a courtroom trial where the jury has heard only the arguments from the prosecution, our inquiry has entirely neglected the other side. Perhaps some companies, like Multifab, mix profits and social responsibility only to be destroyed on the rocks of economic reality. But are Multifabs the rule or the exception? And what about the invisible hand, whose once privileged status is now coming under spirited attack? The next chapter will construct the argument for the defense.

SUGGESTED SUPPLEMENTARY READINGS

ARROW, KENNETH J., *Social Choice and Individual Values.* New York: John Wiley, 1967.

BROZEN, YALE, and ELMER JOHNSON, and CHARLES POWERS, *Can the Market Sustain an Ethic?* Chicago: University of Chicago Press, 1978.

DANIELS, NORMAN, ed., *Reading Rawls.* New York: Basic Books, 1975.

DEANE, PHYLLIS, *The Evolution of Economic Ideas.* Cambridge: Cambridge University Press, 1978.

DOBB, MAURICE, *Political Economy and Capitalism.* Westport, Conn.: Greenwood Press, 1972.

DWORKIN, GERALD, and GORDON BERMANT, and PETER BROWN, eds., *Markets and Morals.* Washington, D.C.: John Wiley Press, 1977.

FLEW, ANTONY, "The Profit Motive," *Ethics,* 86 (July 1976): 312-21.

FREEDMAN, BENJAMIN, "A Meta-Ethics for Professional Morality," *Ethics,* 89 (October 1978): 1-19.

FRIEDMAN, MILTON, "The Social Responsibility of Business Is to Increase Its Profits," *The New York Times Magazine,* September 13, 1970.

———, *Capitalism and Freedom.* Chicago: University of Chicago Press, 1962.

———, "The Methodology of Positive Economics," in *Essays in Positive Economics,* ed. Milton Friedman. Chicago: University of Chicago Press, 1953.

GOUGH, J. W., *The Social Contract.* Oxford: Clarendon Press, 1936.

HAYEK, FRIEDRICH, *The Constitution of Liberty.* Chicago: University of Chicago Press, 1972 (first published 1960).

———, *Law, Legislation and Liberty: A New Statement of the Principles of Justice and Political Economy.* Chicago: University of Chicago Press, 1973-1976.

HILL, IVAN, ed., *The Ethical Basis of Economic Freedom.* Chapel Hill, N.C.: American Viewpoint, 1976.

HIRSCHMAN, ALBERT O., *The Passions and the Interests.* Princeton, N.J.: Princeton University Press, 1977.

KRISTOL, IRVING, *Two Cheers for Capitalism.* New York: Basic Books, 1978.

LAWSON, F. H., *Introduction to the Law of Property.* Oxford: Clarendon Press, 1958.

LOCKE, JOHN, *The Second Treatise of Civil Government and a Letter Concerning Toleration.* Oxford: Basil Blackwell, 1948.

LOWE, ADOLPH, "The Normative Roots of Economic Values," in *Human Values and Economic Policy,* ed. Sidney Hook. New York: New York University Press, 1967.

McKENZIE, RICHARD, "The Economic Dimensions of Ethical Behavior," *Ethics,* 87 (April 1977): 208-21.

MILL, J. S., *Principles of Political Economy.* London: Longmans, Green, 1926.

SAMUELS, WARREN J., "The Political Economy of Adam Smith," *Ethics,* 87 (April 1977): 189-207.

SAMUELSON, PAUL R., *Collected Scientific Papers,* ed. J. Stiglitz. Boston: M.I.T. Press, 1966.

SCHMITT, RICHARD, "The Desire for Private Gain: Capitalism and the Theory of Motives," *Inquiry,* 16 (Summer 1973): 149-67.

SCHUMPETER, JOSEPH, *Capitalism, Socialism and Democracy.* New York: Harper and Brothers, 1942.

———, *The Theory of Economic Development.* Cambridge, Mass.: Harvard University Press, 1934.

SHAW, P. D., "Self-Interest and the Theory of Demand," *Philosophy of the Social Sciences,* 7 (1977): 77-89.

SMITH, ADAM, *An Inquiry into the Nature and Causes of the Wealth of Nations.* 1776; Reprinted in the *Glasgow Edition of the Works and Correspondence of Adam Smith,* ed. R. H. Campbell. London: Oxford University Press, 1976.

WINCH, D. M., *Analytical Welfare Economics.* Baltimore: Penguin, 1971.

CHAPTER 5

Counterarguments

E nglish economist John Maynard Keynes wrote:

I think that capitalism, wisely managed, can probably be made more efficient for attaining economic ends than any alternative system yet in sight, but that in itself is in many ways extremely objectionable. Our problem is to work out a social organization which shall be as efficient as possible without offending our notions of a satisfactory life.[1]

A citizen of Eastern Europe is reputed to have said: "Under capitalism, man exploits man. Under communism, it is the other way round." His statement suggests that no economic system is immune to shortcomings of its members and that the failings of one system must be weighed against those of another. As we saw in the last chapter, the special strength claimed by capitalism is the capacity to harness the inevitable, though perhaps regrettable, selfishness of people and direct it toward the public good. The system thus promises to free itself from the need to depend unrealistically upon the uncertain moral virtues of its participants.

But to what extent does the system succeed in justifying corporate amoralism? If corporations forget about human issues and concentrate simply on profits, will they fulfill the terms of the social contract outlined in Chapter 3? Imagine the president of a bicycle manufacturing firm wondering: "Am I justified in spending my time simply cutting costs and increasing sales? In buying tires, rims, and headlights as cheaply as I can? Even when they aren't as safe as I would want on *my* child's bike?" Answering such questions means confronting head-on the two major sets of arguments: deontological and teleological.

---

[1] John Maynard Keynes, *The End of Laissez-Faire* (Hogarth Press, 1926).

CRITICISMS OF DEONTOLOGICAL ARGUMENTS

In the last chapter we examined three specific deontological arguments, each of which attempts to justify corporate policies of profit maximization and moral disinterest by showing how they reflect the existence of basic rights and liberties. Critics argue that when moralistic producers decide not to market a product for moral reasons, the consumer's freedom to choose has been violated. They argue further that the rights of free association and of property give stockholders the right to adopt whatever profit-maximizing, nonmoral policies they choose. Again, they assume stockholders must avoid policies of outright fraud, deception, and lawbreaking, but beyond this, presumably, anything goes.

The argument asserting that corporations that decide not to market products for moral reasons thereby infringe on consumer freedom appears to be the weakest. It seems to neglect the freedom of the producer to act on his or her own moral beliefs. Government, of course, is different. If the school board of a small South Dakota town decides (as actually happened) to throw all the copies of *Catcher in the Rye* in the school incinerator because the book "implicitly refers to homosexuality," or if the federal government imposes prohibition on alcoholic beverages, then people's freedom has been violated. We affirm that government has a special obligation to provide people with meaningful choices. But corporations are not government organizations. Not only do they lack the power to make law, but, like individuals, they are granted certain freedoms. So long as market transactions are voluntary and so long as one group of sellers is unable to dictate conditions for others, each market transaction represents a free choice by both the buyer and the seller. A customer's decision to buy roller skates is presumably matched by an equally voluntary decision on the part of the store owner to sell them. For this reason, a movie producer's decision not to market a blue film, or Dow Chemical's decision not to market napalm, fails to infringe on the freedom of blue film or napalm users, so long, of course, as other producers are free to make and sell them. Perhaps the film rejected by the producer had redeeming qualities. Perhaps the producer was just being priggish. No matter. He, like the buyer, presumably has the right to refuse to engage in a capitalistic act.

In contrast, the arguments that rely on the rights of association and property are formidable. In an important sense the two arguments may be treated as one, because the force of the association argument depends on that of the property argument. The association argument claims that rights of association, i.e., the rights to form organizations and to establish policy, entail the right to form corporations and establish their policies, including policies of profit maximization and moral disinterest. The property argument claims that the rights of property ownership entail the right to use corporate property as one wishes, including using it in accordance with policies of profit maximization and moral disinterest. If the property argument fails, the first argument is made insignificant: for what is the use of being able to set policies if the policies cannot be carried out? The rights of association are insignificant unless stockholders are able *also* to control the property of the corporation. And showing *that* is the job of the property argument.

For this reason, understanding the property argument is the key to evaluating both arguments. To do this, let us begin by reviewing the concept of property itself.

The Property Argument

The concept of property. If an enterprising Martian were to visit our planet to discover the meaning of the term "property" (having heard it over his intergalactic radio), he would probably be disappointed after talking with the average person. Imagine the Martian landing in a Midwestern cornfield and asking the resident farmer, "What do you mean by property?" "Why," says the farmer, "*this* is my property (pointing with his finger) and my section extends to a line drawn in the middle of that far stream." "What's more," he adds, "I can kick you off if I want. That's what property means." The Martian would be puzzled. He would neither see a "line" in the middle of the stream nor understand how the farmer could demand his exit. To remove the alien's confusion, the farmer would need to explain about the map in the county courthouse which indicates boundaries of the property, and about the sheriff who carries a gun and who would ultimately expell an unwanted intruder. The concept of property is vastly more complicated than it appears; it requires reference to an entire social system for its explication, and it assumes different meanings in different cultures.

Few would deny that people possess at least some rights associated with property. In the United States the Constitution enshrines the right to property in Article IV of its Amendments. The United Nations does the same in its U.N. Declaration of Human Rights. Any country recognizing corporations must affirm property rights, since whatever else it may be, the corporation is a means for allowing the joint ownership of property. Even in socialist countries certain property rights exist, e.g., people may own clothing, tools, and autos (although their rights do not extend to such things as land or factories). Alan Donagan defines property broadly when he says it is "the system of rules agreed upon by its members as to rights to dispose of the various material things individually and collectively under their control, and the distribution among them of those rights."[2]

As a first approximation, let us affirm that the concept of property is applicable to the modern corporation and that this implies at a minimum the existence of rules prescribing:

1. The right of a corporation and its stockholders to own property.

2. The right of a corporation and its stockholders to sell property in accordance with the terms of voluntary agreements (e.g., to sell products to wholesalers or to sell corporate stock).

3. The right of a corporation and its stockholders to buy additional property or hire labor in accordance with the terms of voluntary agree-

---

[2] Alan Donagan, *Theory of Morality* (Chicago: University of Chicago Press, 1977), p. 94.

ments (e.g., to purchase raw materials or equipment, and to employ workers).

4. The right of a corporation and its stockholders to use property in the manner both find acceptable.

Now assuming that corporate policies of profit maximization are simply viewed as an aggregate of the activities represented by these rights, then it can be argued that policies of profit maximization are justified through the rights listed above. The assumption itself has initial plausibility since when General Motors pursues a policy of profit maximization, it does not seem to perform a *single* action describable as "profit maximization." Rather it buys steel as cheaply as possible, pays its workers as little as necessary, and sets prices for its automobiles which maximize net income. Thus, if General Motors is justified in performing all these individual acts, then *ex hypothesi* it is justified in its overall action of profit maximization.

Justifying property rights. But to be fully successful such an argument must defend its underlying concept of the right to property. The most commonly used defense, one familiar to most philosophers, is offered by John Locke in his *Second Treatise on Government*. There Locke postulates a "state of nature," by which he means a state before the appearance of government where all things are owned by God. Now in such a state, Locke reasons, anyone who mixes his or her labor with nature has a right to the resulting fruits. This can be shown by beginning with the assumption that a person in the state of nature owns his own body, and that in turn he should own both the actions of his body and the products of those actions. The three steps of the argument are:

1. A person owns his own body.
2. A person owns the activity of his body (i.e., his labor).
3. A person owns that with which he mixes the labor of his body.

Thus, if in the state of nature one enters the forest and picks berries or clears land, he may be said to own the berries or land. Or at least he may be said to own them *so long as* the following two conditions obtain:

1. After a person appropriates property, there is "enough and as good left over for others."
2. A person does not appropriate any more property than will spoil.

If we add the assumption that people may freely trade, give away, acquire, and divest themselves of their property, then we have the basis for Locke's broad classical justification of the rights of property.

Criticisms of the Property Argument

So far, the story told about property appears simple, straightforward, and with an obvious moral: whoever owns property can adopt whatever policies regarding it he or she wishes. But, as political philosophers know, property is an explosive issue. "Nothing says more about a person's politics," someone once said, "than his view of property." For the other side of the story, let us begin by looking at criticisms of Locke.

Are original appropriations of property fair? Any argument using a concept of property must be prepared to defend its concept. But although the traditional interpretation by Locke appears to justify a system of property by making it rely upon our intuitions about the fairness of "mixing labor," those intuitions can be questioned. To begin with, why should mixing labor with unowned land necessarily result in *gaining* the land? Why not, logically speaking, *losing* one's labor? Mixing does not always imply a gain; when someone constructs a lean-to in a public park it becomes the property of the park, not the builder.

The main attacks on Locke's interpretation, however, have centered on his crucial proviso that "enough and as good be left for others." The proviso is too vague for some tastes, and even Locke's defenders, such as the contemporary philosopher Robert Nozick, find it necessary to express the proviso differently. Nozick suggests a stronger proviso: that a person attempting to acquire a property right in a previously unowned thing will not do so if "the position of others no longer at liberty to use the thing is thereby worsened."[3] He allows, however, that a person might worsen the position of another so long as he provides adequate compensation.

Nozick's formulation of the proviso is no doubt an improvement over the vagueness of Locke's "enough and as good" formulation, and may entail many of the consequences Locke intended. For example, on either Locke's or Nozick's formulation it is true that a person may not appropriate the only water hole in the desert (or the only oil well) and charge what he will.[4] And on either formulation, a person's capacity to appropriate property is limited by the effects such an appropriation has upon others.

One obvious question arising in connection with Locke's justificatory scheme concerns the availability of unowned property. Outside the hypothetical state of nature is there—or was there ever—"enough and as good left over for others" to appropriate? When it was pointed out to Locke in the eighteenth century that the land in England was already appropriated, he replied by pointing west to the New World, to America, where homesteading was allowed. But today the same question could be asked about America. Is not all land already appro-

---

[3] Robert Nozick, *Anarchy, State, and Utopia* (New York : Basic Books, 1974), p. 178. See also *Justice and Economic Distribution,* ed. John Arthur and William Shaw (Englewood Cliffs, N.J.: Prentice-Hall, 1978), p. 77.

[4] Nozick, *Anarchy, State, and Utopia,* p. 180.

priated? Locke *could* respond by pointing south to Peru, where one can even today homestead land on the Alto Plano on the eastern side of the Andes Mountains. Whether this answer solves his underlying problem, however, is doubtful. What happens when nothing is left to homestead? In this context, Nozick's "not worsen" proviso (with its possibility of compensating those injured by an appropriation) appears preferable to Locke's "enough and as good" formulation, since Nozick's escapes the necessity of always pointing elsewhere on an increasingly crowded planet to unowned objects suitable for appropriation.

A Locke-Nozick justificatory schema for property has obvious implications for corporate morality. Nozick explicitly claims that his theory is compatible with laissez-faire economic systems, and says "I believe that the free operation of a market system will not run afoul of the . . . proviso. . . ." "If this is correct," he adds, "the proviso will not . . . provide a significant opportunity for future state action" [i.e., government intervention].[5] Thus, if we believe corporations possess the ordinary rights of property, then according to Locke and Nozick they are justified in freely selling, buying, and giving property, even when these actions are part of an overall policy of exclusive profit maximization. The Locke-Nozick schema interpreted in this way appears to provide moral justification for corporate moral disinterest.

But a crucial issue is whether the Locke-Nozick schema *is* ultimately successful. Philosophers and political scientists have undertaken lengthy investigations of the issue, and although the sheer bulk of output on it precludes adequately discussing it here, three particular problems identified with Locke and Nozick deserve mentioning. The first concerns the determination of when and to what extent a person's position has been "worsened" in the context of Nozick's proviso.

If a person, A, has appropriated a piece of land, then it may be that another person, B, suffers a loss from not owning it. Yet B may *also* suffer from not being able to use the property in the future, say, for acquiring additional wealth. Property frequently breeds wealth, and failing to own it is a disadvantage in this regard. It also is doubtful whether the full loss of not owning property could ever be accurately calculated. Hillel Steiner, among others, has asserted there is a special problem involved in calculating B's net loss of well-being as concerns B's loss of *use* of the object.[6]

The second problem concerns the same issue, i.e., determining how those appropriating property "worsen" the position of others, but is identified with difficulties surrounding the impact of property appropriations on future generations. The Locke-Nozick proviso is intended to apply to future generations as well as present ones. But could it have been determined in the past whether, and to what extent, our situation today is worse than it would have been if some person had *not* appropriated a given piece of property? The difficulty is magnified when we realize that such a determination would require that one know the *number* of

[5] Nozick, *Anarchy, State, and Utopia,* p. 182.

[6] Hillel Steiner, "Nozick on Appropriation," *Mind,* 92 (January 1978), 109-10.

all future individuals and how each one's level of well-being would be affected by a given appropriation of property.[7] The problem seems overwhelming.

Third, problems may persist even supposing one could determine the extent to which the situation of others is worsened. Suppose one person's appropriation of property worsens the situation of another, and compensation must be paid. How would the dollar amount of the compensation be calculated? Nozick suggests using market prices, but market prices reflect an existing structure of property holdings and may not correspond to personal values. In other words, the amount of money needed to compensate a propertyless person in society for his or her lack of ownership may not correspond to the prices at which those who *do* own property happen to buy and sell it.

Finally, even if Locke's belief that investing labor should have a property payoff is correct, why stop with investments in the hypothetical state of nature? Why not include modern-day investments, at least when the value of the invested labor exceeds the rate of reimbursement? Some have argued that corporate employees who labor for years to create a corporate reputation should acquire certain property rights in the corporation. A corporation's good reputation is worth money, and accountants list it as an asset under the heading of "goodwill." But, critics assert, the amount listed as "goodwill" was not *created* by stockholders, nor does it belong to them. Rather, a corporation's earned reputation, considered as an asset, should belong to those who "labored" for it: the employees.

An alternative concept of property: the three-termed view. The Locke-Nozick scheme may entail considerable discretionary power for property owners; but alternative schemes, interestingly enough, deny such power. Consider the "three-termed" view advanced by the contemporary philosopher Joyotpaul Chaudhuri. A three-termed concept of property, he explains, construes all property as a three-way relationship among owner, object, and other people. For example, my ownership of an automobile is a three-way relationship involving me, the automobile, and other people. Moreover, and most important, rights and obligations extend in all directions inside this triad. My ownership of an auto entails an obligation on your part not to damage my auto, but I *also* have obligations to others to refrain from driving at breakneck speed.

Chaudhuri grants that owning property is a right, and he agrees with Locke that it is the business of government to protect that right, but he disagrees with Locke over how the various rights of property are to be specified. Locke viewed the right to property as God-given and existing before the invention of human society; thus, the Greeks possessed the same rights of property that we do (whether they recognized them or not). Chaudhuri, however, views property rights as part of a detailed constellation of rights and obligations, all of which require endorsement in a political state by a democratic process. "Consent," Chaudhuri remarks, "gives life and legitimacy to the abstract, three-termed construct of

[7] Hillel Steiner, "The Natural Right to the Means of Production," *The Philosophical Quarterly*, 27 (January 1977), 47.

property." People in democratic France may decide to build different rights and obligations into the concept of property than people in democratic England. Thus, for Locke, the right to property is simple and eternal, whereas for Chaudhuri it is complex and changeable.[8]

The three-termed concept of property is said to resolve problems that Locke's version cannot. Since, according to it, the obligations associated with property are forever being specified and refined, the shifting structure of property laws can be justified. The view appears to explain, say, why corporations today are required to file environmental impact statements whereas in 1910 they were not. If correct, the theory implies that corporations not only have specific *rights* associated with property, such as to hire, fire, contract, sell, and make profits, but also specific *obligations*. The precise nature of these obligations is subject to specification through democratic processes: corporations today may be required to demonstrate that they do not discriminate against women or blacks; fifty years from now, when a more racially and sexually balanced work force exists, this requirement may be dropped. In turn, another obligation may be specified in the future: say, to use energy and natural resources more responsibly, or to place public directors on corporate boards.

Radical criticisms of property. Most radical criticisms emerge from examinations of society's concrete institutions. The resulting attacks on property frequently reject even reformulated theories of property, such as the three-termed view. They tend to permit the existence only of "personal" property such as clothes, automobiles, and toothbrushes, while stressing the abolishment of property in the form of land, steel mills, textile factories, railroads, and refineries. Only by removing such critical tools of production from the grip of owners, according to these critics, can the injustice which property creates be blocked. Why does one man pick lettuce in an insecticide-ridden field while another keeps polo ponies? Why does one child buy the latest in prep-school fashions while another carries a knife to school for protection? Equality of opportunity, decent health care, and a fair distribution of wealth are a few of the casualties, say many radicals, of a system of private property.

The radical critique of property is detailed in its analysis and massive in its scope; certainly it deserves more attention than we can give it here. Two of its underlying claims, however, bear stressing: the first is its assertion that the rights of property provide the basis for an enormous concentration of political power, especially in the corporate sector. This power is said to block legislation and administrative reforms inimicable to corporate interests. Business refuses at every step to allow any limitation of its power, and it steadfastly opposes regulation, corporate taxation, workers' rights, and programs of social welfare. We are reminded that Josiah Wedgewood, the founder of Wedgewood Pottery, testified against the

---

[8] Joyotpaul Chaudhuri, "Toward a Democratic Theory of Property and the Modern Corporation," *Ethics,* 81 (July 1971), 271-86.

proposed child labor laws in nineteenth-century England, on the grounds that it would blunt the efficiency of business.

Traditional radical theorists locate power directly with the owners of property, such as rich financiers and stockholders, whereas many modern radical theorists locate it with an emerging class of professional corporate managers, or "technocrats." In either case, however, the point of the radical criticism is the same: power is used to authorize the ultimate exploitation of the powerless.

The second claim is that abstract discussions of freedom or property rights tend to obscure rather than clarify economic problems. Everyone may be "free" to own property in the sense that each *could* own something if only he or she had the wherewithal to acquire it. But this is little solace to a mother of five children with no food, or a peasant farmer without adequate land or farm equipment. "To every mouth God sends a pair of hands" someone once said. "True enough," remarked the economist Joan Robinson, "but He does not send a combine harvester."[9]

Even to conceive of the marketplace as a series of abstract relations among property owners, radical critics insist, suggests a distorted "same-level" view of reality. All economic activity is reduced to a series of property exchanges: one person trades soybeans for money, another labor for money. Everyone at bottom is the same, so General Motors is seen on a par with the boy selling lemonade on the corner; the lathe operator is seen on a par with a Rockefeller. But when the lathe operator sells his labor for a modest salary, the situation is remarkably different from when a Rockefeller invests in the stock market and receives dividends. The worker has honestly contributed something of value, his labor, whereas Rockefeller has merely performed the service of allowing the corporation to be owned by him. Still more important, add the critics, while the worker is a political pawn in society, Rockefeller helps create its very rules.

If the radical critique of property is on target, then the very existence of corporations is suspect, for corporations owe their legitimacy to property, and if property is corrupt, then so by definition are corporations. Clearly also, if the radical critique is correct, the argument from property for profit maximization and moral disinterest is bankrupt.

A conflict between property and normative standards. Property, some say, should not be abolished but reformed, especially in ways that will eliminate conflicts between it and traditional values of meritocracy and democracy. If, as these critics assert, existing notions of property are out of step with such ideals, then the moral force of the arguments we are considering is drastically reduced, since any argument should avoid constructing a moral defense using assumptions that are themselves morally indefensible.

Is the exercise of corporate power under existing canons of property in conflict with democracy or meritocracy? Consider an argument from those defending "economic democracy": Democracy, by definition, they say, means "rule by the many," and "rule by the many" implies that those directly affected by deci-

---

[9] Joan Robinson, *Economic Philosophy* (New York: Watts Publishing, 1962).

sions ought to play a role in making them. But whereas political elections follow the rule of "one person, one vote," the marketplace does not. Even assuming that laissez-faire capitalism allows each person equal access to marketplace transactions, the vote there is not "one person, one vote," but "one dollar, one vote." And since some clearly have more dollars, the result is an economic system in which events are controlled by the few—by an aristocracy.

The same lesson extends to corporate governance. Boeing, Gulf Oil, and U.S. Steel employ millions of workers and affect millions of consumers; but if the principle of democracy is that those affected by decisions have a right to participate in them, where is the participation from Boeing, Gulf, and U.S. Steel workers?

The ideal of a meritocracy, similarly, can be used to critique the prerogatives of property. The word "meritocracy" refers to the principle that those who possess the most merit, either through talent or innate capability, deserve advancement before those who are rich, lucky, or well-born. Merit, not money, should count. Yet if property conveys unlimited rights to use the property, and if property can be transferred from one person to another through inheritance, does this not convey the power of property to those of questionable merit? If stockholders have the *power* of ownership, what guarantees their corresponding *merit*? Or consider a corporation adopting a policy of profit maximization and moral disinterest. What guarantees that employees will be advanced for merit? It may appear they will be automatically: since profits depend upon productivity, it appears that profit-maximizing managers will automatically promote the most productive employees. But even this seemingly obvious conclusion overlooks a logical snag. The philosopher Norman Daniels illustrates it in the following example:

> Jack and Jill both want jobs A and B; and each much prefers A to B. Jill can do either A or B better than Jack. But the situation . . . in which Jill performs B and Jack A *is more productive* than Jack doing B and Jill A.[10]

So if Jack and Jill work for ABC corporation, and Jill is not only a better secretary but also a better account executive than Jack, then ABC's pursuit of profit may under certain circumstances dictate that Jill serve as secretary, not account executive, despite her higher qualifications.

Property rights in conflict with other rights. A final criticism relies on the concept underpinning the property rights argument itself: that of a right. To say that stockholders have property rights overlooks the simple truth that the right to property—or to anything—must at a minimum be compatible with other rights. Furthermore, when rights conflict one right may be overridden by another. (These points were made in Chapter 3.) Now, the exercise of the right to property may be argued under certain circumstances to infringe upon other rights. Henry George suggested that property rights can even diminish people's personal freedom: "Place

---

[10]Norman Daniels, "Meritocracy," in *Justice and Economic Distribution,* ed. John Arthur and William Shaw (Englewood Cliffs, N.J.: Prentice-Hall, 1978), pp. 166-67.

one hundred men on an island from which there is no escape," he remarked, "and whether you make one of these the absolute owner of the other ninety-nine or the absolute owner of the soil of the island, it will make no difference to him or them."[11]

Philosophers Michael Hoffman and James Fisher have noted that the ownership of property is normally understood to confer the privilege of benefiting from the use of that property, so that if one owns X, one is entitled to benefit from, say, renting X or selling X. But they point out that the other side of this coin is that a person also is liable for certain bad consequences of X. The people such a person harms thus have a right to be compensated. Consider a man who owns a tiger. He may rightfully claim to collect money when the tiger is exhibited in a circus. But imagine that the tiger escapes and mauls livestock in the local community. Can the owner then say, "I hereby renounce ownership?" No, simply because ownership entails respecting the rights of others, and when those rights are violated, ownership carries liabilities instead of benefits. This conclusion has immediate application to the world of business, since if corporations (say, in the nuclear power industry) claim benefits through owning property, they must not subsequently renounce their liabilities when their property harms society (say, from a Three Mile Island disaster).[12]

Hence, considered as owners of private property, the stockholders of the corporation itself must observe the obligations connected with private property and must respect the rights of others. Although the precise nature of these obligations is a matter of dispute, few would deny that at a minimum, corporations are obliged not to violate the traditional rights guaranteed by the U.S. Constitution and Declaration of Independence, among which are the rights to life, property, and freedom. Furthermore, these obligations extend not only to the present generation but to future ones.

The implications of the fact that property entails obligations are numerous. Because people possess the right to property, it follows that corporations' activities must be compatible with their property rights. If U.S. Steel is contaminating the air with sodium dioxide and trioxide in amounts sufficient to deteriorate marble statues and buildings, then it is damaging the property of others and may not have lived up to one of its moral obligations—to respect the property rights of others. At a minimum, U.S. Steel may be said to be passing off one of its costs of doing business to others, and it is morally bound to compensate those whose property it damages. Moreover, because people possess the right to life, it follows that corporations are obliged not to create unreasonable dangers to life either through the products they manufacture or through the working conditions they establish for employees. When the Paydozer Company designed an earth-moving machine which provided no rear view for its operator, so that people standing behind the machine

[11] Henry George, *Progress and Poverty* (1905; reprinted New York: Henry Schalkenback Foundation, 1955), p. 347.

[12] An article which focuses on the liabilities of property ownership is "Corporate Responsibility: Property and Liability," by W. Michael Hoffman and James V. Fisher, in *Ethical Theory and Business*, ed. T. Beauchamp and N. Bowie (Englewood Cliffs, N.J.: Prentice-Hall, 1979), pp. 187-97.

were sometimes backed over and killed, it was morally unjustified in renouncing its liability to the victims.

Finally, because the rights of future generations as well as present ones must be respected, it follows that corporations are obliged not to create present situations that infringe on those rights. Using this rationale, a drug company is obliged to refrain from selling to pregnant women a pain reliever that endangers the future health of the fetus. Such obligations appear to constitute a minimum set of moral requirements upon corporations. They derive, interestingly enough, from the very concept of the right to property itself.

Beyond this minimum some have argued that corporations have obligations to respect certain rights even when the rights are not *legally* protected. For example, philosophers such as Alan Donagan have argued that people, including members of future generations, possess the right to have the aesthetic qualities of the environment protected. The strip mining of coal has been claimed by some to violate this right insofar as it produces unsightly gouges in what once was natural countryside. Other philosophers have argued that there is a right to a "livable environment" and that this right bars corporate contamination of air or water. If such a right exists, then modern corporations may be violating the rights of residents in places like Los Angeles or Mexico City when the air pollution reaches visible and eye-watering levels. Whether corporations will ever come fully to recognize such rights is uncertain, but whether they do or not is irrelevant to the underlying point: the ownership of property, either by an individual or corporation, involves the obligation to refrain from infringing on the rights of others—however those rights are defined.

Final Remarks on the Deontological Argument

Having sketched out these criticisms, what of our central question: Do property rights justify corporate policies of profit maximization and moral disinterest? The final criticism, perhaps, is telling. Apart from the radical critique of all systems of property—which cannot thoroughly be treated or evaluated here— each of the remaining criticisms overlaps with the final one dealing with rights. For if existing concepts of property rely on unfair original appropriations, or if they fail to recognize the true obligations of ownership, or if they infringe on valid principles of meritocracy and democracy, then they may be said to violate certain rights: e.g., a right to be compensated in the absence of fair appropriations, or a right to have access to democratic procedures. And, more important, whatever the truth value of the first four criticisms—which must be left to the reader to decide— the final criticism appears persuasive. Rights must be respected by property owners *however* those rights are defined, since defending property rights commits one to defending other valid rights.

We may conclude that even if the radical critique of property ultimately fails, a policy of profit maximization and moral disinterest could be morally defensible only if *all* the actions a corporation performs are describable merely as "selling," "buying," "contracting," and so forth. *These* actions are arguably covered by the rights of the ownership of property. But often the same action has alternative descriptions, as when a man can be described as pulling the trigger of a gun or committing a murder, and the actions of a corporation can be similarly equivocal. Insofar as a corporation performs an action correctly describable as "violating another's rights," our discussion indicates that the corporation is morally obliged to refrain from performing it (even if it happens to be *legally* permissible). If the Firestone Tire Company markets a steel-belted tire designed so poorly that it regularly explodes, then Firestone has not lived up to its moral obligations to respect others' rights to life. Although the company's actions may be permissible under the description, "selling a product," etc., they are not permissible under the description, "marketing a dangerous product which threatens a person's right to life."

It follows that the deontological arguments that rely upon the concept of property fail to justify corporate policies of moral disinterest. Because the argument in terms of property rights fails, so too does the argument from rights of association, for as shown in the beginning, the latter argument depends upon the former. Although the property rights argument may demonstrate the permissibility of buying, selling, negotiating contracts, and hiring employees, all in line with a policy of profit maximizing, it cannot justify a morally disinterested policy of profit maximization because it is logically possible that acts required by the policy sometimes will be correctly describable as acts that violate the rights of others.

CRITICISMS OF TELEOLOGICAL ARGUMENTS

When Carl Kotchian, the President of Lockheed Aircraft, delivered suitcases stuffed with cash to Japanese government officials, he violated no existing U.S. law. The justification Kotchian offered for the bribes was teleological: he argued that although they cost Lockheed millions, the bribes succeeded in landing a highly lucrative Tri-Star Jet contract with Nippon Airways.

Similar cases have prompted skeptics to wonder whether profit maximizing really exhibits the work of an invisible hand. Despite the teleological arguments examined in the last chapter—arguing that a single-minded pursuit of profit automatically transforms corporate self-interest into social welfare—critics are convinced that logical inconsistencies infect the free market concept and that a policy even of long-range profit maximization is a poor prescription for corporate responsibility.

Criticisms of teleological arguments are numerous. We shall examine some of the most important.

Conceptual Difficulties with Pure Competition

The thread of the strongest moral defense of profit maximization lies in the enormous gains to consumer satisfaction promised through free competition. But the notion of "competition" is crucial here, and notoriously elusive.

Clarence Walton, a modern business theorist, defines "perfect competition" as a "type of price competition with homogenous products and perfectly free access of all forms to the market."[13] Notice first of all how very narrow this definition is: it refers not to all product competition, but only to competition among homogenous products; and it refers not to all aspects of competition, but only to that which concerns price. In other words, the definition covers competition between Pepsi and Coke, but not between Pepsi and lemonade; and it covers competition related to the relative *price* of Pepsi and Coke, but not to the relative *quality* of the two. As far as the definition goes, Pepsi and Coke never compete with each other for higher quality soft drinks. The reasons for this narrowness stem largely from difficulties of information gathering. It is easy to chart and measure prices, but measuring quality is a slippery task, something like measuring the aesthetic value of a Picasso versus a Rembrandt.

Another peculiarity of the definition is that it describes a fiction. Pure competition, like the perfectly ordered world of Plato's Republic, represents an ideal. There has never been nor will there ever be a market that maintains "perfectly free access" to itself (including access by consumers and producers). Such a market would contain supremely rational consumers who know immediately about the introduction of a new product. They would not require a TV ad to tell them that a cheaper mousetrap had been built, nor to tell them that the traditional makers of mousetraps had heard the news and lowered their prices. In a world of perfect competition, producers would respond to consumer preferences instantly. If on Monday consumers began to want smaller, cheaper automobiles, then producers would have them ready on Tuesday. The ideal of competition is said by some to be so lofty in its abstraction that it yields absurdities: it implies that self-interested consumers, godlike in their ability to reason about their self-interest, confront similarly endowed corporations in a world in which the ordinary limitations of time and space do not apply.

The problem of dishonesty. Among the conceptual difficulties alleged to afflict pure competition is one concerned with dishonesty. The participants in the world of pure competition are presumed to be supremely rational—but *not* supremely honest. Indeed, because they are supremely rational about maximizing their own interests, both as producers and consumers, one seemingly must predict they will be dishonest in a situation in which it pays to lie. Aside from the moral reservations one has about dishonesty, there are unfortunate consequences for the presumption that free competition maximizes social welfare. If you or I bid to buy a table or chair, then our self-interest dictates that eventually we make honest bids, that we eventually say truly what the product is worth to us. Otherwise we will pay too much, or not get the furniture we were willing to buy. But consider a case where *both* of us can use the same commodity, say a road or a weather forecasting service. Now, when it comes time to estimate what the road is worth to us, it is in our self-

---

[13]Clarence Walton, *Conceptual Foundations of Business* (Homewood, Ill.: Richard D. Irwin, 1969), p. 345.

interest to underestimate, or lie. For if somehow we can pass our obligations off to others, we become that much richer while still retaining use of the commodity. But because everyone else is also smart enough to realize this, everyone will underestimate, and the total payment will be inadequate to maximize social welfare.

Timelessness. Because both producers and consumers know instantly about which products and markets are available, and because they can both produce and buy instantly, it seems that in the world of pure competition there can be no profits. As soon as I market oranges at 50 cents each, you lower your price to 49 cents. In the same instant that consumers begin to buy at 49 cents, they notice that I have in turn lowered my price to 48 cents. This process continues, both of us competing for the lowest price, all in the same instant, until we both reach rock-bottom price, namely, the price below which each of us takes a loss. That rock-bottom price is one of *zero* profit. Pure competition allows no profits. Yet was it not the lure of profits that was to supply the muscle behind the invisible hand?

Internal contradictions. Some critics claim to spot outright contradictions in perfect competition. Consider the claim advanced by contemporary theorists Martin Hollis and Edward Nell that perfect competition's assumptions of perfect rationality and perfect information are at loggerheads. Perfect competition implies "perfect rationality" in the sense that all market participants are assumed to act intelligently to advance their interests. If, despite knowing better, market participants mistakenly pick worse products over better, the invisible hand will obviously be blocked. Similarly, it will be blocked if participants lack information, for this would mean consumers lack knowledge about which products are superior to others. But can perfect knowledge and perfect rationality co-exist? Assuming that acquiring information bears a cost—assuming, that is, that gathering information about dishwashers, razors, or stock options demands spending time which could be spent profitably elsewhere—the "rational" market participant will not waste all of his or her time acquiring "perfect" information. Hence, it appears, perfect rationality excludes perfect knowledge.[14]

The same is said about "perfect information" and "perfect mobility." A perfectly competitive market requires perfect mobility in the sense that resources must be free to shift from one line of industry to another. If there is a chance for a killing in widgets, then producers must have the mobility to shift to widget production; otherwise widgets will carry an inflated price. But if perfect mobility prevails, the chance for a killing in widgets will draw *every* producer into widgets. A landslide would occur. In fact, however, by possessing perfect information some market participants know that others cannot leave their existing activities, and that they, not the others, should take the plunge. But this means that perfect information

[14] Martin Hollis and Edward Nell, *Rational Economic Man* (London: Cambridge University Press, 1975), pp. 228-33.

includes knowledge of market *im*mobilities; hence perfect information seems to preclude perfect mobility.[15]

Do Free Market Assumptions Match Facts?

Reality never fits ideals, and the ideal of competition is no exception. But incongruencies between the actual and the ideal market may affect teleological arguments, since if the arguments rely upon ideal concepts, then insofar as reality misses the ideals, the conclusions of the arguments are suspect.

Some imperfection in existing markets can be, and are, blamed on government. A strong message from those defending free markets is that if the corporation is prevented by the government from playing, it will become sluggish and inefficient. In other words, when government interferes with corporate competition, the cost is passed on to society. In 1976 one economist pointed out that because of massive government grants to hospitals, the nation had a surplus of at least 90,000 hospital beds. The federal General Accounting Office acknowledges that despite a rapidly escalating demand for lumber, more than 6 billion board feet of timber in national forests die each year because corporations are prevented by government from harvesting it.[16] Corporations could be more efficient, they could sell lumber cheaper, and they could accommodate patients without wasting beds, market defenders claim, if only they were left to compete on their own.

Yet many market imperfections appear to be something other than the mistakes of government.

Institutional detail. The defense of the free market is alleged to overlook crucial institutional details. By seeing all behavior as the outcome of profit maximizing decisions, the theory may fail to utilize relevant sociological data. When blacks in the United States confront the job market, their confrontation reflects the effects of over a century's worth of discrimination. The market may not "maximize" successfully in their case; racist store owners may pick lazy whites over industrious blacks.

Free market theory assumes that all market exchanges are fundamentally alike. Lettuce has a price and so does capital. But the power to withhold savings, and to demand the optimal price, is more easily exercised than the power to withhold labor. The gardener must work or his family starves, but the investor in municipal bonds is free to withhold her savings until offered the appropriate price.

The real market, in contrast to the ideal one, also manifests significant differences in the degree to which market behavior is "productive." According to the model of the free market, whatever sells is productive, that is, whatever sells must contribute to consumer interests. But critics charge that corporations can sometimes maximize profits when they *refrain* from selling the best product. There

---

[15] Hollis and Nell, *Rational Economic Man*, pp. 228-30.

[16] *Saturday Review*, July 10, 1976, p. 25.

may be conflict between the engineer who designs light bulbs, whose task is to make them burn for eternity, and the sales manager whose task is to keep customers frantically replacing bulbs.[17] Thus critics assert that sometimes it is profitable for an entire industry to promote built-in obsolescence. This has inspired some critics to formulate what is called the "Neo-Greshamite" law, namely: "Other things being equal, in the long term, under realistically competitive conditions, worse products will drive out better."[18]

False predictions may also arise from the assumption that maximization of profit is the simple motive force of economic behavior. In the ideal market this assumption holds good by definition. In the real one, large corporations may have motives different from those of small ones, upper-level managers may have motives different from those of middle-level ones, and married workers' motives may be different from those of single ones. While the motives of a rising young executive may be a higher salary, a big office, and membership in the local country club, those of a seasoned vice-president may be more time for his family and a better industry-wide reputation.

Corporations themselves may have goals other than profit. The economist Kenneth Boulding first suggested this when he wrote about the homeostasis mechanisms in corporations. Boulding was referring to the feedback mechanisms used to maintain equilibrium and keep corporate accounts in balance. In other words, a corporation's balance sheet is designed to reflect financial equilibrium, and when sales exceed inventories, it becomes necessary to replenish inventories to restore equilibrium. Even such an obvious accounting device as this affects corporate behavior. Profit is only *one* factor, says Boulding, and nonprofit factors may even become dominant. When forced to choose between maximizing profit and enhancing liquidity (i.e., enhancing *usable* capital, such as cash or securities, in contrast to *frozen* capital, such as buildings or machinery), a corporation may prefer liquidity. Montgomery Ward for years protected its liquidity at the expense of profits. Since Boulding introduced this criticism, others have added to the list of nonprofit corporate motives. These include desires for: security, expansion, technological advance, avoidance of failure, group loyalty, and organizational diffusion of responsibility.[19]

We noted earlier that the assumption of perfect information may clash with the assumption of perfect rationality. The perfect information assumption may also spell trouble when it comes to assessing the fruits of actual markets. The market transforms self-interest into public good only insofar as each market participant is well informed. Ill-informed consumers bungle even the pursuit of their own self-interest: they buy unsafe cars believing them superior, or worthless patent medicine believing it effective. But a substantial amount of market ignorance may be the rule rather than the exception. How much does even the intelligent consumer know about the chemistry of cough medicines, the tensile strength of car

[17] Hollis and Nell, *Rational Economic Man*, pp. 215-17.

[18] Hollis and Nell, *Rational Economic Man*, pp. 218-22.

[19] Christopher D. Stone, *Where the Law Ends* (New York: Harper & Row, Pub., 1975), p. 236.

doors, or the wing design of a DC-10? As noted already, acquiring information carries a price; and in lieu of good information, consumers often must trust what they learn from advertising. Again, if the teleological criticism of corporate responsibility rests with showing how the informed pursuit of profit produces maximal welfare, then insofar as participants are ill-informed, the criticism will fail.

Say's Law. John Maynard Keynes sparked an economic revolution when he challenged Say's Law. Say's Law, a rule derived from the concept of perfect competition, states that for the economy as a whole, supply necessarily creates demand of a similar magnitude. In other words, in an ideal market not only do prices rise when supply falls relative to demand, and prices fall when supply rises, but *whatever* the level of supply, there will be some matching demand. If the supply of refrigerators rises, refrigerator prices will fall. But Say's Law assumes that people *will continue to buy* all the cheaper refrigerators. This is what Keynes questioned, and the Great Depression seemed to bear him out. With a multitude of unsold inventories and with prices crashing, buyers stayed home. Free market defenders argued that it was a short-run anomaly and that in the long run Say's Law would prevail. To which Keynes made his famous reply: "In the long run we are all dead."

Whether Keynes was correct in his solution—that governments should ensure aggregate demand by regularly pumping money into the economy—is not crucial for our purposes. More important is the consequence of Keynes' denial of Say's Law upon teleological arguments. If Keynes is right, markets may spiral into catastrophic depressions because of the very activity of the invisible hand.

External costs. A free market implies a system of voluntary exchanges. Smith trades with Jones and Jones trades with Smith, *only* if both agree. But what about Brown, the third party? In a voluntary trade between Smith and Jones, both are presumably better off after the trade. But suppose that Smith and Brown own adjacent land and that Smith sells his land to Jones, who constructs a steel mill. What happens to Brown? Once in operation, the mill spews forth sulfur dioxide and soot. Now since such pollutants generate bad odors, slowly deteriorate steel structures, and damage living organisms, Mr. Brown, as well as everyone else in the area, is worse off than before. Moreover, he and others have absorbed what can be called an "external cost," i.e., a cost of production borne by someone other than the producer. By all rights, those external costs should be made "internal," i.e., borne by Jones. However, left to its own, the free market seems to lack a mechanism for bringing this about.

Imperfect competition. Some critics assert that natural forces in the market hamper market freedom. In addition to the fact that profit-motivated entrepreneurs sometimes push for monopolistic benefits, the market itself may embody inner tendencies toward monopoly and oligopoly. One of the first to suggest this was Piero Sraffa, who recommended scrapping theories of pure competition in favor of more realistic, impure ones. The assumption of pure competition, according to Sraffa, is that buyers are indifferent to sellers and will buy from, whomever offers the lowest price. In fact, he points out, buyers are not indifferent at all and rely heavily upon factors of tradition, special packaging, personal acquaintance, location, brand name loyalty, and credit facilities. It matters little that such preferences are irrational. They exist, and they refute assumptions of pure competition. Instead of speaking of *one* market in which all producers compete equally, we should speak of *many* markets, each with its own quasi-monopolistic domain.

In order for a competing firm to crash through the market of a rival firm, it must woo consumers away from their buying habits and loyalties, and this requires considerable expense for advertising and goodwill. Indeed, doing so is costly enough that existing producers should be seen both as having partial monopoly control of the market and as being able to charge additional monopolistic prices. If corporations avoid becoming greedy and charging superinflated prices, they can effectively block outside competition.[20] Thus, through moderate restraint, Coca-Cola, Inc., can effectively block competition from Vess Cola or Canfield Cola, while at the same time charging prices that are higher than the market ordinarily would bear.

Closely related is the problem of oligopolistic development. An oligopoly occurs when a firm holds a market with a relatively small group of other producers. The oligopoly can be caused by factors that lie beyond the control of the market, such as economy of scale. Building automobiles or producing steel efficiently is subject to economies of scale; building Volkswagens or casting ingots in one's back yard is not cost-effective, and production must be left to those few with massive capital reserves. Once two, three, or at most four large manufacturers have entered auto production in the United States, the national market will be saturated, and the results will be oligopolistic advantages for a few firms. Even if these firms do not fix prices directly, *indirect* price-setting mechanisms can be employed. For example, all firms may follow the pricing moves of an industry leader. Free market theories can be and are reconstructed to help one understand monopolistic or oligopolistic tendencies, but critics charge that the negative effects of the tendencies persist.

Long-range profit maximization. We saw in Chapter 4 that many market defenders champion long-range rather than short-range profit maximization. The former, not the latter, presumably coincides with a corporation's social responsibility. Thus, Johnson, Inc., misled the public when it advertised Ultra Sheen as "cool" and "gentle" because the product contained lye; but it would have been more responsible *and* eventually more profitable had it warned the consumer. In the long run, the argument goes, it is unprofitable for corporations to be immoral, because consumers will recognize immorality and refuse to buy. Once the consumer knows lye is in Ultra Sheen, or knows Firestone Tires are unsafe, or that

[20] Piero Sraffa, "The Laws of Return under Competitive Conditions," in *Readings in Price Theory,* ed. George Stigler and Kenneth Boulding (Homewood, Ill.: Richard D. Irwin, 1952).

lettuce growers exploit their workers, then sales of Ultra Sheen, Firestone tires, and lettuce will fall.

The argument's unique strength is its reliance on consumer perceptions; but critics say this is also its fatal weakness. Because people presumably refuse to buy if they *perceive* moral problems, the connection between long-range profits and morality breaks down when consumer perceptions are inaccurate or when their perceptions fail to influence future sales. Commodities such as soft drinks, beauty products, coffee, and automobiles are highly visible in contrast to ball bearings, tanned hides, electric motors, and industrial furnaces. The latter make up a healthy segment of the economy but are often bought by purchasing agents who are unconcerned about the companies' reputations for social responsibility— except, perhaps, about their reliability in business transactions. Or, consider a situation in which consumers are making a *one-time,* never-to-be-repeated purchase. A Florida company, Blood Plasma International, once bought blood for pennies a pint from African natives and then charged 150 times that amount to victims of a Nicaraguan earthquake disaster. The victims' perception of Blood Plasma International—understandably dismal—was not a blow to Plasma International's future profits, because for most of the victims it was the only time they would buy blood.

The long-range argument may also rely unduly upon product factors that are of immediate interest to consumers, such as safety. Consumers will balk at buying a hair-care product when they know it contains lye. But will they also balk if they hear that Ultra Sheen exploits its workers? Equally important, would they even *know* if Ultra Sheen exploited its workers? Consumers usually know more about the product itself than the working conditions under which it is made.

Finally, can corporate managers be expected to *believe* that long-range profits and morality always coincide? Consider a corporation on the brink of bankruptcy. Can the president be expected to reject a morally objectionable but potentially lucrative last-minute gamble to save the company on the grounds that, because it is immoral, it will be unprofitable in the long run? He may reason that *unless* he gambles, there will be no long run.

Normative Problems for Free Competition

Even if the free market were perfectly realized, and even if it invariably generated a bounty of high-quality and inexpensive products, it might remain suspect on normative grounds; i.e., it might fail to square with valid moral principles. As Keynes' remark at the beginning of this chapter implies, even a fully efficient system might "offend our notions of a satisfactory life."

Creating secondary needs. Free market theories assume that goods and services satisfy consumer preferences. Consumer preferences dominate market supply; this is what the expression "consumer sovereignty" means. But for some observers, goods exist that carry their own wants with them, and that, as a result of persuasive advertising, create the very wants they satisfy.[21] Without the help of Madison Avenue, we might fail to realize that neckties should narrow and widen every so often, or that the length of women's skirts should go up and down. Thus critics ask whether it is right for the market not only to satisfy primary needs for food and shelter, but also to create "secondary" needs for hair spray, electric knives, and foot deodorizers. Would we not be as well off *without* the goods, *without* the wants, and *with* our money?

Justice—accommodating need. Someone once said that the problem with the free market is that it allows the winners to feed their pets better than the losers feed their children. From the standpoint of such critics, the market rewards productivity but not need. Marxists, for example, advocate rewarding need through the slogan "from each according to his ability, to each according to his need." Yet, more than Marxists attack the market on the issue of need.

Professional philosophers are familiar with John Rawls' analysis of distributive justice in his book *A Theory of Justice*. Though not a critic of capitalism per se, Rawls implies that need must be a factor in any just theory of distribution, and that a system of unbridled competition fails the test. We shall have time only to glance at his imposing theory, and then only at the part concerned with need.

Rawls points to the accepted fact that money breeds money. Even in a free market the son of a banker has a better life prospect for gaining wealth than the son of an unskilled laborer. It seems unjust that an accident of birth could create such inequality of opportunities. Yet Rawls is not ready to label such a case injust—*until* it is shown that this inequality proves to be a detriment to the son of the laborer. Two people would not complain of injustice if a wealthy philanthropist gave them large sums of money, even if the sums were unequal, because both would be better off than before. In the same sense, it is possible that the benefits of a free market system are great enough and create sufficient additional wealth for society for it to be fair for some to get more than others. Referring to the benefits of the free market, the wealthy industrialist Andrew Carnegie once claimed, "The poor [now] enjoy what the rich could not before afford. What were the luxuries have become the necessities of life . . . [and] the laborer now has more luxuries than the farmer had a few generations ago. . . . The price which society pays for the law of competition . . . is . . . great; but the advantages of the law are greater still. . . ."[22] Does wealth really trickle down from the top and benefit even the laborer as Carnegie claims it does? Rawls is at least ready to admit the possibility, and if so, then the inequality in life opportunities between the son of the laborer and the son of the banker is not necessarily unjust. For Rawls, inequalities fostered by social institutions are tolerable *so long as they work to the advantage of everyone, including the worst off.*[23]

---

[21] Joan Robinson, "What Are the Rules of the Game," in *Property, Profits and Economic Justice,* ed. Virginia Held (Belmont, Calif.: Wadsworth, 1980), p. 142.

[22] Andrew Carnegie, "Wealth," in *Ethical Issues in Business,* ed. T. Donaldson and P. Werhane (Englewood Cliffs, N.J.: Prentice-Hall, 1979), p. 151.

[23] John Rawls, *A Theory of Justice* (Cambridge, Mass.: Harvard University Press, 1971).

But though the inequalities in opportunity which prevail in the free market may fail to produce injustice (because of the trickle-down possibility), according to Rawls the free market creates clear injustices in another area. Because the market distributes goods and services in relation to consumer demand, it obviously provides more goods where demand is higher, and fewer where it is lower. But "demand" is like "pure competition." It is a technical term and does not mean "what people demand" literally, but rather what they demand *and are able to pay for.* If I demand cream for my coffee, it makes no difference to the market unless I can pay for it, and the same goes for food, cars, housing, and medicine. Now the capacity to pay in a free market is linked to two basic factors: (1) one's inherited wealth, and (2) the market value of one's labor. Neither of these factors makes reference to the factor of one's *need,* and it follows that need is not a force in patterning the distribution of wealth in a free market. As Rawls puts it, "A market economy ignores the claims of need altogether."[24] Thus if I am crippled, or if I am mentally ill, or if I have skills that are no longer demanded by the market, it makes no difference to the market. It makes no difference how much I *need* food, shelter, or medicine, because the market operates not on need, but on "demand."

The injustice stemming from the market's neglect of need may be corrected, Rawls believes, but only at the expense of a certain amount of market freedom. Government, through its "transfer branch," must "take into account the precept of need and assign it an appropriate weight with respect to other common-sense precepts of justice."[25] In practice this means, for example, coercively requiring (through taxation) wealthier citizens to give some of their money to those who need it: the old, the handicapped, and the unemployed.

It should be noted that many theorists disagree with Rawls' general theory of justice and with his conviction that the government must consistently intervene in the market to ensure justice. Two men whose views we have already looked at, Robert Nozick and F. A. Hayek, offer elaborate critiques of Rawlsian theory and argue that despite its flaws a free market system maximizes justice and minimizes injustice. The very concept of distributive justice is said to assume that the wealth of society is like a pie on a table waiting to be carved up. We ponder questions of distributive justice when we ask, "How shall we cut the pie?"

But for the critics the staringly obvious fact is that wealth is not like the pie at all; instead of sitting on a table waiting to be divided, it is already divided and distributed. We must thus consider not only *to* whom the pie is to be given, but *from* whom it is to be taken. Because it is unjust to take property from someone who rightfully owns it, the very idea of "distributive justice," according to these theorists, appears to contain the seeds of injustice.

Interestingly enough, Rawls' assertion that a free market cannot in itself accommodate the claims of need may hold good even if his critics are right that a competitive market maximizes justice. Nozick does not claim, nor does Hayek, that a market system eliminates *all* injustice, and each allows that the needs of the aged,

---

[24] John Rawls, "Distributive Justice," in *Ethical Issues in Business,* ed. T. Donaldson and P. Werhane (Englewood Cliffs, N.J.: Prentice-Hall, 1979), p. 223.

[25] Rawls, "Distributive Justice," p. 230.

the handicapped, and the unemployed should be accommodated, albeit by government action or by individual charity. Thus, even if Rawls' larger thesis about the free market's requiring constant government intervention turns out to be wrong, his arguments may identify a flaw in the market, though perhaps a correctable one: namely, that the market fails to distribute goods and services in a way that recognizes need.

Neglecting the role of cooperative rules. The consequences of unrestrained competition in the real world are subject to dramatic fluctuations, and instead of yielding maximum social welfare, they create, according to critics, a "tragedy of the commons." The tragedy occurs when each economic unit, whether a corporation or individual person, attempts to maximize self-interest in a context where the combined effects of such maximizing works against the common good.

Consider a hypothetical situation. A host of individual sheep owners graze their sheep on the same land. No single person may be said to own the land; rather it is common property. From the perspective of each individual, it is profitable to add more sheep to his flock, and that is true even when the net effect of everyone's doing so is to ruin the grazing land. Suppose each owner stands to profit most by limiting his herd to 100 sheep, since the maximum number of sheep the land can adequately support is 100 times the number of owners. But if one owner limits his herd to 100 and another expands to 500, the former is a clear loser. It is in the self-interest of each to expand, despite the fact that the net effect of all doing so is eventual tragedy. The simple answer is that each must abide by a rule to limit herd size and that the rule must be enforced. But this is not free competition, nor does the theory of free competition explain the need for such rules.

The moral of this story is not limited to sheep. One of its most striking applications is to cities such as Los Angeles, where drivers confront smog and pollution. From the standpoint of each driver her self-interest is not maximized by her cutting down on driving, or even paying for unleaded gasoline. She correctly calculates the effect of her own particular sacrifice as next to nothing. Yet when everyone arrives at the same rational, self-interested conclusion, the result is an inevitable smog-choked, eye-watering atmosphere. Even fervent defenders of competition such as Milton Friedman acknowledge this difficulty under the label of the "neighborhood effects" problem. They cite as examples cases where companies dump waste into the air or waterways. In such instances even Friedman allows that regulations must be imposed on the free market.

Theorists dispute the seriousness and extent of the problem. Some say it is a minor but persistent thorn in the side of the free market; others believe it spells the ultimate ruination of capitalism. At a minimum, the problem of cooperative rules extends to issues such as ocean dumping, oil spills, the use of private autos versus public transportation, and the disposal of nuclear waste.

Small is beautiful. According to some critics, we suffer from the idolatry of giantism; people have tended to seek bigger houses, bigger cars, and ever-growing Gross National Products. The tendency itself may be rooted in the concept of a free market. Since the time of Adam Smith, economists have claimed that the forte of the free market is economic growth. But is "more" always "better"?

E. F. Schumacher, the author of *Small Is Beautiful,* leads a growing movement which challenges the assumption that "more is better."[26] "An attitude to life which seeks fulfillment in the single-minded pursuit of wealth," Schumacher writes, "does not fit into this world because it contains within itself no limiting principles, while the environment in which it is placed is strictly limited." Any gain in Gross National Product is considered a gain by the free market; yet a growing GNP is almost certain evidence of a shrinking supply of natural resources. With every additional gas-guzzler, the GNP grows but there is a corresponding unregistered waste of petroleum. The Gross National Product reflects not only the costs of the giant oil tanker that carries Middle Eastern oil, but the millions spent cleaning coastlines after a spill. The GNP reflects the production of feminine deodorants, designer jeans, "Saturday night specials," and baby seal fur coats. But are these *contributions* or *hindrances* to the general welfare?

Small-is-beautiful defenders advocate a return to basics. They claim that people are losing the vital capacity to work with their hands and that although we cannot turn back the clock to the Medieval era of craftsmanship, we can adopt technology to humans rather than vice versa. The workplace should be humanized; it should be designed to meet human needs and human values, and its technology must be scaled to needs of society as a whole. Especially underdeveloped countries, such as India or Colombia, should refuse to waste technological resources that provide a handful of people with high-technology jobs. They should refuse to allow a fraction of the population to build dishwashers in a fully automated factory while 40 percent of the rural population remains unemployed. Finally, these critics argue, we must redefine the very concept of "efficiency." An industrial system that uses 40 percent of the world's primary resources to supply less than 6 percent of the world's population, says Schumacher, could be called efficient only if it obtained strikingly successful results in terms of "human happiness, well-being, culture, peace, and harmony." Needless to say, Schumacher doubts that the present system attains such striking results.

A full discussion of the small-is-beautiful criticism cannot be undertaken here. For our purposes, the criticism's crucial challenge is to the free market's traditional emphasis on economic growth. Hundreds of years ago Adam Smith described the invisible hand as the answer to increasing the wealth of nations; this same insight appears to underlie many of today's arguments for profit maximization and corporate moral disinterest. But Schumacher and others charge that increasing the wealth of nations carries hidden costs: namely, shrinking resources, pollution, and threats to personal values.

Fairness and rights. A final criticism of the market is that it creates unfair advantages sometimes to the point of violating rights. We looked earlier at the

[26] E. F. Schumacher, *Small Is Beautiful: Economics as if People Mattered* (New York: Harper & Row, Pub., 1973), pp. 13-79.

charge that the market fails to distribute in accordance with need. Other critics assert that it is guilty of equally important, though related failures: that it offers built-in advantages to the rich but built-in disadvantages to the poor. Despite Rawls' claim that inequalities are acceptable if they work to the benefit of everyone, someone may wonder whether the enormously greater life prospects of the son of a rich financier, in contrast to those of the són of a coal miner or American Indian, are fair.

A free market is said to generate such inequalities because it concentrates wealth and power through free market transfers; it allows participants to trade and transfer unhindered, even when this means distributing wealth and privileges to undeserving people. Burdens as well as benefits may be unfairly distributed. When the market dips into a recession or a depression, thousands become unemployed, discouraged, and financially destitute. Yet those who suffer most are always the same: the poor, the black, the aging, and the handicapped.

Will the activities of a free market go so far as to violate people's rights? Robert Nozick, for one, denies it. According to him, so long as one acquires property in accordance with just principles of acquisition, or through just principles of transfer, one is entitled to the property. Voluntary market agreements are naturally consistent with a doctrine of rights because the agreements themselves reflect the most crucial right of all: freedom.

However, arguments from other theorists take issue with Nozick and conclude that a system of free and fair exchange can violate rights. Let us examine two such arguments, one from A. H. Goldman and the other from Peter Singer. Goldman asks us to consider a case in which the market reveals aggregate public preference for cheap electricity. Even if the majority of consumers are willing to take the risks involved in generating electricity by unsafe nuclear reactors, he asks, and even if independent utility companies are willing to build them, does not doing so violate the rights of a minority by subjecting it to risks and severe harm?[27]

In a similar vein, Peter Singer asks us to consider what happens when the market commercializes a previously noncommercial process. Consider a market in blood. In a country such as England, where all donations of blood are handled by the government and all donations are free, no one is paid for his or her blood, and consequently every donor must be motivated by charity rather than gain. Now it might be presumed that the absence of a market in blood denies the right of people to sell blood. But in fact, says Singer, just the opposite is true; the introduction of a market, as in the United States, violates the rights of donors to give their blood free of charge to those in need. Without the marketplace, people rightly worry that without contributions those needing blood would die: with the market, they are less concerned. Most important, with the market, the act of an individual donor loses much of its significance; he knows, among other things, that his blood will be

[27]Alan H. Goldman, "Business Ethics: Profits, Utilities, and Moral Rights," *Philosophy and Public Affairs,* 9 (Spring 1980), 275.

sold, not given, to the recipient. The net effect of a market in blood, Singer concludes, is ironically to deny people the right to donate blood outside the market.[28]

Modern Adjustments to the Free Market

The cogency of the preceding criticisms is a matter of dispute. If correct, however, they identify an impressive collection of free market problems which some critics of the invisible hand have labeled the "invisible foot." Society thus may be helped by the invisible hand, only to be kicked by the invisible foot.

Although few would embrace all of these criticisms, a surprising number of economists, including free market theorists, have accepted some. The majority of Western economists have stopped short of abandoning the free market entirely but have made crucial adjustments: economists no longer speak of the free market without tacitly referring to a host of qualifications on the meaning of "free," and many have developed theories to pinpoint market imperfections or to show the consequences of imperfections in actual practice. Optimistic observers compare these adjustments to the calculations of the physicist, who uses the concept of a perfect, frictionless plane to explain physical movement but who must also have theories of the "imperfection" in the real world. Pessimistic observers, on the other hand, compare them to a hasty patch job in which the theory of free competition is patched up for service but falls apart whenever applied.

One consequence of acknowledging market imperfections has been the acceptance of more government activity in the marketplace. Since the Great Depression, Western governments have accepted to varying degrees John Maynard Keynes' pronouncement that the market has no automatic mechanism to ensure that all goods produced at full employment will be bought (an outgrowth of the rejection of Say's Law). Businesspeople themselves worry that lagging demand can force suppliers to cut production, thus triggering a downward economic spiral of lower employment, lower demand, and lower production—into depression. Despite their traditional skepticism toward government, most businesspeople now accept and even endorse certain efforts by government to ensure effective demand. These take such forms as special policies of corporate taxation, control of the money supply, and the regulation of interest rates. The U.S. government also plays an increasingly active role in helping corporations meet other crucial objectives. It attempts to stabilize wages and prices, encourages continued technological innovation by spending public money on research and development, and gives large sums to universities to produce the engineers, accountants, chemists, lawyers, and other professionals that corporations hire. E. H. Carr once remarked that "the twentieth century . . . has substituted the cult of the strong remedial state for the doctrine of the natural harmony of interests."[29]

---

[28] Peter Singer, "Rights and the Market," in *Justice and Economic Distribution,* ed. John Arthur and William Shaw (Englewood Cliffs, N.J.: Prentice-Hall, 1978), pp. 207-21.

[29] E. H. Carr, *The New Society* (New York: Macmillan, 1951).

But the government has entered the free market to do more than help business. It also has attempted to rectify some of the problems stemming from the market's failure to distribute wealth in accordance with need. People who need goods and services but who fail to compete successfully in a free market have become a special concern of the modern welfare state. One well-known economic theorist said recently that "The welfare state, however inadequate in actuality, is now a generally accepted model for all industrial societies, bringing with it a considerable degree of socialism in the form of guaranteed incomes, family allowances, public health insurance, educational access for low income groups, and the like."[30] The persistent presence of government in what once was a more autonomous market system has led some observers to refer to the modern era as "Postcapitalism."

Thus, free market theories have undergone significant criticism and change in the twentieth century. Not only have they been criticized on conceptual grounds for their inability to predict monopolistic tendencies and other market forces, but in the real world their application has been diluted through a mixture of government planning, taxation, and control. Whatever the peculiar benefits of the classical free market, they must be weighed against such realities.

A Reformulation of the Teleological Argument

If the previous arguments have merit, then the work promised by the invisible hand is threatened by the invisible foot. But we have also seen that most existing economic systems refuse to trust the invisible hand completely. With this in mind, it may be worth returning to the original argument—the claim that the free market justifies profit maximization and moral disinterest—and reformulating it in light of existing realities. Consider the following series of claims:

1. Modern capitalistic economic systems (such as those in the United States, England, and Germany) embody, however imperfectly, free markets.

2. The free market component of such systems is responsible for their capacity to satisfy consumer interests better than any other alternative (nonfree market) system.

3. An assumption of free market theory is that participants will merely maximize profits.

4. Therefore, corporations should merely maximize profits.

This version escapes many of the difficulties of the former argument: most important, it refers to actual rather than ideal institutions. But it too has problems. To begin with, the second premise is controversial. On the one hand, there is no doubt that the economic systems of England, France, Germany, and in short, all of

---

[30]Robert L. Heilbroner, *Business Civilization in Decline* (New York: W. W. Norton & Co., Inc., 1976).

Western Europe plus the United States and Japan, have attained levels of material wealth superior to those of the rest of the world. The hypothesis that their remarkable success stems from their capitalistic economies has much in its favor. Yet, even if supported by good reasons, the hypothesis lacks the degree of certainty found in the proposition, "2 plus 2 equals 4," or "I see a glass on the table." This is because of the multitude of variables that figure into the creation and maintenance of modern economic systems. One analyst points to the fact that most highly productive countries such as England and the United States have capitalistic economic systems. But another analyst, less impressed with the connection between a given economic system and level of productivity, points to the relatively high level of education and technology existing in these countries *before* capitalism emerged. Another, still unconvinced, points to the role of work habits, religion, and family in economic success. Certainly a variety of factors, including type of economic system, level of technology, and cultural habits, play roles; the real question is, how much does each play?

Many economists today tend to emphasize historical factors and to see people as being more firmly prisoners of national histories than before. George Dalton, a contemporary anthropologist-economist, writes:

> Traditional attributes of culture and social organization will count more than capitalist or socialist institutions in determining success or failure of third world nations to industrialize or develop; that communist China will do better than communist Cuba for the same reasons that capitalist Japan has done better than capitalist Philippines; that semi-socialist Israel will continue to do better than socialist Egypt and Syria . . . and that socialist Guinea and Tanzania will not do any better than capitalist Ivory Coast and Nigeria.[31]

Dalton's suggestion may be doubted, but it cannot be dismissed out of hand, since like any economic hypothesis, it arises from a confusing labyrinth of facts. In the laboratory the scientist isolates variables; she separates salt from one test tube and leaves it in another. But in the world of economics the scientist must study her elusive subject as it is.

A deeper problem, however, lies in the link between the first three premises and the conclusion. Do 1-3, if true, imply that corporations should merely maximize profits? Notice the wording of 3: it states that an assumption of free market theory is that participants will merely maximize profits. As we saw earlier, this is not quite true: corporations do pursue goals besides profits, but for now we shall let that pass. More important is that the premise states participants *will* maximize profits, not that they *should* do so. A crucial question, then, is how the "should" in the conclusion is derived.

Professional philosophers will recognize the problem here as one of deriving an "is" from an "ought." Few problems have vexed philosophers more, or ship-

[31]George Dalton, *Economic Systems and Society* (Kingsport, Tenn.: Kingsport Press, 1974), p. 197.

wrecked more of their arguments. Clearly, from the claim that people *are* selfish, or *are* warlike, or *are* aggressive, it is difficult to conclude they *ought* to be. However, if facts do not support values, what can? Without attempting to solve this thorny problem, let us note that even those philosophers who do believe an "ought" can be extracted from an "is" also believe doing so is tedious and requires both special circumstances and detailed explanation.

The argument as it stands, then, is inconclusive. To succeed, it must explain the move from the assumption that market participants *will* simply maximize profits to the conclusion that they *should*. Most likely, this will involve, at a minimum, specifying the moral merits of a free market system, for example, how a free market contributes to human welfare. But this, unfortunately, means returning full circle to the original free market arguments, and these arguments, as we have seen, are highly controversial. Thus, the reformulated argument appears to make no genuine advance over the earlier ones. Its merits, whatever they are, are the same merits emphasized by the original teleological arguments—and open to the same doubts.

Thus, the teleological argument is only as strong as the response it can muster to its numerous criticisms. But though the final evaluation will be left to the reader, the burden of proof appears to lie with those defending the argument, with those who claim that policies of profit maximization and moral disinterest are justified through free market theory. The burden rests here because in the absence of arguments to the contrary, few would presume that moral deliberation automatically can be bypassed by either individuals or corporations. The burden, moreover, is a formidable one: for although flaws appear when the numerous criticisms are examined individually, when considered as a group they form an impressive challenge to any would-be exoneration of pure profit maximizing. Nothing said thus far, then, succeeds in demonstrating that corporations are *excused* from deliberating about moral issues. Neither the teleological nor deontological arguments escape shadows of significant doubt.

This is not at all to demean the free market; it is only to suggest that it lacks omnipotence. Despite the enormous advantages it promises—and appears to deliver—a system of free enterprise cannot absolve persons of the need to confront moral problems. And what it cannot do for individual people, it cannot do for corporations.

To persist in defending unadulterated profit maximization tends to generate a vicious circle. If corporations neglect moral issues, society will look outside the corporation for remedies to corporate immorality, for remedies to product safety violations, to dishonesty, and to employee problems. Invariably it will look to government, since the government alone has sufficient power to control corporations. But this means governmental interference in business, which the theory of the invisible hand opposes. Thus there is a vicious circle: the free market is used, as it were, as a weapon against itself. This problem has led many observers to suggest that instead of discouraging corporate morality, free market theory actually establishes its necessity.

Let us be clear: nothing has successfully demonstrated that the primary goal of a corporation should *not* be profit. As we saw in Chapter 4, the market system is designed to promote efficiency, entrepreneurship, and economic development by utilizing the motive of profit. This suggests that the profit motive may play a peculiarly moral role in capitalistic systems and that corporations that pursue profits are, however ironic it sounds, involved in a *moral* pursuit. As Peter Drucker once remarked, "Even if archangels sat in the corporate boardroom instead of businessmen, they would still have to be concerned with profitability."[32]

But as we have seen, the invisible hand should no longer be counted upon to perform society's dirty work. This asks more of the theory than it was designed to deliver. Even the discoverer of the invisible hand, Adam Smith, believed that moral rules were necessary aspects of a society in which the marketplace could function properly and that market solutions are not always socially optimal. For them to be optimal, he believed, morality itself must be a force in the marketplace.

SUGGESTED SUPPLEMENTARY READINGS

BECKER, LAWRENCE C., *Property Rights.* London: Routledge & Kegan Paul, 1978.

———, "The Labor Theory of Property Acquisition," *Journal of Philosophy,* 73 (1976): 653-664.

CHAUDHURI, JOYOTPAUL, "Toward a Democratic Theory of Property and the Modern Corporation," *Ethics,* 81 (July 1971): 271-86.

COHEN, G. A., "The Labor Theory of Value and the Concept of Exploitation," *Philosophy and Public Affairs,* 8 (Summer 1979): 338-60.

DALTON, GEORGE, *Economic Systems and Society.* Kingsport, Tenn.: Kingsport Press, Inc., 1974.

GIBBARD, ALLAN, and HAL VARIAN, "Economic Models," *Journal of Philosophy,* 75 (November 1978): 664-77.

GOLDMAN, ALAN H., "Business Ethics: Profits, Utilities, and Moral Rights," *Philosophy and Public Affairs,* 9 (Spring 1980): 260-86.

HAHN, FRANK, and MARTIN HOLLIS, eds., *Philosophy and Economic Theory.* Oxford: Oxford University Press, 1979.

HARRINGTON, MICHAEL, *Socialism.* New York: Bantam Books, 1970.

———, *The Twilight of Capitalism.* New York: Simon & Schuster, 1972 (first published 1953).

[32] Quoted in David Ewing, *Freedom Inside the Organization* (New York: McGraw-Hill, 1977), p. 66.

HELD, VIRGINIA, *Property, Profits and Economic Justice*. Belmont, Calif.: Wadsworth, 1980.

HOLLIS, MARTIN, and EDWARD NELL, *Rational Economic Man*. London: Cambridge University Press, 1975.

KEYNES, J. M., *The End of Laissez-Faire*. London: L. & Wolf, 1926.

LOEVINSOHN, ERNEST, "Liberty and the Redistribution of Property," *Philosophy and Public Affairs*, 6 (Spring 1977): 226-39.

MACPHERSON, D. B., *Democratic Theory*. Oxford: Oxford University Press, 1973.

MILBRAND, RALPH, *Marxism and Politics*. Oxford: Oxford University Press, 1977.

NOZICK, ROBERT, *Anarchy, State, and Utopia*. New York: Basic Books, 1974.

RESCHER, NICHOLAS, "Economics vs. Moral Philosophy," *Theory and Decision*, 10 (1979): 169-79.

ROSEN, FREDERICK, "Basic Needs and Justice," *Mind*, 86 (1977): 88-94.

SCHUMACHER, E. F., *Small Is Beautiful: Economics as if People Mattered*. New York: Harper & Row, Pub., 1973.

SCHWEICKART, DAVID, "Capitalism, Contribution and Sacrifice," *The Philosophical Forum (1976): 260-75.*

SEN, AMARTYA, *On Economic Inequality*. Oxford: Clarendon Press, 1973.

———, "Rational Fools: Critique of the Behavioral Foundations of Economic Theory," *Philosophy and Public Affairs*, 6 (1976-1977): 317-44.

SMITH, ADAM, *The Theory of Moral Sentiments*. London: Henry Bohn, 1853 (first published 1759).

SRAFFA, PIERO, "The Laws of Return under Competitive Conditions," in *Readings in Price Theory*, ed. George Stigler and Kenneth Boulding. Homewood, Ill.: Richard D. Irwin, 1952.

WOLIN, SHELDON, *Politics and Vision*. Boston: Little, Brown, 1960.

CHAPTER 6

Responsibility in Corporate Bureaucracies

"**M**an is born free, but everywhere he is in organizations." Whoever altered Rousseau's famous slogan might have been thinking of life in large, modern corporations. Large corporations are succumbing to the pressures of bureaucratization and experiencing the problems typical in bureaucracies. Their transition carries direct implications for the issue of corporate responsibility, because the extent to which people are submerged in and controlled by bureaucracies is the extent to which ordinary individual responsibility is threatened. The clerk who works for a multibillion dollar corporation behaves in accordance with a system of rules—but he does not make the rules, and he is not directly accountable for their consequences. Chapter 2 revealed that in order to attain the status of moral agency, a corporation must possess a decision-making process which is genuinely moral. One of the principal aims of the present chapter is to unravel the problems for developing such a process which are posed by the complexities of modern bureaucratization.

THE ELEMENTS OF BUREAUCRACY

As organizations become larger, they become more bureaucratic, and modern corporations are clearly becoming larger. The same share of manufacturing assets that was controlled by the largest 1,000 corporations in 1946 was controlled by the largest 200 corporations in 1973. More important, changes in basic structure are occurring; modern corporations look less like the traditional model, with clearly defined authority and accountability structures, and are becoming more complicated and impersonal. The demands of technology have forced the development of a corporate technostructure and have in turn blurred traditional demarcations of authority and responsibility. We shall see that the resulting problems of moral responsibility are logical as well as empirical. There are logical difficulties in assigning responsibility to corporate structures that divorce the responsibility to account for moral error from the capacity to control events.

Determining the locus of responsibility is more difficult in a bureaucratic corporation. Contrast the ease with which accountability may be understood in a small, simple organization, with the difficulty of understanding it in an enormous one. How, for example, does one sort through the tangled skein of accountability problems which culminated in a Firestone "500" or a Three-Mile Island disaster?

The increasing bureaucratization of the corporation has threatened meaningful corporate responsibility. Three specific tendencies constitute the overall movement toward bureaucratization: (1) the increase of impersonal rules; (2) the move toward centralized decision-making, and (3) the isolation of strata in the corporate hierarchy.[1] Each shall be examined separately.

The subjugation of the individual by the organization is an old fact. While examining the modern corporation, it is well to remember that only two centuries ago conformity in organizations was obtained through direct means, often with a great deal of open coercion. Nothing less than complete devotion was demanded of members of the Jesuit order or the Prussian Grenadiers. In such organizations leaving was equated with treason.[2] Yet modern methods of generating conformity have an equally effective, though more subtle impact. Of special importance is the ongoing deterioration of systems of direct supervision in favor of elaborate systems of impersonal rules and regulations. Although rule-bound work relieves people from the watchful eyes of their superiors, it causes special problems in morale and accountability.

Organizational theorists agree that increasing bureaucratization of the corporation results in an increase in impersonal rules. Max Weber maintains that the evolution toward large-scale organizations is unrelenting, and he identifies an increase in rules as a necessary feature of that evolution. In order to achieve increasing efficiency, expertise, rationality, and predictability, organizations must not only develop effective control structures, but specify spheres of competence and increase the number and the impact of rules.[3] In an efficient organization, individual people must be replaceable without provoking crisis, and this means that decision-making must depend on rules, not people. Other forces also prompt systems of impersonal rules. The subordination of one individual to another creates a predictable tension (especially in societies where the ideal of individual freedom is strong) and these tensions can be alleviated by imposing impersonal bureaucratic standards. But a vicious circle develops. Impersonal rules perpetuate the very tensions that

---

[1] These represent three tendencies which Michael Crozier identifies in *The Bureaucratic Phenomenon* (Chicago: University of Chicago Press, 1964).

[2] Crozier, *Bureaucratic Phenomenon*, p. 184.

[3] For Max Weber's account of the paradigmatic organization, see his *The Theory of Social and Economic Organizations*, trans. Am. Henderson and Talcott Parsons (New York: Macmillan, 1947); and *Basic Concepts in Sociology*, trans. H. Secher (New York: Philosophical Library, 1962).

generated them: such rules reinforce low motivation, which in turn creates a need for close supervision.

The immediate consequence of the emergence of impersonal rules is that responsibility becomes submerged in rules. We noticed that a special advantage of rule structures is that they are more permanent than people; they relieve the organization from a dependence on particular individuals. Yet from the standpoint of moral responsibility this advantage becomes a disadvantage in that rule-bound individuals refuse accountability for their own actions. "I only follow the rules," is the typical, threadbare, bureaucratic response. If the antagonisms between worker and manager are severe, the curious phenomenon of ritualism may even develop. We all know of the stubborn clerk who makes a point of following the regulations to the letter, even when doing so involves ignoring realities and frustrating the very goals of the organization. Members of a labor union may, in a similar manner, defy management by "working to rule," that is, only working up to the level explicitly stated in the union contract—*even when* exceeding that level is easier.

If in a bureaucracy responsibility is submerged in rules, then it follows that ultimate responsibility should attach to those who make the rules. But though this implication is logical, it neither simplifies nor resolves the problem. Rules outlive their makers, and it is often impossible to hold a single person accountable for a bad rule, or for the exceptions an otherwise good rule should allow. Furthermore, individuals in a bureaucracy seldom make rules alone: committees or informal groups usually make them, with the result that these groups become the logical locus of accountability. This is problematic, however, since the committee or group is at a distance from the clerk or employee who follows its directives, and since such groups can *account* for their activities only when they are in session.

In addition to impersonal rules, corporate bureaucracies generate centralized authority. As Paul Kurtz remarks, "The logic of the organization is essentially conservative. Thus there is a standardization and consistency of behavior. Increasingly there is a tendency for individual responsibility to give way to corporate responsibility, and the individual denies he is responsible for what the corporation does."[4] The elimination of discretionary personal power in lower corporate ranks pushes that power up the ranks. Commands then flow from the pinnacle of the bureaucracy to its base, and when the bureaucracy is large, the lines of accountability become overextended. John Lachs characterizes the resulting problem as one of "psychic distance." When the Japanese General Yamashita was tried (and eventually executed) for war crimes following World War II, he protested that the atrocities his soldiers committed in the Pacific Islands were so distant from the center of his organization that they occurred despite his good intentions. Lachs observes that the centralization inherent in large bureaucracies demands that responsibility be assigned to the center; but this assignment is weakened by the

---

[4]Paul Kurtz, "The Individual, the Organization, and Participatory Democracy," in *Problems in Contemporary Society,* ed. Paul Kurtz (Englewood Cliffs, N.J.: Prentice-Hall, 1969), p. 193.

fact that the psychic distance between center and periphery is often so great that effective control vanishes.[5]

Closely connected to the problem of impersonal rules and centralization is the problem of the isolation of different strata in the corporate hierarchy. When authority is converted into impersonal rules, and when ultimate power is transferred to the center of the corporation, the result is a separation of strata in the authority hierarchy. Impersonal rules obviate the need for face-to-face authority relations, and this in turn means a separation of subordinate and superordinate structures. One always obeys the rules, but it no longer is necessary to submit to the whims of individual people. If there is no need to yield to higher authority, the importance of peer pressures increases. Nevertheless, the peer pressures to which people submit are not, either by accident or design, ones which assume moral responsibility for the actions of the organization. Peer pressures and impersonal rules eliminate day-to-day decision-making in a corporate bureaucracy, but neither promotes genuine moral responsibility.

Because of the isolation of the various strata, it often happens that the center of the organization, i.e., its decision-making nucleus, is isolated from the peripheral areas at which the organization has its direct contact with the public. Here the problem of isolation of strata overlaps with that of centralization. Executives at the center of a corporation often find it difficult to respond effectively to, and be responsible for, actions at the periphery. In his classical analysis of General Motors in 1946, Peter Drucker identified one of that company's greatest problems as the isolation of its top executives from the sentiments of the general public, and he pointed out that it was an isolation which resulted in poor public relations and bad investment decisions.[6]

THE PROFESSIONAL

We have seen that because a bureaucratic organization does not allow for initiative at the periphery, decisions must be made and responsibility must be located where the power is located, at the center. There is one exception to this rule. Modern corporations require one kind of employee whose actions stubbornly resist being reduced to impersonal rules—the professional. The professional is a species of expert whose services are often required because of increasingly technological demands or increasing complexity in the surrounding social and legal climate. Yet as an expert he is presumed to know best about his area of work. His expertise makes him unique in the bureaucratic world. His activities cannot be fully directed from the main office through impersonal rules, because only he is qualified to direct his own work.

[5] John Lachs, " 'I Only Work Here': Mediation and Irresponsibility," in *Ethics, Free Enterprise, and Public Policy,* ed. Richard De George and Joseph Pichler (New York: Oxford University Press, 1978), pp. 201-13.

[6] Peter Drucker, *Concept of the Corporation,* rev. ed. (New York: John Day Co., 1972), p. 88.

Two important consequences follow. First, the professional, unlike other bureaucratic employees, is faced with two sets of standards used to evaluate his behavior, and the two are not always mutually compatible. He is faced on the one hand with the standards of the organization, which dictate success in terms of organizational goals; and he is faced on the other with the standards of his profession. The professional feels this dilemma most acutely when thrown into the role of organizational administrator. The professor who becomes dean of her college suffers when forced to make important decisions which are supposed to *both* enhance the future of the university and satisfy professional academic standards. The closer the professional comes to the power center of the organization, the sharper the conflict.

Second, in a bureaucratic world which tends to reduce all authority relationships to impersonal rules, the relative status and power of the professional increases. "The position of experts," Crozier remarks, "is much stronger in an organization where everything is controlled and regulated."[7] This is true, of course, so long as his own task cannot be reduced to rules. It follows that as corporations become more bureaucratic, the power of the professional increases in relation to that of the nonprofessional. Thus, a bureaucracy transforms specialized expertise into political power.

In addition to the traditional categories of professionals, modern corporate life creates new ones. The data systems analyst, the marketing specialist, the labor negotiator, the management theorist, and the public relations expert are necessary ingredients in the modern corporate success formula. These new professionals possess most of the traditional characteristics associated with professionals: they rely on a theoretical store of knowledge, are graduated from research-oriented institutions, apply their knowledge to practical problems, and subject their work to review and criticism from colleagues.

Many of these new "technocratic" professions, however, lack a key characteristic associated with traditional professions. With the professions of medicine, law, or teaching, we associate a spirit of altruism or service; but the new technocratic professions often lack this characteristic and thus raise special problems of moral responsibility. We associate the goal of healing with the physician, and of knowledge with the professor (no matter how mercenary doctors or professors may be in fact), yet there are no corresponding goals for the marketing specialist, the public relations manager, or the advertising expert. The standards of the new professional do not explicitly include moral standards, in part because his or her profession does not recognize an altruistic element in its overall goals. The old professions have frequently failed to apply the moral standards articulated in statements of their professional goals; but the new professions fail, it seems, because they do not even attempt to articulate moral standards.

With the power and status of professionals rising in proportion to the degree of bureaucratization of the organization and the degree of technological

[7]Crozier, *Bureaucratic Phenomenon,* p. 193.

efficiency required, the need for moral reinforcement through one's profession also increases. Henry Ford used to make virtually every decision about the design and production of the Model T. Today the demands of technology reserve authority for the technocrat. At Ford Motor Company important decisions are reserved for such specialists as the production expert and the design engineer. But the added authority for the new professional requires added responsibility: those who design and produce Ford products today are obliged to avoid catastrophies like the Pinto's exploding gas tank. That is why, when considering the modern corporation, many critics stress a need for an improvement in professional ethics.

When in 1970 Peter Drucker returned to General Motors nearly twenty years after an earlier study, he complained that G.M. had failed to solve the basic problem of balancing its own needs with "concern for its environment and compassion for its community." Drucker concludes that much of the blame for this failure lies at the door of the new professional. "General Motors' success is clearly the success of the technocrat," he remarks, "but so is General Motors' failure."[8]

BUREAUCRATIC COMPLEXITY

So far we have identified four fundamental accountability problems stemming from the increasing bureaucratization of the corporation. These are related to:

1. The increase of impersonal rules.
2. The increase of centralized decision-making.
3. The increase of isolation between hierarchical strata.
4. The increase in the relative power of professionals, and a failure, especially of the new professions, to embody standards of moral responsibility.

The fifth and final problem which deserves consideration is that of aggravated complexity in bureaucratic decision-making. Bureaucracies are frequently faced with decision-making complexities more severe than those faced by human individuals, and sometimes these frustrate even the combined capacities of the bureaucracy. Greater complexity means decreased control, and this in turn means problems for organizational accountability.

Ordinary human beings confront a maze of facts with each decision. Making an ordinary decision to buy groceries requires knowledge of a multitude of facts, e.g., when stores open and close, which products are available, how to find transportation, and which selections will fulfill intended needs. These complexities are multiplied enormously in corporate decision-making. When General Motors plans to purchase parts from a supplier, it may need three or four years of discussion, the talents of thousands of employees, and enough information to fill a good-sized computer. Even then it may not avoid a purchasing disaster.

[8] Drucker, *Concept*, p. 468.

Three specific factors heighten the complexity of bureaucratic decision-making: technology, organizational structure, and mediation. First, technological problems accelerate complexity. The more a task is reducible to routine, other things being equal, the simpler it is; but the ongoing needs for technological improvements rule out routinization. With the need for constant improvements in drugs, automobile engines, and audio equipment, technocrats who design these products must constantly rethink their own decisions and must constantly modify product designs and modes of production. Today, Zenith, Inc., would fail if it attempted to market the same stereo system it designed in 1975. Another factor increasing complexity is the tendency of technology to require a variety of skills. Although the problems inherent in a simple task, such as mixing chemicals, may call only for the expertise of a single chemist, the successful design and manufacture of the latest hair dryer or typewriter can require the skills of metallurgists, organic chemists, electrical engineers, and safety experts. When more people are added to a single task, its complexity increases, not only because the efforts of each must be coordinated with the others, but because when technological skills are combined, each expert is ignorant, practically speaking, of the knowledge possessed by the others. The plastics expert must coordinate his efforts with those of the organic chemist and of the electrical engineer, but none of them knows much about each other's skills and approaches.

Second, organizational structure itself compounds complexity. Groups do not make decisions as individuals do, and when organizational mechanisms are complex, as often happens, the complexity spills over into decision-making problems. For example, companies typically separate "line" from "staff" functions. Line organizations are characterized by a hierarchical authority structure (the plant manager reports upward to the division manager, and so on) while staff organizations are characterized by the special functions they serve in the overall organization (examples would be corporate accounting divisions and departments of research and development). Most modern corporations embody both kinds of structure. Yet although personnel from both ultimately report to the president, authority relationships *between* the two are typically vauge. Furthermore, personnel from each are expected to cooperate in corporate projects, but facilitating such cooperation can be complex and frustrating.

Add to this the fact that corporations often depend upon groups rather than individuals for decision-making. The variables generating a decision increase with an increase in the number of people making the decision; thus group decisions increase complexity. Not only do different group members hold divergent views, but when considered as a whole, the group is less inclined than an individual person to display consistency over the long run. Members of committees, for example, change, and often the changing ideas of even existing members combine in surprising ways. The larger the group, the greater the number of changing variables. As leaders of totalitarian countries have discovered to their frustration, commitments from democratic governments are subject to modification, precisely because of the vicissitudes of large-group decision-making.

The phenomenon called "mediation" constitutes the third and final factor compounding complexity in corporate bureaucracies. A constraint on corporate decision-makers is that their decisions must be communicated to the individuals and groups who implement them. In contrast to the individual who carries out his or her own decisions, corporate decisions are often mediated through hundreds or even thousands of people. Not only do breakdowns in communication occur (as in the case of the Japanese General Yamashita) but in large organizations such breakdowns are *predictable;* that is to say, they are sufficiently frequent that the decision-maker must actively consider their possibility. The marketing team in a publishing company that designs procedures for advertising and distributing text-books must anticipate that some sample copies will fail to be distributed by field representatives in accordance with its directives. Anticipating the problems arising from mediation makes the tasks of bureaucratic decision-making significantly more complex; since one does not have full control over the outcome, one must choose against a formidable backdrop of uncertainties.

As Aristotle observed in his classical formula for voluntary action, if a decision-maker is unaware of the consequences of his action, his act is involuntary. This also means that he is not morally responsible for his act, since an action must be voluntary before we consider it subject to praise or blame. (We excuse people from first-degree murder when they didn't know the gun was loaded.) Now, because the problems of technology, organizational structure, and mediation combine to inflate decision-making complexities in corporations, they seriously threaten assignments of responsibility. With multiplied uncertainties, superhuman intelligence is demanded for anticipating outcomes. The dilemma of unforeseen consequences is magnified, and with it the dilemma of establishing genuine accountability.

LESSENING BUREAUCRATIC PROBLEMS

When accountability disasters erupt in U.S. corporations, one or more of the problems we have discussed frequently are involved. Consider, for example, the much publicized aircraft brake scandal which occurred in the B. F. Goodrich Corporation in the late 1960's. During the month of June 1968, Air Force A7D planes equipped with new B. F. Goodrich brake assemblies landed at Edwards Air Force Base during experiments to test the brakes. The Goodrich brakes failed repeatedly. During a particular landing one brake welded shut, sending the plane skidding 1,500 feet before it came to a halt. Luckily, no one was killed. After the plane was jacked up and its wheels removed, the faulty brakes had to be pried apart with metal bars. Most remarkable was the fact that this disaster occurred after months of tests at B. F. Goodrich had already shown that the brakes were faulty. (The brakes overheated in simulated landings and failed on each occasion to pass requisite Air Force standards.) Nearly ten Goodrich employees had helped to doctor and falsify the test reports.

It is possible to pass off the disaster as a mere failure on the part of individual Goodrich employees, and to think each employee succumbed to pressures that most people would have overcome. But in this instance, none of the employees had histories of misbehavior. All were good citizens as well as respected corporate employees. Why did these employees falsify the report?

The answer may lie with the bureaucratic factors we have been discussing. At B. F. Goodrich, as at other major corporations, impersonal rules, centralized authority relationships, and isolation of organizational strata are standard features. Indeed, the isolation between strata was so severe at B. F. Goodrich that the strata at which engineering decisions were made had little contact with the strata at which major policy decisions were made. The decision to go after the Air Force brake contract "at all costs" was made by the corporate hierarchy and laid unceremoniously at the door of the engineering department. No communication occurred between the two which might have clarified the meaning of the "at all costs" proviso. Upper management had no idea how its directives were being interpreted and was not informed that the brakes were faulty until the scandal broke. Meanwhile, the employees who were courageous enough to complain about the faulty design found themselves caught in a maze of overlapping line and staff structures. Nobody wanted to hear the complaints, partly because nobody knew *whose* responsibility the complaints were. At lower levels, individuals were reluctant to blow the whistle because they saw their obligation as simply doing their jobs and "following the rules." The official supervisor for the engineering department turned a deaf ear to complaints. Not having an engineering degree himself, he was compelled, he said, to trust the professional skills of the designer. The moral timidness of Goodrich personnel played some role in the B. F. Goodrich brake scandal, but clearly the scandal was aggravated by the character of the Goodrich bureaucracy.

To solve problems of bureaucratization, one may turn to traditional answers, namely, to the government or to unions. However, the government finds it difficult to control the professional for the same reason corporations do: the acknowledged expert in the professional's area is the professional himself. Unions in turn are often more concerned with the welfare of their members than they are with consumers or society at large. A final consideration is still more damning. How can the problems stemming from the bureaucratization of the corporation be solved through the government or the unions—which are *themselves* large bureaucracies?

Society demands that corporations be morally accountable for their actions. As we saw in the analysis of the social contract, society requires that corporations behave responsibly toward employees, consumers, and the general public. They must adhere to certain norms of, for example, product safety, use of natural resources, hiring policies, environmental impact, treatment of employees, and relations with Third World nations. Moreover, society assumes that when corporations fail to meet these standards, moral criticism is appropriate.

We have seen that bureaucratization weakens the accountability of the individual with respect to corporate actions, so it appears reasonable to suggest that society's demands might be satisfied by development of *institutional* mechanisms which do not depend on individuals. This solution is analogous to the institutional solutions embodied in liberal democracy and laissez-faire economic theory. Our constitutional and institutional arrangements in a liberal democracy are designed to prevent individual abuses of power by balancing opposing political interests; and the laissez-faire system of economics, as we saw in Chapter 4, lessens the need to rely on individual virtue by automatically converting economic self-interest into public welfare. Whether these mechanisms are thoroughly effective is not at issue; they suggest a strategy for reforming the modern corporation.

But though such mechanisms promise a better fit between corporate behavior and social well-being, few would do much for corporate responsibility per se. Including representatives of the public on corporate boards of directors, or instituting "social audit" committees composed of consumers, or giving towns-people "voting shares" of corporate stock—to mention only a few of the current institutional proposals—may limit corporate harm, but if so, it is not because of increased *responsibility,* but because of a better balancing of competing interests. Protecting people against themselves is not equivalent to making them more responsible. To increase moral responsibility, there must be an increase in the tendency for individuals and groups themselves to direct their behavior according to moral norms.

What, then, is the solution to the problems of moral responsibility in bureaucratic corporations? Here we enter unexplored territory with few empirical guideposts and no proven strategies. Fortunately, in recent years such problems have attracted sufficient attention to generate a number of proposals for corporate reform. A few of these bear directly on problems of corporate bureaucratization and may be grouped into the following classes:

1. Attempts to restore individual responsibility in bureaucracies.
2. Attempts to enhance the accountability of professionals in bureau-cracies.
3. Attempts to improve bureaucratic decision-making.

Restoring individual accountability. The first set of proposals contains potential remedies for the problem of individuals who are stripped of individual responsibility because of bureaucratic routinization. This problem especially afflicts individuals who, like the clerk or assembly line worker, lie at the bottom of the corporate pyramid. We saw that a vicious bureaucratic circle develops: impersonal rules are imposed to solve problems of immediate authority relationships, but they only lead to a deterioration of morale, which in turn demands stronger immediate authority relationships. A saying common among French bureaucrats describes the resulting attitude: "We are here to write reports; our service to the public is only a by-product."

Some means must be discovered to restore the individual accountability that is destroyed by the bureaucracy. Two options present themselves. First, corporate organizations might be encouraged to return to their historic origins and reinstitute direct authority relationships among individuals and among corporate strata, thus relieving the need for impersonal rules and reuniting disjoined accountability segments. Second, corporations might be encouraged to push toward a wholly new *democratic* model of accountability, in which individuals would participate through institutional structures in the management of the bureaucracy. These two alternatives correspond roughly to Dorothy Emmet's distinction between mechanistic and organic organizations, "mechanistic" referring to organizations with a hierarchical system of control, authority, and communication, with information and knowledge located at the center of the organization, and "organic" referring to organizations with lateral rather than vertical directions of communication, with continual adjustment and redefinition of individual tasks, and mutual decision-making.[9]

The first model is a return to classical, pyramid-shaped organizations. For this reason it seems an unlikely candidate, since it is reasonable to assume that the same forces that led to the breakdown of the traditional organization will do the same today. The second is appealing but sounds dangerously utopian. Can the ideal of participatory democracy survive in the brutal environment of modern business?

The philosopher Paul Kurtz has argued that the participatory model is the only means of restoring genuine accountability to bureaucratic institutions. "We need," he says, "an organizational bill of rights, an emancipation proclamation by means of which we can build a plurality of democratic institutions."[10] Although he is not specific about the form such an emancipation might take in the corporation, we may assume that corporate employees would participate in decisions that specify corporate goals and define systems of corporate rules (although their participation might be limited). Thus, although features of bureaucratization would remain, such as the existence of impersonal rules, the fact of employee participation would imply that those generating the rules would be accountable for their form and impact. Individual accountability for the application of impersonal rules would be enhanced, since those applying them would also be responsible for their generation. At the same time, participatory mechanisms would mitigate accountability problems flowing from centralization and isolation of corporate strata. Participation implies a reversal of the tendency toward centralized, hierarchical decision-making, and knowledgeable decision-making implies that participants from one strata of corporate life are acquainted with the facts of life in other strata.

Despite the benefits of the participatory model, there are also costs. Participation denies employees the luxury of separating themselves spiritually from their work. When one helps make the rules, it is harder to say "I just follow the rules." It is harder, in short, to keep one's soul aloof from the organization, and surprisingly, those living in societies that prize individualism are often eager to

[9]Dorothy Emmet, *Rules, Roles, and Relations* (New York: St. Martin's Press, 1967), pp. 118-215.

[10]Kurtz, "The Individual," p. 195.

maintain such an aloofness. Another cost is that participation from the periphery of an organization does not mean less work for those at the center; it typically means more. When everyone participates in a promotion decision, the pressure to design complex procedures and to cope with delicate political problems increases for the administrator.[11] As chairpersons from thoroughly democratic academic departments realize, democracy can be messy. Then there is the standard dilemma of all democratic social action; participatory control is possible only through bureaucratic structures, and bureaucratic structures can be destructive of democratic values.

There is evidence that increased worker participation in the design of work conditions yields greater productivity, but the evidence is slight and must be weighed in terms of the "Hawthorne Effect."[12] (The Hawthorne experiment showed that production tends to increase *whenever* management alters work conditions, regardless of the change.)

Nevertheless, the ultimate moral justification for attempting to solve accountability problems by introducing participatory mechanisms is not greater productivity. It is that our moral ideals require accountability whenever actions are taken affecting the well-being of large numbers of people. And corporations do affect large numbers of people.

Despite problems, participatory mechanisms seem worth the cost of experiment. We have seen that the bureaucratization of corporations tends to weaken ordinary accountability, and increasing individual participation would allow increased individual accountability. Although designing and implementing participatory mechanisms are tasks laden with difficulties, it would be unwise to assume their unworkability from the outset. Chapter 7 will examine some of the current experiments with employee participation systems, especially those falling under the heading of "quality of work life."

There might be halfway measures of employee participation, stopping short of full employee control, which could be implemented immediately and would receive blessings from many managers. One such measure calls for corporations to institute a right of dissent or whistle blowing for employees. That is to say, some argue that employees should be given the right to complain about dangerous products or unsafe working conditions without suffering penalties. More will be said about this topic in the chapter dealing with employee rights; for the present, however, it is worth noticing that such a right would encourage employees to participate by way of relieving the pressures *against* doing so. Employees who would meekly prefer silence when faced with corporate retaliation might be heartened in the context of such a right to step forward. In the B. F. Goodrich case, the engineer who finally blew the whistle on Goodrich's cover-up scandal risked his job. (He later left the company, while those directly involved in the scandal were pro-

---

[11] Emmet, *Rules,* pp. 195-96.

[12] Richard Sennett, "The Boss's New Clothes," *The New York Review of Books,* February 22, 1979, p. 44.

moted by Goodrich to higher positions.) No doubt, he would have gone to the public sooner if Goodrich had a formal policy endorsing the right of whistle blowing.

Strong resistance to such policies can be found among some top corporate officials. The former chairman of General Motors, James M. Roche, once expressed his opinion on the issue of whistle blowing. "However labeled," he said, "—industrial espionage, whistle blowing, or professional responsibility—it is another tactic for spreading disunity and creating conflict."[13] In sharp contrast to this attitude, some critics find it surprising that a right to whistle blowing has failed to emerge, especially in industries such as nuclear power, where minor safety problems can have disastrous human consequences.

Employees at the bottom of the corporate hierarchy might also be encouraged to assume greater responsibility if allowed to develop greater self-respect. Men and women who work daily on assembly lines, whose jobs are reduced not only to rules but to a set of specified bodily motions, can become bitter toward their employers. When General Motors opened its showcase Vega assembly plant in Lordstown, Ohio, years ago, assembly line workers discovered that the speed of the conveyer belt was so rapid that they could not leave to drink water. Workers rebelled by undertaking assembly line sabotage. People such as these, who suffer injuries to their self-respect and whose lot is mechanized and impersonal, will take little moral responsibility for what they produce. Sometimes their bitterness goes beyond a mere hatred of the company. One industrial psychologist remarks that workers can feel a "level of downright hostility—not just to the employer, but to the entire society, which as they see it, has cast them in a role barely above, perhaps subordinate to, machines."[14]

Enhancing the accountability of the professional. A second class of remedies aims at providing professionals in corporations, especially the members of the new professions, with ethical skills. More power should mean more responsibility; yet, as we have seen, the technological needs of corporations combined with the impossibility of subsuming the professional's activities under rules, increase the professional's power without at the same time promoting increased responsibility. Many observers recommend that professional education include an ethical component, so that people who are graduated from schools of engineering, law, medicine, and business will have exposure to ethical problems likely to arise. Thus, business professionals would be better prepared to meet predictable ethical challenges arising in corporations.

That some professional challenges are predictable is clear: lawyers can forecast that ethical problems will accompany decisions to withhold or divulge information about clients; accountants can predict that ethical issues will arise in their decisions to accept or reject claims for tax expenses; and engineers can

---

[13] "The Whistle Blowers," *Time,* April 17, 1972, p. 85.

[14] Christopher D. Stone, *Where the Law Ends* (New York: Harper & Row, Pub., 1975), p. 235.

predict that ethical problems will arise in the design of products when trade-offs must be made between cost and safety. Ethical training seems especially plausible in the context of so-called "new" professionals, such as market analysts and computer programmers, whose professions lack traditional altruistic commitments. For example, computer specialists take no Hippocratic oath, face no disbarment from professional organizations when they are guilty of corrupt practices; yet their skills lend themselves to corrupt practices as easily as those of doctors or lawyers. Years ago, people discovered to their horror that Equity Funding, Inc. had made millions of dollars by borrowing money and using as collateral imaginary insurance contracts it had supposedly concluded with customers. The scandal that ensued revealed that Equity simply invented the names of tens of thousands of customers. Equity Funding defrauded its creditors by co-opting both accountants and computer specialists who regularly examined Equity's books. These experts fed names into the computer, just as if the names were real. When professional skills confer special power, it can be argued, professional education should include training in professional ethics.

Many critics even push for specific controls on professionals. Citing cases such as the B. F. Goodrich scandal, Christopher Stone proposes that special credentials be required of people assuming sensitive corporate positions. In the Goodrich case, for example, the head of the engineering department lacked a degree in engineering and consequently failed to understand complaints about the safety of the brakes. If B. F. Goodrich had required an engineering degree as a condition for the job, the eventual disaster might have been avoided.

Refusing to allow errant professionals to practice their trade for a certain time is also suggested as a means of enhancing professional standards. A case in point is the Lockheed Shipbuilding Corporation, which contracted to build a tunnel in the San Fernando Valley of California. Despite repeated warnings and complaints from employees, engineers refused to add equipment to detect dangerous gas pockets. The inevitable happened; on July 23, 1971, gas ignited and injured four of the men. Workers refused to return to the mine until a monitoring system was installed, but the company persisted. The next day more gas was found and the mine exploded. Seventeen people were killed, three wounded.[15] The judge rendering the decision against the company and its two safety engineers remarked it was incredible that anyone "could stand by and watch almost identical circumstances develop on the night of the fatal explosion as developed the night before. . . ."[16] Both engineers, however, were free to resume the profession of safety engineering, even while still on probation. Professor Stone asks the obvious question: Should such professionals be allowed to make the same mistakes over and over again?

Improving bureaucratic decision-making. A final class of proposals attempts to block the bureaucratic tendency toward decision-making errors, a tendency which, as we observed, is increased by the lack of communication between organi-

[15] Stone, *Where the Law Ends,* p. 194.
[16] Stone, *Where the Law Ends,* p. 194.

zational strata and by the inherent complexity of bureaucratic process. Here, too, Christopher Stone provides us with a ready supply of proposals, including the following:

1. Adding to boards of directors staff personnel who would locate and pass on information to the board and who would conduct investigations authorized by the board.

2. Establishing information networks to guarantee that ethically sensitive information reaches the board of directors (e.g., requiring engineering departments to forward information about significant failures in product safety testing).

3. Establishing a corporate information office to assist managers in collecting information and in specifying needed kinds of information.

4. Requiring the storage and filing of all ethically sensitive information, including test data, executive memos, and letters of complaint from customers.

5. Requiring that test reports be signed personally by those conducting the tests.

6. Improving "downward" information flows so that ethically relevant information reaches those at lower corporate echelons (e.g., making sure that employees are aware of corporate policies toward bribery).[17]

These proposals are suggested as ways to mend the corporate "information net." Although Stone advocates enforcing their adoption through legal means, they also could be implemented voluntarily through the initiative of corporate executives. Such measures are designed especially to improve the problems of fragmentation and complexity inherent in the corporate bureaucracies. They promise to achieve for the corporation what improving one's memory or perception achieves for the individual: to strengthen the accuracy and reliability of decision-making. Consider the proposal to add a staff to corporate boards of directors. Most board members, especially those who are not employees of the corporation, devote a fraction of their time to board duties. They lack the time necessary to collect relevant information, conduct investigations, and study federal regulations. A full-time staff could handle these functions and, in turn, enhance the moral sensitivity of corporate decision-making. In the B. F. Goodrich case and similar scandals board members probably would never have tolerated the actions that prompted the scandal—had they only known about them.

Can any of these proposals lessen the bureaucratic problems that threaten corporate responsibility? It is well to be cautious. Whether the proposals will prove effective or not is largely an empirical matter, to be settled by empirical methods;

[17]Stone mentions other proposals which, for want of space, are not included.

companies must test such proposals and see what happens. There is no shortcut to success in the real world.

Even so, the strategy that underlies the proposals is attractive. Since bureaucracy tends to destroy individual accountability, there is a prima facie reasonableness in attempting to rebuild individual accountability. Since bureaucracy tends to enhance the power of professionals, there is a prima facie reasonableness in attempting to unite moral responsibility with professional pride. And, because bureaucracy tends to impede the efficient flow of information, there is a prima facie reasonableness in attempting to improve the information function in corporate decision-making. (This last point is merely an extension of Aristotle's principle that one's moral responsibility is grounded upon one's capacity to know what one is doing.) In short, although endorsing specific proposals without having tested them is unwise, one can construct a blueprint for lessening bureaucratic problems which recommends *enhancing individual responsibility, motivating professional responsibility, and improving the information functions of corporate decision-making.* Improved responsibility involves, in short, a blocking of the very tendencies discussed earlier which constitute the bureaucratization of corporations.

CORPORATE RESPONSIBILITY:
THE BUREAUCRATIC MODEL

Chapter 2 showed that the issue of moral agency in corporations arises primarily with large corporations, that is, with the massive organizations whose behavior lies beyond the control of a few individuals. The conclusions of that chapter are confirmed by our discussion of bureaucracy in this chapter. Large, bureaucratic corporations cannot be treated simply as "moral persons" because the bureaucratization of corporations raises problems of accountability for corporations unlike those faced by human individuals. This chapter has shown that the crucial features of bureaucratization (i.e., rules, strata isolation, centralization, professionalism, and complexity) create problems for corporate responsibility, and these problems are clearly different from those of individuals. This, in turn, suggests that for large corporations we must be satisfied with a different and more complex model of responsibility than for individuals.

To begin with, the corporate model must encompass as subjects of moral judgments not only the overall actions of the corporation, but also its structure. The closest corporate analogue to a person's mental structure is a corporation's decision-making structure. But although we do not hold people accountable for their mental structures (something they have no control over), we do hold corporations accountable for their decision-making structures. As we saw in the last chapter, any corporation that qualifies as a moral agent must have control over its decision-making structure. A corporation whose structure is so diffuse and fragmented that communication between its segments is virtually nonexistent and which has no means to remedy the problem is a corporation acting blindly. One part does not know what the other does, and the corporation fails even to qualify as a moral agent. Moreover, any corporation that *does* qualify as a moral agent should not have the luxury of renouncing responsibility, as B. F. Goodrich attempted to do, on the grounds that faulty structures could not accommodate routine communications. Our model of corporate responsibility must be sufficiently complex, then, to allow responsibility for overt acts *and* for creating and maintaining structures necessary to bring about such acts.

A model for responsibility in bureaucratic corporations also requires a more complex concept of "intelligence." Some ethicists claim that in order to be morally praiseworthy an individual's decision need only be motivated by love. Thus, the motive of love is required; erudition is not. Even if this is true for individuals, it is certainly not for large corporations. Corporations can and should have access to practical and theoretical knowledge which dwarfs that of individuals. When Westinghouse Inc. manufactures machinery for use in nuclear power generating plants, it should use its massive resources to consider tens of thousands of possible consequences and be able to weigh their likelihood accurately. Which human errors might occur? How are they to be handled? How might espionage occur? How should human systems interface with mechanized ones? And so on, and so on. Whether nuclear machinery should be built in the first place is a separate issue (and also one which Westinghouse should consider). Good intentions for Westinghouse are not adequate. Westinghouse must have, in addition to good intentions, superhuman intelligence.

Ironically, many of the same considerations necessitating higher than normal standards of corporate knowledgeability necessitate lower standards in other areas. When an individual decides to refuse a bribe, it is usually an easy step from decision to act. When a corporation decides to act, bringing about the act is usually difficult. For example, when the U.S. Steel Company decides to refuse to allow its salespeople to accept gifts from customers, implementing the decision is hampered by extended lines of communication, the habits of customers, and the attitudes of reluctant salespeople. Thus, an adequate model of corporate responsibility may require lower standards for bringing about intended acts than for an individual. If, after deciding to refuse gifts, U.S. Steel is discovered to have eliminated *most,* but not all, gifts to its salespeople, it may still receive high marks for responsibility.

A model of corporate responsibility also entails out-of-the-ordinary standards for assigning praise and blame. Accountability in a corporation requires internal as well as external criteria. Whereas it is tempting to construe corporations as large persons, and to think that only their *external* acts should be subject to praise and blame, this assumption is self-defeating. It is true that in the case of individuals it is the external behavior and not the internal behavior, i.e., mental acts, that constitutes the locus of responsibility—even though we assume they *are* able to control their mental behavior. But if one holds a corporation accountable merely for the products it produces, the contracts it endorses, and the public statements it makes, the internal acts of the corporation, many of which give rise to the overt ones, escape scrutiny. Firestone Rubber Co. is morally accountable, and should hold *itself* accountable, for undertaking a long-term analysis of the durability of tire components and for treating its employees with respect, as well as for marketing durable tires. And practically speaking, if Firestone does not praise, blame, punish, and reward in accordance with moral criteria at the level of *internal* behavior, it will not do well at the level of *external* behavior.

This point is similar to the earlier claim that corporations must be held responsible for their decision-making structures; yet it is also subtly different. The earlier claim insists that among the internal events over which corporations should exercise control is the formation of decision-making structures. We never hold individuals responsible for their decision-making structures, for they have no control over them; but corporate moral agents must have such control. The second point, however, is that corporations are responsible for a wide range of internal behaviors in addition to decision-making structures, such as treatment of employees, quality control procedures, and selection of executives. Here there is no issue of control. Individuals have significant control over internal mental events, and corporations have significant control over internal behaviors. But though we tend to refrain from blaming a person for what he or she thinks, we should—and must—blame a corporation for what it does internally.

Finally, one must settle for a model of corporate responsibility that sometimes divorces the capacity to answer for behavior from the capacity to control events. A crucial ingredient for accountability, as noted in Chapter 2, is the liability to *answer* for one's actions in moral terms, that is, to offer a moral account of one's actions using reasons that are moral in character. In ordinary cases, the obligation to answer for behavior is contingent upon the capacity to control it: we do not hold someone answerable for consequences of a muscle spasm. But in the corporation it often happens that the man or committee who influences a course of action is not equipped to answer to the general public, especially when communicating to the public is a task assigned to a specialist. Also, as we have seen, single individuals, or even single committees, cannot fully control corporate behavior. When Douglas Aircraft markets a new jet, the action is a composite of thousands of smaller decisions, of design, of choice of materials, of intended markets—over which no single person or committee has full control. Thus in corporations answerability can be divorced from control in two ways: (1) those who must answer may not be those who control, and (2) even those who have control and who must answer (e.g., key committees or the president) may have only *partial* control over the actions for which they must answer.

In all these senses, then, the model of responsibility in large corporations differs from that of ordinary individual responsibility. What this means for the issue of corporate moral agency is that although large corporations can be moral agents, they are agents of a different kind than are individual persons. One way to understand this difference is to ask how the responsible corporation differs from the responsible individual. The picture of the responsible corporation, in contrast to that of the individual, must make reference to structural design, to information flow and retention, to internal and external accountability, and to mechanisms of interpersonal control. Such a corporation also, considered as a unit, must "know" more both practically and theoretically than the responsible individual, yet its capacity to control its own behavior will be less. The problems of accountability inherent in the bureaucratization of corporations are shared only by other large bureaucracies. Thus despite being construed by the law as artificial persons, large modern corporations must recognize their special moral status and the special moral problems they face because of it.

In this chapter we have examined the way bureaucratization tends to weaken the capacity for responsible decision-making. Bureaucracy entails rules, centralized decision-making, isolated strata, decision-making complexity, and an increase in the relative power of the professional. All these raise problems for corporate moral responsibility, and the problems can be divided into two major kinds. First there is the problem of a corporation's merely *qualifying* as a moral agent. As Chapter 2 showed, in order to qualify, a corporation must be able to use moral reasons in decision-making—that is, it must be morally accountable—and it must have control over the structures of the decision-making process itself. When the problems of bureaucratization are sufficiently severe that fragmented communication, isolated strata, and complexity destroy accountability, then such problems might prevent the corporation even from qualifying as a moral agent. In this instance the corporation would be similar to someone who is suffering from mental disease and whose mental systems do not permit accountability. Society may, however, wish to hold the *individuals* in such a corporation responsible for the failure, or even to revoke the corporation's charter.

Second, even when problems are insufficient to suffocate moral agency, bureaucracy can interfere with corporate responsibility. Despite the best of policies, and despite the most enlightened of executives, a corporation suffering from severe bureaucratization may fail to execute its good intentions. Such a company's first responsibility is to rethink and reform its patterns of bureaucracy.

This chapter has also canvassed general strategies for lessening bureaucratic strain and has proposed a new model for responsibility in large corporations. The general strategies attempt to (1) restore individual responsibility, (2) enhance the accountability of professionals, and (3) improve bureaucratic decision-making. The new model for responsibility exhibits specific differences between individual moral agency and corporate moral agency.

Problems, however, remain. Even if the snares of bureaucratization can be overcome, others with equally serious implications arise. The corporation is an artifact, not a product of nature. Unlike persons, it has no built-in "directedness" toward morality, no inherent desire to be moral. We can, given the appropriate conditions, deem it a moral agent. But can we expect corporations—even when they qualify as moral agents, and even when they have overcome problems of bureaucracy—to adhere to laudatory standards? Even mastering problems of bureaucratization is no guarantee of responsible behavior.

This chapter has advanced a new model of responsibility for large corporations—one that is marked by the idiosyncrasies of bureaucratic structure—and has shown that this model is different in kind from that of individual responsibility. But the model fails to specify, nor is it designed to specify, means of improving corporate moral behavior. Corporate bureaucracies, as we have seen, function in accordance with a unique moral logic. The remaining chapters will explore this logic to see whether it can, and should, accommodate major moral readjustments.

SUGGESTED SUPPLEMENTARY READINGS

BAUM, R., and A. FLORES, *Ethical Problems in Engineering.* New York: Rensselaer Polytechnic Institute. London: Routledge & Kegan Paul, 1965.

CROZIER, MICHAEL, *The Bureaucratic Phenomenon.* Chicago: University of Chicago Press, 1964.

EMMET, DOROTHY, *Rules, Roles, and Relations.* New York: St. Martin's Press, 1967.

HASKELL, THOMAS L., "Professionalism as Cultural Reform," *Humanities in Society,* 1 (Spring 1978): 103-14.

KANTER, ROSABETH, *Men and Women of the Corporation.* Basic Books, 1977.

KURTZ, PAUL, "The Individual, the Organization, and Participatory Democracy," in *Problems in Contemporary Society,* ed. Paul Kurtz. Englewood Cliffs, N.J.: Prentice-Hall, 1969.

McGREGOR, DOUGLAS, *The Human Side of Enterprise.* New York: McGraw Hill, 1960.

WEBER, MAX, *The Protestant Ethic and the Spirit of Capitalism.* New York: Scribners', 1958.

———, *The Theory of Social and Economic Organization.* Glencoe, Ill.: Free Press, 1947.

CHAPTER 7

Employee Rights

Ⓗow can large, bureaucratic corporations escape the problems that threaten meaningful responsibility? The last chapter isolated problems peculiar to corporate bureaucracies and demonstrated that a new model, one different from that of human personal agency, is required to understand corporate agency. If accountability inside the corporation is to be realized, the forces prompting bureaucratization must be curtailed. One of the most pernicious of those, as we saw, was the tendency to suffocate individual moral accountability by loading rules upon employees, only to define the responsibilities of each in terms of those rules. Thus the clerk is caught in a web of rules and forgets about a deeper sense of accountability to the customer. The behavior of the clerk, the mechanic, or the safety inspector in a bureaucracy is seemingly excused from the normal canons of morality, for he can always account for his behavior by saying "I only follow the rules."

According to some theorists, the best way to relieve bureaucratic forces which threaten individual accountability and to extricate the employee caught in the bureaucratic machine is formally to recognize and protect employees' rights. The expression "employee rights" has gained considerable currency in the past decade and is now applied to a variety of loosely allied proposals which aim to recognize the central role, and inherent worth, of the employee. Among the rights defended are:

1. The right of an employee to complain about dangerous products or practices without being penalized.
2. The right of an employee to participate in political activities outside the workplace without being penalized.

3. The right of an employee to refuse lie-detector tests without being penalized.

4. The right of an employee to a hearing before being fired.

5. The right of an employee to refuse immoral orders without being penalized.

This list is incomplete (other proposed rights will be mentioned later) but it indicates the character of moral reforms urged by defenders of employee rights. Such rights are meant to apply not only to employees in corporations, but to those in private and government organizations as well. Investigating the issue of employee rights, of how employee rights are justified, and of how they can be implemented is the task of this chapter.

THE PRESENT STATUS OF EMPLOYEE RIGHTS

The last 200 years have brought revolutionary changes in the way employers treat employees. Once forbidden even to organize into unions under the threat of "conspiracy" laws, most employees now possess the legal right to unionize, a right protected by sweeping federal legislation such as the Taft-Hartley Act. Once treated with the personal domination typical of highly structured family life, employees now may sue their bosses for a variety of misbehavior. Today one would never see a sign posted in the workplace like that in an 1878 New York carriage shop, reading:

> It is expected that each employee shall participate in the activities of the church and contribute liberally to the Lord's work. . . . All employees are expected to be in bed by 10:00 P.M. Except: Each male employee may be given one evening a week for courting purposes. . . .[1]

Still, today's boss has enormous prerogatives. David Ewing, perhaps the foremost defender of employee rights, argues that the rights U.S. citizens possess through the Constitution are "left at the door" when employees enter the workplace. There is a constitutional right to free speech, but Ewing points out that employees who complain about dangerous products can be fired for their trouble. Consider the following cases:

CASE I: Louis V. McIntire, a technical worker for Du Pont Co., published a novel in which a character, "Marmaduke Glumm," is depicted as a victim of corporate mismanagement. The fictitious company for which Glumm works bears a strong similarity to Du Pont. In the novel Glumm argues that technical employees should unionize and push for employee-oriented federal legislation. When Du Pont management learned of the novel, it fired McIntire, despite his good record

---

[1] Quoted in David Ewing, *Freedom Inside the Organization* (New York: McGraw-Hill, 1977), p. 120.

of over fifteen years. When he in turn sued Du Pont for damages, the court dismissed his claim that his right to free speech had been violated.[2]

CASE II: George Geary, an employee at a large steel corporation, complained that tubular steel casing being sold by the company was faulty and dangerous. None of his superiors would listen and they responded curtly that the casing had been tested adequately. When he finally went to the vice-president, he was fired, and the Supreme Court of Pennsylvania said no to his attempt at reinstatement.[3]

CASE III: Shirley Zinman, a secretary at a small corporation, refused her boss's demand to tape telephone calls with clients. She would not record such calls, she said, unless the clients were informed. For this, she was forced to resign. Although legal authorities granted her the right to qualify for unemployment insurance, they refused to acknowledge any right to retain her job.[4]

Such cases have prompted heated attacks upon managerial insensitivity and have brought critics to recommend an employees' "Bill of Rights." Only a formal policy, it is said, can counter the tendency of management systematically to place organizational goals before employee interests. Certainly labor unions are able to pressure management on behalf of employees, and they have been instrumental in gaining safer working conditions, more humane employee treatment, and higher wages. But unions are not, in the eyes of critics, the solution to employee rights problems, since historically unions have tended to be less concerned with issues of rights and freedom and more concerned with wages and fringe benefits. Higher wages bring the capacity to pay higher union dues, thus benefiting union management, but enhancing employee rights offers no clear payoff for union management and receives low priority. Even if unions could be persuaded to take rights seriously, critics say, the overall changes they could effect would be slight, for the vast majority of U.S. workers are nonunionized: of all U.S. workers, only one in five is unionized.

In most instances, employers have the legal power to fire employees at will. As the legal theorist Lawrence Blades puts it, "Employers may dismiss their employees at will . . . for good cause, for no cause, or even for cause morally wrong, without thereby being guilty of legal wrong."[5] In one celebrated case an employer fired an employee for reasons which later were challenged by a court of law. The employer rehired the employee, then promptly fired him again, and this time the court upheld the firing decison. The rationale behind the law's unwillingness to restrict employers' firing prerogatives lies largely in the law's long-standing reluctance to interfere with the voluntary agreement between worker and employer. The worker voluntarily agrees to work, while the employer agrees to pay specified

---

[2] Ewing, *Inside the Organization,* p. 99.

[3] David Ewing, "Sunlight in the Salt Mines," *Harvard Law School Bulletin* (Fall 1977), p. 133.

[4] Ewing, *Inside the Organization,* p. 116.

[5] Lawrence E. Blades, "Employment at Will vs. Individual Freedom: On Limiting the Abusive Exercise of Employer Power," *Columbia Law Review,* 67 (1967), 1405.

wages; but unless otherwise specified, their agreement can be broken at will by either party. Whether the sanctity of voluntary agreements is sufficient to justify purely arbitrary firings by employers is an issue that will be examined later.

Employees complain about their lack of rights. The absence of employee rights is felt more acutely, many contend, because in modern society work itself is dehumanizing. Employee rights are needed to counter the dehumanizing tendencies of mechanized routine and boredom brought on by technology and economic necessities. A long-time observer of the work scene, Studs Terkel, begins his book *Working* with the following observation:

> This book, being about work, is by its very nature about violence—to the spirit as well as to the body. It is about ulcers as well as accidents, about shouting matches as well as fistfights, about nervous breakdowns as well as kicking the dog around. It is, above all (or beneath all) about daily humiliations. To survive the day is triumph enough for the walking wounded among many of us.[6]

If much work is dehumanizing, then divergent explanations are possible: either such work is dehumanizing because it is inherently so (as, by analogy, running is inherently tiring); or such work is dehumanizing because of certain contingent features of the workplace or of managerial behavior, and if one removes these features, then the dehumanization will cease. If one holds the former view, then one is barred from believing that introducing employee rights will relieve problems of dehumanization: it is impossible to make work something it is not. If one holds the latter view, however, there is hope that changes such as the introduction of employee rights can bring to the worker a sense of autonomy and self-respect and, in turn, can lessen the problems of dehumanization.

Taking the second alternative, many view the introduction of employee rights as part of the same historical evolution that brought improved working conditions and higher pay for workers. Extending the concept of evolution one step further, some theorists view employee rights as a natural and inevitable occurrence of the evolutionary process which brought legal and constitutional rights to citizens in the political arena. In presumably the same way kings were forced to step aside for democratic governments that protected citizens' rights, so corporate executives must give way to more worker-centered corporations which protect employee rights. The only prerequisite for the appearance of employee rights is said to be a firm foundation of legal and political rights. Thus, employee rights will not arise in countries until after more basic rights, such as freedom of speech or voting, are secured. One would look for employee rights to emerge only in countries with long traditions of rights, such as the United States, England, and Sweden, but not in countries with short or nonexistent traditions such as Argentina, Spain, or the Soviet Union.

Whether or not such grand evolutionary expectations are justified, the direction of change in recent employee law is toward a greater recognition of

[6] Studs Terkel, *Working* (New York: Avon Paperbacks, 1975). p. 1.

employee rights. A review of law affecting employees in the United States from the 1950's until today shows that at the beginning of the period employers had few legal restraints upon their handling of employees. According to sections 383 and 385 of the Restatement of Agency (as revised in 1958), an agent (employee) has a duty to obey all "reasonable" directions of the principal (employer). Although this implies that an employee can refuse to perform any illegal or unethical act—presumably because the acts are "unreasonable"—it means only that the employee is free to quit. It does not, in the event he refuses an unethical order, give him the right to keep this job. Section 387 also reinforces the prerogatives of the employer by noting that in agent-principal relationships, the agent "is under a duty not to speak or act disloyally."

Today, although the legal right of employers to fire for good reason, bad reason, or no reason continues to exist, exceptions are recognized. In the well-known case of *NLRB* v. *Jones and Laughlin Steel Co.,* the court reasserted the employer's "normal" right to discharge employees, but insisted that employees had a right to unionize, a right that could not be blocked through employers' arbitrarily discharging pro-union employees.[7] During the 1970's, new laws designed to prevent dangerous corporate practices placed further restrictions on employers. The Coal Mine Safety Act, passed in 1974, specifies that no employee can be penalized for reporting alleged violations of the Act. The Occupational Safety and Health Act (OSHA) likewise prevents the penalizing of employees who complain about health and safety violations, and the Water Pollution Control Act blocks the penalizing of employees who complain about water pollution violations. By the end of the 1970's large-scale legal machinery was in place to protect employees' rights to free speech; most of it, however, protected only narrow rights relating to the enforcement of specific regulatory acts.

DEFINING EMPLOYEE RIGHTS

Proponents of employee rights want much more than the general right to complain about regulation infractions. They want broadly interpreted rights for employees, such as the right to complain about any unethical practices, to participate in political activities outside the workplace, and not to have private conversations monitored by corporate officials. But how are we to interpret the claims for such rights? Rights proponents often speak as if such rights are to be understood merely as extensions of *political* rights and assert that since employees apparently leave their political rights at the door when entering the workplace, the solution is to extend them into the workplace.

But surely this is a mistaken interpretation. Employees are not denied their *political* rights when they enter the workplace, although one may claim that they are denied certain *employee* rights. It is wrong to equate political and employee rights. For example, people have the same political, First Amendment rights

---

[7] Ewing, *Inside the Organization,* p. 32.

at work that they have at home, and they are free to speak their minds in either place without suffering government reprisal. No law prevents them from proclaiming Marxism or from complaining about unethical practices, and they cannot be threatened with fines or a jail sentence for doing so. But the First Amendment says only that people are free to speak; it says nothing about whether, having spoken, corporations are required to keep them on the payroll. Thus, it is not an infringement upon one's *political* right of free speech to be fired from a corporation for complaining about unethical practices. If it is an infringement upon one's rights at all, it is an infringement upon one's *employee* right.

How, then, are *employee* rights different from, or similar to, other rights? We hear about political rights enshrined in the Declaration of Independence and Constitution, such as the "God given" and "inalienable" rights to "life, liberty, and the pursuit of happiness." We also hear about *human* rights (especially in the context of U.S. foreign policy), such as the right to national self-determination and the right not to be tortured. We hear too about *civil* rights, involving equal treatment for women, blacks, and other minorities. What, if anything, do these rights have in common?

Philosophers disagree over which properties are common to all rights, or in other words, how to define the concept of a right. One popular definition asserts that a right is a "valid claim *to* something and *against* someone which is recognized by the principles of an enlightened conscience."[8] In other words, any right makes a claim *to* something, as a right to free speech is a right to speak freely, or a right to equal treatment is a right to be treated as all others would be in relevantly similar situations. At the same time, any right makes a claim *against* someone, in the sense that my right to free speech must also be a claim against those who are obliged to allow me to speak, or my right to equal treatment is a claim against those who are obliged to treat me equally.

Another definition interprets a right not as a claim but as an *entitlement* to do, have, enjoy, or have done something. In this definition, it is not necessary to specify whom the right is *against;* rather, rights are things that entitle people to certain things—e.g., to freedom, to life, to associate with people of one' choosing—without necessarily imposing specific obligations on others for seeing the rights fulfilled.[9] Still another definition interprets rights as "trumps" over collective goals, or in other words, as considerations which get first priority even in the face of pressing collective needs.[10] This means that a right is to be given first priority even when it appears that violating the right might enhance public welfare. Thus, the right to privacy is said to have higher priority than the CIA's claim that national welfare will

---

[8] This definition, philosophers will recognize, comes from Joel Feinberg. See Feinberg, "Duties, Rights and Claims," *American Philosophical Quarterly,* 3 (1966), 137-44. Also Feinberg, "The Nature and Value of Rights," *Journal of Value Inquiry,* 4 (1970), 243-57.

[9] H. J. McCloskey, "Human Needs, Rights and Political Values," *American Philosophical Quarterly,* 13 (1976), 1-11.

[10] Ronald Dworkin, *Taking Rights Seriously* (Cambridge, Mass.: Harvard University Press, 1977).

be enhanced by the clandestine tapping of private phone calls. The right to privacy here is seen as the "trump" over a collective national goal.

Although not sharply inconsistent with each other, the definitions stress different characteristics as being central to the concept of a right. Unfortunately, there is insufficient space to settle the important question of which definition is best. So, let us merely stipulate that a "right" is a *valid claim or an entitlement, which imposes some burden of restraint or obligation upon others (though perhaps upon unspecified others) and which frequently functions to block threats to individual interests made by collective goals.* This definition, which is a mixture of currently competing definitions, will be adequate for our purposes.

The next step is to distinguish among different kinds of rights. *Moral* rights, for example, are distinct from *legal* rights. The former exist without the formal endorsement of the law, whereas the latter require it. The right to vote is, at least in the United States, a *legal* right which is specified in official documents such as the U.S. Constitution, while the right to be told the truth (assuming such a right exists) is a *moral* right and consequently has no legal specification. If my friend lies to me, she may have violated my right to hear the truth, but she has broken no law; nor in such instances do we believe my right should be legally enforced.

Another useful distinction may be drawn between traditional rights, modern rights, and manifesto rights. Unlike the distinction between legal and moral rights, these distinctions turn on how recently the rights have been promoted. *Traditional* rights have been promoted and accepted in most Western countries for over a century and include familiar items such as the right to own property, to worship freely, and to vote. *Modern* rights, on the other hand, have been promoted more recently, and although they have become generally accepted, they often fail to appear in national constitutions. Modern rights such as the right to an elementary education, or to not be discriminated against in hiring or firing decisions, or to receive social security, are not specifically mentioned in the Bill of Rights, but we accept them nonetheless.

Manifesto rights are the newest and least accepted of all rights. The term "manifesto right" was coined by Joel Feinberg and refers to rights that are proposed by reformers and that leave unspecified to *whom* falls the obligation of policing the right. Manifesto rights have a progressive social character and typically call upon people to recognize human interests heretofore neglected, such as the right of all people to a job, to medical care, or to a decent standard of living. In order for these to become full-fledged modern rights, it would be necessary to determine *who* has responsibility for protecting these rights. For example, it would be necessary to determine that, say, the government is responsible for protecting the right to a job by ensuring that there are enough jobs for all. Manifesto rights are subjects of intense controversy, despite the fact that many are listed in the United Nations Declaration of Human Rights (along with traditional and modern rights), and some theorists deny they actually exist.

Critics claim that manifesto rights conflict with traditional and modern rights, for although manifesto rights leave unspecified who is responsible for satisfying them, clearly the obligation must fall on someone and whoever it is may be burdened unfairly. For example, if the United States took the right to a job seriously and elevated it to the status of a *legal* right, then the financial burden of providing jobs to the unemployed—some of whom might be lazy or bad workers— would fall to the financially better off. But this would interfere, some claim, with the right of people to do with their money as they please. Defenders of manifesto rights disagree. They refuse to believe that manifesto rights impose unfair burdens and point to the historical evolution of rights in which even traditional rights, such as the right to liberty, were once disputed on the grounds that they would inconvenience a privileged minority. For example, the right to liberty was once claimed to be an unfair burden upon slaveholders.

Our discussion indicates that if there are such things as employee rights, then they should be classified as moral rights and as manifesto rights. They must be *moral* rather than *legal* rights because at the present time they are not enforced by legal authority. Sometime in the future they may be converted to legal rights, but such conversion is not essential for their maintaining the status of genuine rights. (Some defenders of employee rights vigorously deny that employee rights should *ever* aspire to becoming legal rights, claiming that to do so would transfer the responsibility of enforcing them from its proper locus, the employer, to the government.) Further, employee rights must be classified as *manifesto* rights for the obvious reason that they are not generally accepted at the present time and are formulated with reference to a need for reform in present-day organizations.

JUSTIFYING EMPLOYEE RIGHTS

The next question to ask is how the defenders of employee rights might attempt to prove that such rights exist. Critics will certainly deny that the existence of employee rights is self-evident. How can they be persuaded? What is the logic underlying the concept of an employee right? Who is to say *which* rights should appear on an authoritative list of employee rights? These are challenges defenders of such rights can ill afford to ignore. Without a theoretical justification, it appears that rights are being postulated *ex nihilo.*

The need to offer justification is more acute because the very issue of employee rights touches sensitive nerves in the corporate consciousness. When critics claim that workers have rights to blow the whistle, they are in effect attacking all corporate executives who have failed to allow whistle blowing. The executives may reply that talk of employee rights is merely a camouflaged attempt to rob indviduals and corporations of rightful authority and that it will breed chaos and inefficiency. Thus a challenge is posed to the defenders of employee rights: to provide a theoretical foundation from which these rights can be supported.

Some theoretical support for employee rights can be found in the social contract (discussed in Chapter 3). The social contract, we remember, specified that productive organizations have an obligation to "minimize montony and the dehumanization of the worker." Thus, the social contract encourages certain standards of treatment of employees by corporations, especially in the areas of potential worker monotony and dehumanization, and such standards carry implications for the nature of employee rights. Unfortunately, the language of the social contract is too imprecise (at least as formulated) to bring the issue of employee rights into relief. What counts as "dehumanizing," for example? Are employees who are denied the right to blow the whistle on corrupt corporate practices "dehumanized"? This can be a matter of dispute. A need exists, then, for a more tightly structured defense of employee rights.

Critics of employee rights point out that *employers* as well as employees may have rights. Some even argue that employers should have the right to fire or penalize employees at will. Such a right, obviously, is in direct conflict with employee rights, since most employee rights place restrictions on the freedom to fire or penalize. Broad employer rights are usually defended through the doctrine of *freedom of contract,* which construes the relationship between employee and employer as a voluntary agreement, on the model of a contract, which may be terminated at will by either party. When Jim Smith works for the Acme Corporation, presumably both he and the company have freely agreed to live up to the changing expectations of each other until such time as one party calls it quits. (Contracts *can,* however, be more specific, as union-negotiated contracts typically are.) If the company begins harassing Smith, then Smith is free to leave; and if Smith begins causing trouble to the company—say by complaining about dangerous products—then it is free to terminate Smith. In a free enterprise economy, restraints upon voluntary agreements must be eliminated, and employee rights, it is said, entail such restraints. The doctrine of freedom of contract, thus, seemingly spells trouble for employee rights.

Some defenders of employee rights respond by arguing that the freedom of contract doctrine is unfair because the two parties making the agreement, namely corporation and employee, are unevenly matched. Freedom of contract is fine for the powerful corporation, but what about the relatively powerless employee? Do not employees find it more difficult and costly to find a new job than the corporation finds it to replace them? An employer advertises and hires a new employee, but the employee lacks the resources to canvass potential openings, and frequently he must sell his house, relocate his family, and move to a new city. Even granting that a firm must spend money to train a replacement, are the odds not weighted in its favor? The attitude of powerful corporations is said to be like that of the proverbial elephant: "Each for himself, and God for us all," sang the elephant, as he danced among the chickens.

But such criticisms fail to sink the freedom of contract doctrine for the simple reason that the doctrine has never assumed equality of power among contracting parties. Those who, like Adam Smith, defend freedom of contract in the marketplace do so because they believe either that voluntary associations are good in themselves or that such associations breed economic efficiency; moreover they do so knowing that parties will frequently, if not always, possess unequal bargaining power. The doctrine of freedom of contract asserts that a poor woman should sell her wares to a rich one only when the bargain is voluntary on both sides; but no assumptions are made about parity of power. Therefore, lack of parity cannot be adduced as a reason for questioning the doctrine of freedom of contract in the case of employee rights, unless one is prepared to question it in all instances where parity is lacking.

Employee rights are also attacked from a quite different quarter. The establishment of such rights, critics charge, will generate gross inefficiency since it will ensnarl simple employee proceedings with procedural red tape. With special rights, no employee can simply be fired or demoted; he must be given a formal hearing; and to ensure that due process is realized, complicated organizational mechanisms must be established, mechanisms that will require time and effort that might otherwise contribute to productive activities. Such critics envision a straitjacketed corporate management, working in an environment in which penalizing and firing workers is all but impossible. The result, presumably, will be lower working standards, lazier employees, and widespread inefficiency.

To this argument one can reply that employee rights might enhance efficiency rather than harm it, because they will improve employee morale, which will in turn boost efficiency. Whether those making this reply can marshal persuasive evidence, however, is controversial. Reliable statistics on how basic changes in the quality of work life affect long-range productivity are notoriously difficult to obtain. Usually an abundance of variables are in flux at the same time changes in work life are being studied, and thus it is virtually impossible to isolate the causes of increased productivity.

In the face of two such seemingly strong arguments against employee rights, defenders of employee rights appear to have only one escape route. This is to construct a proof for employee rights that demonstrates they exist on an equal footing with full-fledged traditional and modern rights. Once this is demonstrated, the opposition to employee rights as expressed in the two critical arguments should collapse. One could no longer argue that freedom of contract protects corporate prerogatives to fire and penalize at will, for freedom of contract has traditionally been forced to accommodate full-fledged rights. Freedom of contract is interpreted to mean, at most, freedom to contract *within* the range of behavior which is compatible with existing rights. For example, no person is free to engage in a contract that will violate the right of another to life or property (I am not free to contract with someone for the murder of a third party). For the same reason, no person or corporation would be free to engage in a contract that would be in conflict with any employee rights.

Nor, if the existence of employee rights were demonstrated, could it be maintained that considerations of efficiency rule out employee rights, because considerations of efficiency are irrelevant in the face of full-fledged rights. When lawyers defending racially segregated school systems in the 1950's argued that segregation was economically more efficient than integration, their arguments fell on deaf ears. No judge took such arguments seriously because it was not efficiency, but a *right* that was at stake—namely, the right to equal educational opportunity for all races. If employee rights could be proven to have the status of full-fledged rights on an equal footing with other traditional or modern rights, neither considerations of freedom of contract nor of efficiency could overturn them.

Thus we are brought to the philosophical task which for defenders of employee rights is a *sine qua non:* to demonstrate, using logical and persuasive methods, the existence of employee rights. But how are they to accomplish such a task?

Some suggestions are too vague to be helpful. Consider Feinberg's definition of a right as a valid claim that is recognized by the principles of an enlightened conscience. Now one might attempt to use his definition to suggest that employee rights are precisely those acknowledged by an enlightened conscience (Feinberg himself doesn't do this); but over the issue of what counts as an "enlightened" conscience there will be great dispute. Critics of employee rights would no doubt fail to acknowledge such rights in their "enlightened" consciences, while defenders, being equally enlightened, might find them self-evident. The same goes for other attempts to use general interpretations of rights as methods to derive rights. William Blackstone, for example, argues that rights are based upon the capacity of all people for rationality and freedom.[11] But what is meant by "rationality" or "freedom," and how are rights to be derived from such concepts? Or, again, Gregory Vlastos argues that rights are based upon the "equal worth" of all people,[12] and upon their capacity to be happy and free; but again, how can these terms be defined precisely enough to demonstrate the point at hand? All these interpretations of the concept of right may be correct as far as they go, but they are inadequate to place employee rights upon a solid justificatory footing.

What is needed is a method, or set of methods, that will demonstrate (with more accuracy than the above suggestions) the existence of employee rights. Let us consider four areas from which employee rights might be derived:

1. Perfect duties.
2. Basic needs and interests.
3. The right to equal freedom.
4. The right to behave responsibly.

Perfect duties. One strategy for deriving rights is to derive them from duties. That is to say, if a clear duty or obligation may be assumed to exist, then one may be able to infer a correlative right. My obligation to pay you $100, incurred through my promise to you, gives you the right to $100 from me. Of course, this method works only with "perfect" duties, that is, duties owed to a

[11] William T. Blackstone, "Ethics and Ecology," in *Ethical Issues in Business,* ed. T. Donaldson and P. Werhane (Englewood Cliffs, N.J.: Prentice-Hall, 1979).

[12] Gregory Vlastos, "Justice and Equality," in *Ethical Issues in Business,* ed. T. Donaldson and P. Werhane (Englewood Cliffs, N.J.: Prentice-Hall, 1979), pp. 257-70.

specific class of persons under specified conditions, such as the duty to honor promises, and not with "imperfect" duties, such as the duty of charity, which allow considerable discretion as to when, how, and to whom they are fulfilled. Your obligation to be charitable does not give *me* the right to receive your charity.

But one can infer some significant employee rights from the concept of perfect duties—so long, that is, as the duties themselves are agreed to exist. Contract-related rights, i.e., rights that organizational participants possess by virtue of making agreements, are derivable from the duty to honor one's agreements. A worker clearly has the right to expect a certain salary if that is the salary agreed to by his or her employer. One can also argue that the right not to be discriminated against (say, because of race or sex) in firing or promotion decisions, or when salaries are distributed, is derivable from the perfect duty to treat people equally, a duty that is incumbent upon all people, including managers and corporate executives. We may allow the method of inferring rights from perfect duties, then, as an acceptable method of generating at least some employee rights.

Unfortunately, the application of this method to institutional rights is limited for the simple reason that often the relevant duties are as much in question as the rights themselves. Also, as the philosopher David Lyons and others point out, it is likely that some rights do not have ordinary duties as correlatives. For these reasons, the strategy of deriving rights from perfect duties is not typically utilized by proponents of employee rights. Indeed, the reverse is more common. Proponents impose a duty, which they realize is controversial, by *first* establishing a less controversial right. These considerations are sufficient encouragement to search for other possible methods of deriving employee rights.

Basic interests and needs. A second possible method for generating employee rights would be to derive them from basic needs or fundamental interests. Contemporary philosophers such as James Nickel suggest that a good reason for a right is the "existence of a strong or fundamental interest in a thing."[13]

In this sense, a need for such things as food or medical care would constitute the basis for a right to such things. The need or interest in question must be fundamental and of the most nearly universal sort. An interest in becoming a doctor, no matter how keenly felt, will not support the right of all people to become doctors, whereas interests in personal security or in food or shelter would, *ex hypothesi,* be rights supporting. Consequently, this method for validating rights involves discovering fundamental, almost universal, needs and then extrapolating to the relevant rights. Taking a similar approach, Joel Feinberg argues that a natural need (say for food) justifies the existence of a manifesto right. That is, the mere presence of a natural need justifies a claim to food by a hungry person. Feinberg emphasizes, however, that this manifesto right does not become full-fledged until it is clear whom the claim is against, that is, to whom the obligation of fulfilling the right falls.

[13] James Nickel, "Is There a Human Right to Employment?" forthcoming in the *Philosophical Forum.*

Feinberg's hesitation over letting mere needs generate full-fledged rights is relevant to the issue of employee rights. Not all fundamental, nearly universal needs *do* appear to generate genuine rights. Frederick Rosen notes, for example, that meeting basic needs is sometimes more a matter of charity than of rights. "If someone goes hiking for recreation and becomes lost and hungry, we could agree that his basic needs are not being met, but no one could be said to have treated him unjustly."[14] Many would question whether our would-be explorer has a *right* to be rescued, though certainly he would qualify as a candidate for charity. Or consider another problem. Along with food and medical care, sex and aggression have been argued by some (most persuasively by Freud) to be fundamental, almost universal interests. Yet it seems odd to use these interests as a foundation for so-called rights to sex and aggression (not to mention the problem of isolating corresponding duties). Thus, the strategy of using basic needs to generate rights appears confronted with the problem of generating *too many* rights.

The problem of too many rights could be eased, perhaps, if a method for reducing their number could be discovered. One suggestion is to limit the rights to those "most needful of special protection." Thus, a so-called right to breathe air or to be aggressive would not be a true right, because typically there is no special threat to its satisfaction, whereas the right to liberty would be a true right because of its special vulnerability. However, this proviso fails to resolve the problem of too many rights because some most nearly universal interests, such as interests in personal reputation and status, have ongoing threats to their satisfaction yet seem unacceptable as the basis for rights justification. Most people prefer higher-status jobs to lower ones and most are blocked from moving up the status ladder, yet few would argue that people have a *right* to step into high-status jobs.

A final attempt to employ the basic interests approach lies with restricting still further the field of rights through the criterion of "self-respect." One might argue that the only needs or interests that are relevant for generating rights are the kind that, if unsatisfied, result in a large loss of *dignity* or *self-respect.*[15] The basic emphasis is upon a person's inherent worth and the conditions for self-respect. Not fulfilling certain needs promotes loss of self-respect, and hence people have an equal right to have them fulfilled. When those needs can be identified concretely, it then becomes possible to identify corresponding rights. If in the political realm, for example, people were denied the opportunity to vote, it could be argued that their self-respect would be severely diminished because of the implicit suggestion that they lack self-control and need to have their wills subordinated to others. In this case the need for self-determination, whose frustration diminishes self-respect, is used to generate the right to vote.

Let us apply this same strategy to the problem of employee rights. Consider a proposed employee right to privacy, or more specifically, a right to not have one's desk at work arbitrarily searched. Here one could argue that employees have a

[14] Frederick Rosen, "Basic Needs and Justice," *Mind,* 86 (1977), 88-94.

[15] Nickel, "Human Right?" p. 21.

need for privacy which when frustrated through arbitrary searches of their desks results in a significant loss of self-respect. Using the criterion of self-respect in this way, one can make a case for an employee's right not to have his or her desk arbitrarily searched.

Yet other employee rights appear immune to this strategy. To determine whether, say, an employee has a right to criticize management without incurring penalties, one would need to determine whether a nearly universal interest supported such a right and whether a denial of the right would be a severe blow to a person's self-respect. But whose self-respect is at issue? An employee who is fired for criticizing her company may regard her dismissal more as an unjust blow to her pocketbook and security than to her self-respect. Furthermore, it may be argued that employees who are never promoted to higher positions in organizations have a fundamental need which is being frustrated, and consequently suffer a loss of self-respect—yet few would champion the universal right to be promoted. The concept of self-respect must be clarified, then, before it can function as an efficient indicator of some employee rights. Self-respect may generate some employee rights, but it cannot—at least in its present form—generate all of them.

The right to equal freedom. Perhaps the best-known attempt to ground rights on a concept of freedom is that of the twentieth-century theorist of jurisprudence H. L. A. Hart, especially in his well-known article, "Are There Any Natural Rights?" There Hart argues that "if there are any moral rights at all, it follows that there is at least one natural right, the equal right of men to be free."[16] Hart's main argument is deceptively simple; if there are any rights, then these rights give to their holders special claims, which when recognized by others necessarily restrict the others' freedom. (If I recognize your right, I can't do *anything* I want; in particular, I can't violate your right.) Hart is able to extract the crucial assumption implicit in such relationships: the very fact that one even *claims* a right shows that interference with another's freedom requires a moral justification. And this, in turn, commits the claimant to affirming the equal right of all to be free. Equal freedom, thus, is presupposed by the very act of claiming a right since a right is nothing other than a justification for restricting freedom.

Hart offers this agreement in a spirit not unlike that of the classical philosopher Immanuel Kant, who in the *Metaphysical Elements of Justice* argues that rights are specifically concerned with determining when one person's freedom may be limited by another.[17] If rights are grounded on the concept of a right to equal freedom, as Hart suggests, then this fundamental right might be used as a springboard to reach derivative rights, including employee rights. In other words, perhaps

[16] H. L. A. Hart, "Are There Any Natural Rights?" *Philosophical Review,* 64 (1955); reprinted in *Rights,* ed. David Lyons (Belmont, Cal.: Wadsworth Publishing Co., 1979), p. 14.

[17] Immanuel Kant, *The Metaphysical Elements of Justice,* trans. John Ladd (New York: Bobbs-Merrill, 1965).

the right to equal freedom can be used as a tool for deriving specific employee rights.

Despite the power of Hart's view, however, it is affected by a minor oddity. Hart begins by saying "if there are any rights . . . there is the equal right to freedom." But why the "if" at the beginning? Why does Hart not say simply that all men *have* the equal right to freedom? Moreover, how can the right to equal freedom be used to justify employee rights, unless it itself is first justified?

To remedy Hart's problem, the "if" from his argument must be removed. It must be possible to show that people do, as a matter of fact, possess the right to equal freedom. The best accepted method of doing this is to analyze the conditions for moral behavior in general and then show how any moral behavior requires a right to equal freedom. In other words, suppose one asks what is necessary for behavior that is subject to moral evaluation; that is, what is necessary in order for people to behave "responsibly" or "irresponsibly" or "charitably" or "atrociously," etc.? One condition necessary for genuine moral behavior is that people possess the *freedom* to act; for if they were restrained from acting, or if their behavior were under the control of external influences, then we could not evaluate them from a moral point of view. Freedom thus seems to be the indispensable and necessary condition for any moral behavior whatsoever. Thus, one may conclude that any *moral* agent that is considered as a *moral* agent, regardless of personal characteristics, has a right to freedom.[18]

Having placed the right to freedom on a secure footing, the next task is to show how it can generate other rights, especially employee rights. The concept of freedom at first glance seems vague, general, and unsuited to the task of deriving anything. As one philosopher has remarked, the right to be free seems to be a "determinable" right rather than a "determinate" right, in the same way the term "color" is the determinable term for determinate ones such as "red" or "blue." Deriving employee rights from the right to be free, then, seems to have the same problems as deriving the concept of "red" from the concept of "color."

But the concept of freedom may not be so vacuous as it appears. It is true that one could never deduce an institutional right, in a strict sense of "deduce," from the right to be free, but one might deduce—in some weak sense of "deduce"— *some* institutional rights. Consider, for example, Immanuel Kant's argument that because everyone has the right to freedom (the right to be protected from violence and coercion from others), it follows that everyone also has a right to live under a political order that controls violence and protects liberty.[19] Here, according to Kant, a specific right is derived—though not perhaps in the strict, logical sense of "derived"—from a right to liberty. Now the move from Kant's concept of freedom to the right to live in a political order is not, we should notice, a logically necessary one. It is logically possible that other means than a political state might effectively secure freedom (say, the taking of a super, yet-to-be-discovered drug), or that if

[18] Hillel Steiner, "The Natural Right to Equal Freedom," *Mind,* 83 (1974), 194-210.

[19] Kant, *Elements of Justice.*

human nature were different and people were not disposed to interfere with others' freedom, that no steps at all would be needed to secure it. But given human nature now and as it will be in the foreseeable future, the relationship between the right to freedom and the right to live in a political state seems well established.

The logical relationship here is not unlike that of practical inference where the conclusion does not follow with logical necessity but follows with some kind of logic nonetheless. From the premises (1) I desire to be happy, and (2) I believe doing X is a means of being happy, it does not follow that I *must* do X. For doing Y may *also* be a means of being happy. Similarly, from the right to freedom one may not deduce a right to live in a political state, but one may deduce that one has a right to *some* means, practically speaking, of securing one's freedom; and it may be that empirical evidence overwhelmingly supports a right to a political state as the *best* means of securing it. With these considerations in mind we may return to the issue of employee rights to see what if any employee rights may be squeezed from the right to equal freedom in this "weak" sense of deduction.

One fundamental employee right clearly is derivable, namely, a right for employees *to exercise their right to equal freedom.* As abstract as this right sounds, it carries weight for the way in which organizations with employees are to be structured. For if employees possess such a right, it follows that organizations such as corporations, professional organizations, and union organizations must be structured so as to avoid coerciveness and so as to allow participants a certain degree of security of person and property.

Can more specific employee rights be derived from the right to freedom? Here the waters are murky. Any attempt merely to stretch the concept of equal freedom in a crude manner to cover, say, an employee's right to whistle blowing, or to have access to his or her personal files, seems doomed to failure. Of course, granting employees a right to whistle blowing or access to personal files would expand the limits of employees' freedom, but so would granting some other rights that are objectionable. Granting employees the right to lie to superiors without suffering repercussions, or to have access to all of a corporation's financial documents, would similarly expand freedom—yet no one would endorse such rights. Thus merely stretching the concept of freedom into the employee arena is unacceptable, since doing so sparks the familar hazard of too many rights.

Some employee rights are more adaptable to this method. In particular, those that seem also to be affected by other moral considerations, such as the right to engage in political activities of one's choosing outside the workplace (without suffering penalties), seem easier to derive. On behalf of this right, it can be argued not only that such a right expands the limits of employee freedom, but also that, all other things being equal, corporations and employers are less justified in restricting employee behavior *off* the job than *on.* After all, employees are hired and paid for what they do when at work, not away from it. Adding additional moral considerations such as this to the right to equal freedom, then, enhances the possibility of generating specific employee rights.

The right to behave responsibly. None of the methods discussed so far is a likely candidate for generating a right to whistle blowing. But this is puzzling, since among defenders of employee rights the right of whistle blowing is the most talked about and the best accepted. Is there no way of justifying such a right?

Returning to the previous discussion of a right to equal freedom, we remember that a prerequisite for a person's performing any action with moral worth is freedom. This is true whether the act in question is a morally bad or good act. Thus considered as moral agents people have a right to freedom. But if one has a right to what is a prerequisite for behaving responsibly and irresponsibly, then of course one at least has a right to what is a prerequisite for behaving responsibly. To put it another way, if one has an equal right to the conditions for moral behavior in general, including right and at least some wrong actions, then one necessarily has an equal right to the conditions for performing right actions.

But if good moral behavior, or responsible moral behavior, is a species of all moral behavior, then why even mention a right to behave responsibly *in addition to* a right to moral behavior in general? Is not the right to the conditions for responsible behavior already guaranteed through the right to the conditions for all moral behavior—namely, through the right to equal freedom?

Here it is important to distinguish the relative weights of the right to behave in any moral way and the right to behave responsibly. That is, one can argue that the right to behave responsibly is stronger than the right to behave irresponsibly. One can argue that one has a stronger right to speak the truth, or to be charitable, or to demand one's rights, than one has to lie, cheat, or hurt others (assuming one may be said to have a "right" to perform the latter acts). And one can argue, in turn, that one's right to the preconditions for behaving responsibly is stronger than to the preconditions for behaving irresponsibly.

If this is true—and let us assume for the moment that it is—then it becomes possible to attempt a derivation of important employee rights. It becomes possible to attempt a derivation of an employee's right to "behave responsibly in the workplace," and this right, in turn, can be used to derive both:

1. The right to refuse immoral orders from superiors.
2. The right to complain about potentially dangerous products or potentially dangerous practices.

The second right above is roughly what is meant by the right of whistle blowing.

In other words, if all people have a right to the conditions for responsible behavior, then it can be argued that corporations and other employers are obligated to establish conditions that are compatible with responsible behavior. It can further be argued that if corporations fire employees who undertake morally responsible acts such as (1) refusing to obey immoral orders or (2) complaining about dangerous products, then they have discouraged responsible behavior and thus have infringed upon employee rights.

Now this method has the obvious advantage over the earlier method (using the right to equal freedom) of being able to distinguish between the freedom to lie or to perform shoddy work, and the freedom to whistle-blow or refuse immoral orders, for it suggests that one's underlying right to the latter is stronger than to the former. In this way, the method explains why there may be a right to blow the whistle without suffering penalties, but certainly not a right to perform shoddy work without suffering penalties.

The four methods for deriving employee rights which we have discussed are not the only possible methods; others have been suggested by employee rights defenders. Such methods provide potential keys for unlocking the issue of employee rights and for providing a clear view of the philosophical foundations of such rights. In this sense, any method is clearly preferable to merely proclaiming employee rights *ex nihilo,* a strategy sometimes employed by corporate reformers.

Our next step is to turn away from the issue of how employee rights are derived and justified and confront the issue of how employee rights might function in concrete situations. So far, we have talked about what employee rights are and how they might be justified, but we have shied away from talking about what they would mean if, say, they were taken seriously by General Motors or Exxon. Four kinds of rights deserve investigation: rights of (1) freedom of speech, (2) privacy, (3) due process, and (4) employee participation.

FREEDOM OF SPEECH

Under the heading of freedom of speech are lumped two distinct types of employee rights. These are rights concerning speech about (1) affairs of the organization and (2) affairs not directly related to the organization. The first typically concerns whistle blowing while the second concerns political activities outside working hours, such as an employee's campaigning for a political candidate. It is possible, logically speaking, to endorse 1 without 2 or, alternatively, 2 without 1. Among employee rights theorists, the emphasis has been upon 1.

A storm of controversy about employee rights developed in 1975 when the Kennedy hearings for Senate Bill 1210 revealed instances of potential rights abuses by government agencies. One man, working for the Office of Economic Opportunity, was fired when he blew the whistle about arbitrary expenditures of day care funds. Two women working for the Indian Health Service were fired when they mailed a letter to President Nixon showing how patients were mistreated at an Indian hospital. Another woman, working for the Department of Health, Education and Welfare, was penalized for raising questions about possible discrimination in the hiring practices of HEW.[20] Such cases, critics insist, never should have occurred; they prove the need for formal proclamations of employee rights.

Some business executives, of course, do not agree. Emphasizing the potential for employee rights programs to decrease productive efficiency, they deny

[20] Ewing, *Inside the Organization,* pp. 77-78.

that a right to whistle blowing exists. We are reminded of the characterization of whistle blowing by the past president of General Motors, in Chapter 6, as "another tactic for spreading disunity and creating conflict."

Recent legislation has favored the defenders of employee rights. Many states have adopted statutes making it unlawful for companies to fire employees who participate in political activities outside the workplace. In the past it was legal for a corporation to fire all employees who refused to vote for a particular political candidate—and some companies did.[21] Today, threats of this kind are illegal in states such as California, Wisconsin, Missouri, and Minnesota.[22] Though the law's clout is weaker than many would like, a legal trend on behalf of free speech is emerging.

The trend gained momentum in the late 1960's when the U.S. Supreme Court reached its landmark Pickering decision, which reinstated a high school teacher fired for criticizing school policies. The teacher, Pickering, had complained that athletics were emphasized at the expense of academic quality and said so in a letter to the local newspaper. In its decision the Court emphasized the fact that Pickering's remarks concerned matters of general public interest and that the right to discuss such matters was protected by the First Amendment to the U.S. Constitution.

In still another case, *Holodnak* v. *Avco Corporation* (1974), courts moved to extend employee freedom of speech from government organizations (as in the Pickering case) to private corporations whose major contracts were with the government. Michael Holodnak, an employee of the Avco Steel Corporation, wrote an article for a local newspaper accusing both the steel company and the union (the United Auto Workers) of ruining the employees' grievance procedure. Miffed by Holodnak's charges, the union refused to arbitrate his dispute with the company. Although the court acknowledged that private employers were not covered by the Pickering decision, it noted that 80 percent of the steel company's business was with the government—a fact it decided was sufficient to justify its enforcing the right to free speech. The court required Avco to compensate Holodnak.[23] Despite these decisions, most U.S. corporations remain free to fire whistle blowers at will. The major share of business of most corporations is with other private corporations or consumers; thus, they escape the Holodnak decision. For these corporations the issue of whistle blowing remains highly charged.

One can grant that employees deserve free speech, but deny that every instance of free speech should be protected. In his textbook on business ethics, Professor Thomas Garrett argues that free speech should be protected but remarks that "If a vice-president belongs to the American Nazi Party, the situation is differ-

---

[21] Ralph Nader and Mark Green, "Owing Your Soul to the Company Store," in *Ethical Issues in Business,* ed. T. Donaldson and P. Werhane (Englewood Cliffs, N.J.: Prentice-Hall, 1979), pp. 197-207.

[22] Ewing, *Inside the Organization,* p. 123.

[23] Holodnak v. Avco Corporation, Avco-Lycoming Division, et al., Civil Action No. B-15 (1974), U.S. District Ct., Connecticut.

ent, since people may not want to deal with him or with a company that has such a man in a key position."[24] Or, suppose that a marketing executive for a large recording company that specializes in selling records that appeal to the black community boasts—off the job—of his affiliation with the Ku Klux Klan. Is the president morally obligated to keep that executive, even if doing so sends sales plunging?

Such cases are troublesome. Even so, we must be careful, for the simple fact that an executive's political views affect sales may be inadequate in itself to restrict free speech. Suppose that a vice-president's membership in the NAACP turns out to upset customers who are racists. Should the financial reactions of the racists be allowed to justify the firing of the vice-president?

If allowing workers certain rights of free speech (however these rights are defined or limited) tends to spark an increase in organizational friction and disharmony, then are the rights themselves unjustified? Seemingly not, since disharmony and friction sometimes yield positive results. In the political arena we allow freedom of speech even in circumstances in which denying it might reduce friction. We allow Marxists, critics of U.S. foreign policy, and even proponents of racism to express their views, although doing so takes its toll on the peace and harmony of society. A bit of friction, it is said, is the price of meaningful freedom. Without such friction, prevailing ideas would be immune to criticism and hence immune to the improvement which follows on the heels of criticism. The same, perhaps, is true in the workplace: without criticism, corporations would plow ahead, blind to their worst faults, firing and penalizing the very employees who might cure their blindness. The real question is how *much* criticism to allow, and *when.*

For those defending the right of employee free speech, a crucial issue is how to formulate the right itself. Like formulating a right to free speech in the political arena, this issue only appears to be simple; its complexity appears when one realizes that some acts of free speech cannot be allowed, just as in the political arena we cannot allow people to yell "fire" in a crowded theatre. Hence, an employee right to free speech could not be formulated as:

> Employees have the right to say whatever they wish, both on and off the job, without being penalized.

This formulation would allow workers to lie to superiors about routine work matters, or maliciously slander fellow employees, with no fears of repercussions. A better formulation would be:

> Employees are free to criticize dangerous or unjust activities, and to participate in political activities of their choosing off the job, without being penalized.

[24]Thomas Garrett, *Business Ethics* (Englewood Cliffs, N.J.: Prentice-Hall, 1966), p. 68.

This formulation avoids the earlier problems by focusing upon "dangerous" and "unjust" activities. Nevertheless, it is not immune to problems. For example, who is to determine whether the activities in question really are "dangerous" or "unjust"? The organization itself? Might not corporate presidents and vice-presidents, for example, lack the objectivity to make such determinations fairly? Perhaps the problem could be met by establishment of a review committee composed of impartial employees and managers. But even so, problems remain. As formulated above, the right requires an impartial person, or group of persons, that can interpret its application in controversial cases.

The tasks of formulating and interpreting a right to free speech are connected to the task of enforcing the right. If rights are to be meaningful and not mere window dressing, they must be enforced. But the path towards enforcement leads in two mutually exclusive directions. One direction is toward the government and the courts, where external pressure through threats of fines and lawsuits can command corporate obedience. This route ensures corporate compliance but has the drawbacks of multiplying bureaucratic red tape and of aggravating the hostility between business and government. The other direction leads toward corporate self-compliance, or self-compliance coupled with appropriate pressures from unions and professional organizations. Here, corporations would voluntarily implement "bills of employee rights" and enact the necessary procedures and committee arrangements to ensure general compliance. This route avoids the problems of government control and is supported by recent business trends. Many corporations have successfully established bills of rights, and many professional organizations, such as the American Chemical Society, have moved to support the adoption and use of such bills. This route is open to an obvious problem, however: can corporations, even with the aid of unions and professional organizations, be trusted to tackle employee rights without government threats?

Even if corporations instituted safeguards to protect whistle blowing and off-the-job political activities, there is little insurance against informal reprisals against employees who break step with established organizational habits. If John Doe complains about his company's safety procedures or actively campaigns for a socialist party candidate off the job, he may be protected from losing his job or being demoted. But can he be protected from his colleagues who shun him at the office, or from the supervisor who takes his behavior into account when promotions are considered? Formal guarantees are possible, but full protection seems impossible.

PRIVACY

The right to privacy has long been championed in the political arena, but only recently has it been considered as an employee right. Citizens of the United States are notorious for becoming indignant when the government meddles in their private lives, as when the CIA in the late 1960's indiscriminately tapped private phones.

Recently, however, critics have drawn attention to a group of corporate practices they claim violate employee privacy, such as:

1. Supervisors' eavesdropping on employees' private phone calls.
2. Unauthorized searches of employees' desks.
3. Firing or penalizing employees who refuse lie-detector tests.
4. Denying employees access to information in their personal files.

Existing laws permit most of the above practices. David Ewing reports that in all but two states, employers are free to monitor employees' conversations on company telephones without telling employees.[25] Although courts have ruled to block employers from digging through the desks of absent employees on the vague suspicion something interesting might be found, they have allowed the smallest pretext to suffice as justification. A senior manager may not go on an arbitrary fishing expedition, but he or she can prowl through an absent employee's desk "looking for an invoice" or "hunting for a special letter." In the case of lie-detector tests, despite vigorous union complaints many corporations require signed affidavits from job applicants saying that if hired they will submit to lie-detector examinations when ordered by management, and they continue to fire employees who refuse such tests. A federal study reported that in 1974 between 200,000 and 300,000 polygraph. Corporations complain bitterly about the nearly $4 billion lost annually legislation requiring corporations to give employees access to their personal files, many have not. In the mid-1970's Congress enacted the Buckley Amendment to ensure students access to their records on file at universities, but this legislation failed to secure the same rights for corporate employees.

Perhaps the most explosive of these issues is that of the lie detector, or polygraph. Corporations complain bitterly about the nearly $4 billion lost annually through employee theft. The only answer, they conclude, is regular polygraph tests. Employees, who face the problem from the other side, argue differently. Mandated lie-detector tests, they charge, are an invasion of privacy. Even criminals can refuse to testify by pleading the Fifth Amendment. Why cannot employees refuse to submit to a polygraph test? Furthermore, with an accuracy rate for polygraphs estimated by some to be as low as 70 percent, what prevents the ethical employee from losing a job through accident? (Those defending the polygraph credit it with 95 to 99 percent accuracy.) Lee Burkey, an attorney known for his criticism of polygraph testing, is fond of citing the case in which a prospective employee being given a battery of lie-detector tests was asked such questions as "Have you ever been arrested?" "Were you ever fired from a previous job?" The man passed with flying colors. Later it turned out that he had been convicted of second-degree murder.

No court of law has ever permitted polygraph test information to be admitted as evidence without the express permission of the accused, and most

[25] Ewing, *Inside the Organization,* p. 130.
[26] Ewing, *Inside the Organization,* p. 131.

courts refuse to allow such information even with permission. The rationale presumably is that the lie detector is a fallible instrument and may mislead the judge or jury. Why, then, employees ask, are polygraph examinations permitted in business?

Opposition to polygraph testing seems to be mounting at the same time businesses are increasingly desperate to halt employee theft. The American Civil Liberties Union has supported legislation to protect those not already protected by unions, e.g., ordinary job applicants. At the time of this writing, sixteen states prohibit employers from requiring job applicants to take polygraph tests as a condition of employment. In the public sector, legislation has been introduced barring state, federal, and local governments from firing employees (such as police officers and civil servants) who refuse such tests. Yet even in the public sector, employees who refused the tests have been successfully fired—not for refusing the tests, but for "insubordination."[27] In the private sector, corporations have been slow to institute rights with regard to polygraph testing on their own. Without external pressure, it is doubtful they will.

Less explosive, but equally persistent, are issues concerning collection and retention of information about employees. Since 1975 many states have introduced legislation establishing standards for corporate behavior in this area, but the legislation varies from state to state in its character and impact. Various defenders of employee rights have suggested that corporations establish internal ethical principles regarding such matters which would apply whether supported by law or not. Among the principles suggested are:

1. No performance evaluations older than four years should be retained in an employee's files.

2. Employees should have access to most material in their files and should know what type of information is kept there. (Some material may be excluded, e.g., a letter showing that the employee was considered for, but narrowly missed receiving, an unannounced honor.)

3. No search of an absent employee's desk may be undertaken without his or her permission. (Or, alternatively: No search of an absent employee's desk may be undertaken without written authorization from a specified member of upper management.)

4. Employee phone calls should not be monitored without the employee's knowledge.

5. Access to personal files should be limited to a specifically designated few corporate employees.

6. Employees should be notified when and if information from their files is given to outside agencies or individuals.[28]

---

[27] Lee Burkey, from a speech given to the Institute of Industrial Relations, Loyola University, October 1979.

[28] See Ewing's longer list of suggestions in *Inside the Organization,* esp. pp. 133-38.

DUE PROCESS

Connected to every employee rights issue is the subsidiary issue of due process, for without due process or in other words without procedures that tend to ensure just outcomes for internal corporate disputes, no employee right can be meaningfully implemented. As it happens, however, due process itself is typically counted by employee rights defenders as a separate right. Due process is at issue when employees are fired for purely arbitrary reasons—for example, when a female employee is fired for refusing her supervisor's advances. In 1974, to take an actual case, the New Hampshire Supreme Court ruled that a married woman with three children could recover damages if she refused to go on a date with her foreman and was then fired.[29] In another case, the county assessor demanded that his female employees wear dresses and that his male employees have short haircurts. When four men exceeded his haircut standards, he promptly fired them all. Here the court refused to side with the employees.[30]

What is needed, critics contend, is not so much legal action as recognition by corporations of the need for due process. The term "due process" is drawn from the legal system, where the expectations of due process require among other things that accused citizens not be indiscriminately condemned by a single person but that they be judged in public under the protection of certain rights and procedures. Every person has a right to have a trial, to have professional counsel, and to appeal a negative verdict to a higher court. Thus, considerable faith is vested in procedures as well as in the judgment of individual persons. When all these rights and procedures are properly observed, then "due process" has been observed.

A similar need exists, it is claimed, for due process in corporations, but most agree that due process may be implemented using more than one system. One suggestion to ensure due process would require that employees at a certain seniority level be fired only with the concurrence of at least two upper-level corporate officials. (The American Chemical Society has endorsed this idea.) Another suggestion involves the establishment of a formal appeal procedure, not unlike the appeal system in courts of law, through which an employee may contest an adverse decision at a higher level. The H. P. Hood Company in Boston, for example, has a formal hearing procedure whereby employees may appeal decisions to a special panel which reports directly to the president and is composed of five nonmanagement employees chosen at random. The Polaroid Company has a similar committee composed of members elected by fellow employees. In the Polaroid system, employees whose appeals are turned down by the committee may next appeal the decision to an outside arbitrator. If systems like these became common, defenders contend, the number of arbitrary, unjust dismissals would decrease.

[29] Kenneth Walters, "Your Employees' Right to Blow the Whistle," *Harvard Business Review*, 53 (July-August 1975), 1-7.

[30] Ewing, *Inside the Organization*, p. 139.

PARTICIPATION

The last general area of employee rights is by far the most controversial. It concerns the question of an employee right to participate, in some undetermined fashion, in the management of the corporation. Few if any people defend the right of employees to control fully the behavior of the corporation. Most argue that such extreme measures would, in a capitalistic society, conflict with the rights of shareholders. But less extreme proposals, involving employee participation on key committees, or some form of employee access to higher management, are advocated. One person to endorse explicitly the right of worker participation was Pope John XXIII, who in his 1962 encyclical *Mater et Magistra* remarked:

> Like our predecessors, we are convinced of the legitimacy of the workers' ambitions to take part in the life of the undertaking in which they are employed . . . workers must be given an active part to play in the concern in which they are employed.

Support for a right to participation often takes on an evolutionary form, with defenders pointing to the slow but inevitable increase throughout history of citizens' participation in national decision-making. Just as the rigid autocracy of princes and despots was forced to yield to democratic, participatory governments, so, it is said, the fixed structure of corporate authority must yield to new, employee-centered corporate structures. Defenders say the first signs of this coming revolution are visible: many Western corporations have instituted systems for reflecting employee opinions about management; and in noncapitalistic Yugoslavia, in the most radical participation scheme yet existing, workers both own and run factories.

Support also comes from those who argue that there is emerging a new breed of employee who will demand a voice in organizations. Modern employees are surely better educated, and probably more independent, than their traditional counterparts. Once a rarity, the college-educated worker is now common, and he or she is less willing to subordinate personal beliefs to those of the organization. Professionally trained workers such as engineers, accountants, and lawyers are increasing in numbers, and their loyalty often is as much to their professions as it is to their employers.

Theorists have developed new theories to reflect this trend. Today one of the most popular theories of administrative science is called the "cooperative" approach. It sees productivity linked to employee motivation, and motivation in turn linked to cooperative work arrangements. If workers participate in decisions, then they will have higher motivation and work harder, even when the work is inherently distasteful.[31]

[31] Richard Sennett, "The Boss's New Clothes," *The New York Review of Books,* February 22, 1979, p. 43.

The cooperative trend contrasts to traditional approaches to management, which can be divided into the "job contentment" approach and the "scientific management" approach. The first of these, which grows out of the psychological observations of theorists such as Abraham Maslow, emphasizes that the "higher" needs of workers, such as the need for self-respect, require human sensitivity from management. The thrust of the job contentment approach has been to devise strategies for making workers happier, by, for example, piping music into factories and using variable speed assembly lines. The scientific management approach, on the other hand, frequently attempts to apply Skinnerian psychology to the workplace and to promote higher production by designing the proper mix of "rewards" and "penalties." It takes a hardheaded view of human nature, seeing it as reward-oriented and unconcerned with higher values. It sometimes has been called a "theory X" view, in order to contrast it to more humanistic, nonbehavioristic approaches subsumed under the heading, "theory Y." A strategy employed by some scientific management theorists involves "reward clocks," whereby five minutes of high-level production results in five minutes additional paid rest.[32]

The cooperative approach rejects both of its competitors. It denies that all work can be made inherently enjoyable and chooses instead to develop a sense of responsibility through cooperation. It also denies that workers are reward-punishment machines and strives to bring out the natural human tendency for self-control and participation.

The cooperative approach has inspired interesting corporate experiments. The best known is one undertaken by Sweden's Volvo Corporation. In addition to building automobiles through work teams and removing assembly lines, Volvo has placed employee representatives on their board of directors and allowed employee committees access to all corporate information. In the United States, General Motors has achieved success with its "Quality of Worklife Program," which since 1969 has encouraged increased employee participation in decisions affecting working conditions. In G.M.'s Terrytown plant, plant officials worked in close cooperation with the union and established "teams" of workers who were responsible for choosing their own production goals. To date the Terrytown program is said to be highly successful.[33]

Other U.S. companies have solicited employee input through different programs. The Harman-Kardon Company's plant in Bolivar, Tennessee, has introduced worker committees which confront issues such as cost reduction, capital investment, compensation, and working hours. Productivity at the Bolivar plant has increased since the changes, as has worker morale. Less dramatic but equally innovative approaches are taken by Connecticut Mutual Life Insurance Company and American Airlines. Connecticut Mutual offers a free lunch to any worker who will eat at the executives' table, where frank comments and questions are encouraged. American Airlines, relying on the broad coverage of its company news-

[32] Sennett, "New Clothes," p. 43.

[33] A presentation by Stephen Fuller, vice-president in charge of Personnel, General Motors, at Bentley College's Third National Conference on Business Ethics.

paper, devotes a full page each issue to employee criticisms of management. Other companies have developed "hot lines," "open door" policies, and "management-employee" meetings, through which employees can—often anonymously—voice complaints and give advice to management.

Critics of participatory management cite the possibility of inefficiency and a trampling of the rights of stockholders. Managers, not workers, are trained to manage, and if workers are allowed to manage they may throw the entire corporation off course. To decide issues concerned with capital investment one must know about financial trends, predicted market competition, the status of the investment community, and a host of fundamental accounting facts. How can a person who works eight hours a day on a lathe or an assembly line possess such knowledge? How can he or she make good decisions? A further problem is cited in the area of stockholder rights. It is said stockholders invest capital, and risk losses, upon the assumption that corporations will maximize their return on investment; but workers typically have interests quite distinct from stockholders. Is there a danger that participatory management schemes will satisfy workers' interests for higher pay, better working conditions, and increased status at the price of the stockholders' interest in profit maximization?

Just how damning these criticisms are depends on how the so-called "right of participation" is characterized. If characterized as a right "to control, through democratic mechanisms, the activities of the corporation," then it is open to vigorous attack. Are not stockholders to have some say in the running of the corporation? What evidence indicates that democratic control will satisfy the goal of productive efficiency as spelled out in the social contract? If, on the other hand, the right is characterized as a right of workers "to participate in the governance of the corporation," the road is easier. This formulation allows other corporate interest groups, including stockholders and managers, to have an active hand in governing, and indeed it leaves unspecified the level of relative influence which each interest group will have. Thus it is compatible with a division of authority whereby the bulk of decision-making falls to management but a small fraction is reserved by workers. Such a formulation can draw significant support from the social contract itself, especially the section specifying the obligation of corporations to minimize the "lack of worker control over work conditions." Indeed, *some* minimal level of worker input to management decision-making appears to be required by the social contract.

What would a sample "Bill of Employee Rights" include? To begin with, it would include rights falling in the four areas we have discussed: (1) free speech, (2) privacy, (3) due process, and (4) participation. In addition, it might include such other rights as the following:

> The right to refuse unethical directives without being penalized.
>
> The right to be free from "blacklisting" practices (whereby employers make it virtually impossible for employees to find employment elsewhere).

The right to refuse a promotion or relocation assignment without suffering penalties.

A recent study published in the *Harvard Business Review* reveals increasing acceptance of employee rights by businesspeople, especially in the area of whistle blowing. Of those executives surveyed, 61 percent agreed that if a whistle blower "believes sincerely he is acting in the best interests of customers, stockholders, or the community, he should not be penalized."[34] Only one-third believed that if a whistle blower doesn't like the company, he should leave it; and less than one-tenth think the whistle blower should be penalized if there is "factual evidence that the whistle blower is hurting sales."[35] Other rights, such as privacy and participation, are more controversial, but the trend is toward a softer and more sympathetic view of employee rights in general.

This chapter has examined the issue of employee rights from both a theoretical and practical perspective. From a theoretical perspective, the chapter has defended the view that employees have the right to make claims against employers, as well as a right to a variety of freedoms and prerogatives, the most important classes of which are freedom of speech, privacy, due process, and participation. At the present time, these are moral rights only, not legal rights, and are classified as "manifesto" rights in the sense that society is not agreed as to whom the task of policing them should fall. Furthermore, these are rights whose very existence is controversial: employers often argue that the impact of such rights on business practices will be to decrease efficiency and employee loyalty.

Despite the controversy surrounding employee rights, this chapter has proposed a combination of methods for justifying the existence of particular rights. It has indicated that rights such as the right to engage in political activities off the job, to refuse immoral orders from superiors, and to complain about potentially dangerous products, can be derived from more basic moral concepts.

Considered from a practical perspective, employee rights pose problems of implementation. Two obvious means of implementing them are available: implementation from the outside, through courts or government regulatory agencies, or implementation from the inside, relying on corporate initiative and self-regulation. Giant steps have been taken by the courts in recent years to protect employee rights, especially in companies with government affiliations. But the second means of implementation has obvious advantages. Moral suasion, most people grant, is preferable to government coercion. But can rights programs be implemented *voluntarily* by corporations? The answer, it appears, depends upon the overall moral posture of individual corporations and the corporate community. Improving the moral posture of modern corporations is the subject of the next chapter.

[34] David Ewing, "What Business Thinks about Employee Rights," *Harvard Business Review*, 55 (September-October 1977), 91-94.
[35] Ewing, "What Business Thinks," p. 91.

SUGGESTED SUPPLEMENTARY READINGS

DWORKIN, RONALD, *Taking Rights Seriously*. Cambridge, Mass.: Harvard University Press, 1977.

EWING, DAVID, *Freedom Inside the Organization*. New York: McGraw-Hill, 1977.

———, "What Business Thinks About Employee Rights," *Harvard Business Review*, 55 (September-October 1977); 91-94.

HART, H. L. A. "Are There Any Natural Rights?" *Philosophical Review*, 64 (1955), reprint in A. I. Meldon, ed., *Human Rights*. Belmont, Cal.: Wadsworth, 1970.

MARGOLIS, JOSEPH, "The Rights of Man," *Social Theory and Practice*, 4 (Spring 1978): 423-44.

NICKEL, JAMES, "Is There a Human Right to Employment?" *Philosophical Forum*. (forthcoming)

Philosophical Forum. "Special Issue: Work," vol. X, nos. 2-4, 1978-1979.

RICHARDS, NORVIN, "Using People," *Mind*, 87 (January 1978): 98-104.

STEINER, HILLEL, "The Natural Right to Equal Freedom," *Mind*, 83 (1974): 194-210.

WALTERS, KENNETH, "Your Employees' Right to Blow the Whistle," *Harvard Business Review*, 53 (July-August 1975): 1-7.

WERHANE, PATRICIA H., "The Obligatory Nature of Moral Rights" American Philosophical Association Western Division Meeting, Detroit, Michigan, April 29, 1980.

WESTIN, ALAN and STEPHAN SALISBURY, eds., *Individual Rights in the Corporation: A Reader on Employee Rights*. New York: Pantheon, 1980.

YOUNG, ROBERT, "Dispensing with Moral Rights," *Political Theory*, 6 (February 1978): 63-74.

CHAPTER 8

Improving Corporate Morality: Basic Issues

The previous chapters asked questions about the character of moral responsibilities that should be assumed by corporations. They focused upon issues such as the social contract, ethics in the free market, and employee rights. But suppose one has determined to his or her own satisfaction what a corporation's moral obligations *are,* and then asks *how* those obligations can be fulfilled. One might conclude that corporations should improve in the areas of employee rights, product safety, or environmental pollution, and yet wonder how corporations, with their centuries-old preoccupation with economic interests, can ever bring about such improvements. The complex issue of how corporations can facilitate moral improvement is the subject of the remaining chapters. In this chapter the aim is to develop a set of theoretical principles to use in evaluating proposals for corporate improvement. In the final chapter the aim will be to present and evaluate the proposals themselves.

As we saw in Chapter 2 and 6, even when corporations meet the minimal standards for moral agency, they, unlike ordinary moral agents, embody a moral logic of their own. Discovering how to improve corporate behavior is not like discovering how to make Jane Smith stop telling lies or how to persuade John Jones to give up smoking. General Motors confronts problems that John Jones has never dreamed of. To succeed morally, General Motors must develop systems of accountability, and this process, as Chapter 6 showed, often involves overcoming bureaucratic problems that mar accountability, such as fragmented decision-making structures and inefficient information systems. Bureaucratic problems such as these do not exist, except by remote analogy, for individual human moral agents.

Yet despite the unique moral logic of the corporation, its mere status as a moral agent gives rise to many of the same perplexing questions that arise with people. Why do corporations often fail to behave well? What, if anything, can be done to improve their behavior? Even if all the accountability problems could be solved, a corporation, just like a person, could be fully accountable—but accountable to the *wrong* standards. Even if all of a corporation's bureaucratic problems could be eliminated, the corporation might continue to behave badly. Consider the following case which illustrates this point.

The Mead Corporation Case

The Mead Corporation, a large multinational corporation with headquarters in the United States, hoped to expand its paper-making operations in the small town of Escanaba, Michigan, by constructing a large pulp mill. Though Escanaba welcomed the potential boost to its sagging local economy (the area was listed by the Department of Labor as economically depressed), it became alarmed over the prospect of air pollution and the possible "rotten egg" smell associated with a special Kraft pulp process which Mead intended to use. Surrounded by scenic forests and lakes, Escanaba was a popular vacation and retirement spot. The townspeople prided themselves on having the "cleanest air in the country," and shortly after Mead announced its plans, the townspeople formed a group entitled the Save Our Air Committee.[1]

Mead, on the other hand, wanted the new plant in order to capitalize on the growing demand for paper. Business was booming, and the rapid national increase in specialty magazines meant increased demand for strong, lightweight paper. With a new Kraft process mill in Escanaba, Mead would be in an excellent position to beat the competition and capture a larger market share. Although Michigan had pollution control laws, Mead's proposal for the first stage of plant construction had been approved by the Michigan State Air Pollution Control Commission. The company also knew that its political influence in the state capital was formidable and that even in Escanaba it had two Mead employees who were members of the local County Board of Supervisors. The outrage expressed by the citizens of Escanaba bothered Mead, but the company also knew that the political power of a town of 15,000 was slight. Mead pushed ahead. Upper-level management at first said nothing to the townspeople about the Kraft process or possible odor problems, but stressed instead the economic advantages of the mill to the local community.

The townspeople rallied to defend their cause. They demanded assurances from Mead that the air would remain clean, and they held a public meeting, at which four or five hundred people were greeted by teenage girls wearing "Save Our Air" sashes and citizens making speeches.

---

[1] John Collins, "Escanaba A and B," in *Business and Society: Cases and Text,* ed. Robert Hay and Edmund Gray (Cincinnati: South-Western, 1976), pp. 132-46.

They wrote letters to the Michigan State Air Pollution Control Commission and pushed for the development of county laws which would ban the proposed plant. Their efforts appeared to achieve success when the local Delta County Board of Supervisors passed an ordinance which required any new manufacturing plant to meet pollution standards established by the County Board.

Mead Corporation, meanwhile, stuck to its policy of minimum communication with the citizens of Escanaba. It continued negotiating with the Michigan State Air Pollution Control Board and argued that only the Kraft process, despite its odor problems, would be economically feasible. By a vote of six to two, the Board voted to give Mead a permit to build. Mead then announced to the citizens of Escanaba that although it didn't believe the mill would have odor problems, it could make no guarantees.

Mead won in the end. It built the Kraft process mill as planned over the objections of the citizens, and, as might be expected, the townspeople later complained about the "rotten egg" smell from the plant. The law passed by the local supervisors to prevent odor pollution was a failure. The Michigan attorney-general ruled the law was invalid because the county lacked authority to pass such legislation. A quote from the president of the Save Our Air Committee typifies the reaction of the Escanaba citizens: "What I want to say you couldn't put in the paper," he remarked, "It feels like everything we've done just went down the drain."[2]

If Mead failed in its responsibility to Escanaba citizens, it failed through none of the problems discussed earlier concerning accountability and bureaucratization. There was no special failure of its information system, no overburdened technocrat, no problem of "working to rule," and no failure on Mead's part to assume responsibility. Mead performed well in terms of its own standards; the problem was that those standards seemed exclusively directed to securing economic advantages and omitted reference to their effect upon the well-being of Escanaba citizens. Also nothing suggests that Mead forgot its consumers: indeed, each of its actions seemed likely to improve the satisfaction of consumer interests. But its standards seemed to omit reference to the concept of fair treatment, or (using the language of the social contract) to the need to accommodate the demands of *justice*. Mead refused to communicate with the citizenry openly and was guilty of, if nothing else, bad manners. This is true even if Mead provided economic benefits to the area—which it did. But, then, is it possible to improve the standards of a giant like Mead?

Cases such as Mead often stimulate demands for more and tougher laws. Unlike a person, Mead Corporation can neither be shunned by its friends nor be brought to feel guilt. It must be tamed, many argue, by the government.

[2] Collins, "Escanaba," p. 146.

GOVERNMENT CONTROL

But can the law ensure corporate morality? The question requires looking both at existing mechanisms of legal control and at suggestions for legal change. Certainly many existing laws have eliminated or reduced corrupt corporate practices. Consider the old tactic known as "bait and switch," a retail company advertising products at low prices and then conveniently running out of them. After being "baited" into the store, the consumer would be encouraged to "switch" to a more expensive product. This practice is now outlawed in the United States and other Western countries; when supplies of an advertised product are exhausted, retailers are required to provide rain checks to consumers. Similarly, there are now laws applying to advertising practices. The television razor blade advertisements of the 1960's which claimed that one brand would "shave sandpaper"—and then proceeded to demonstrate the fact by shaving a clean swath out of a lathered piece of sandpaper—would now be banned as "misleading" by the Federal Trade Commission. The ads were created by using a clear piece of plexiglas, which was laid on a table, with a television camera aimed from above. The plexiglas was then strewn with a layer of ordinary sand and topped off with shaving cream. Not surprisingly, the razor blade cut a neat swath through the sand. Many such questionable practices have been reduced by the application of law.

To estimate better the power of present law, let us review the major classifications of U.S. law regarding corporate abuses. These are: (1) procedures allowing citizens to bring suit against corporations, (2) laws affecting the relationship between corporations and their stockholders, and (3) legislation establishing special regulatory agencies and policies. All three owe their present form to a tradition of corporate law stretching back to common law practices inherited from the British. After fifty years of laissez-faire, "hands-off" treatment of business by the U.S. government, the spectre of corporate monopolies and labor unrest in the second half of the nineteenth century brought on increasing legal control. Through the Sherman and Clayton Acts, the federal government asserted its right to break monopolistic corporations, and later through a series of individual court decisions it began officially to recognize the rights of labor unions.

The power of consumers to sue corporations for product-related damage increased dramatically during the same period and continues to increase today. In 1853 the doctrine of "privity," which restricted consumers to suing only the party from whom they had purchased a product, was struck down, thus allowing consumers to reach into the deeper corporate pocket. The case prompting this change is instructive. A consumer purchased from a druggist a bottle marked "dandelion"; it had been mislabeled by the manufacturer and actually contained belladonna, a deadly poison. Under the doctrine of privity, only the druggist could be sued, but in this case the judge rejected privity and assigned liability to the manufacturer. Today the requirement of privity no longer exists. Furthermore, today consumers may sue not only when products are defective, but when they are defectively *designed;* thus if a power saw is poorly designed and throws wood chips at the operator, the operator may sue the corporation for damage to his eyes. Under the doctrine of "strict liability," consumers may sue corporations for product-related damages even when they are unable to prove corporate negligence. Sometimes puzzling to philosophers, the doctrine of strict liability confers liability without a corresponding need to prove misconduct; if a consumer buys a can of hair spray which explodes, it doesn't matter that the corporation took all reasonable safety precautions in manufacturing the spray, or even that it used the best available quality control system. It must compensate the injured consumer despite its own reasonable behavior.

The capacity of the public to sue corporations now extends beyond the arena of product liability. People may sue corporations for a wide range of environmental ills: for water pollution, for air pollution, and for the discharge of low-level nuclear radiation. Through "class-action" suits, by which the interests of many people are represented in a single suit, corporations may be sued for these and other social injuries.

The law also has strengthened its control over corporate-stockholder transactions. It has done so largely by emphasizing claims of ownership by stockholders. Through the Securities Act of 1933 and the Securities Exchange Act of 1934 (which established the Securities Exchange Commission [SEC]), the law now guarantees voting rights of shareholders, demands regular disclosure of corporate financial information, and requires that corporate managers fulfill specified obligations to stockholders.[3] As we shall see later, these laws do not hand control of the corporation over to stockholders, but they do ensure that the primary interest of a majority of stockholders, namely maximum return on investment, is taken seriously by corporate managers.

Everyone knows that regulatory agencies have mushroomed in the United States since the 1920's. Few know how dramatic that change has been. At one time the most corporations had to worry about was the Internal Revenue Service; now smaller corporations claim they cannot compete with larger ones because of their lessened capacity to bear the financial burden of coping with regulatory red tape. The list of government regulatory agencies whose principal business is to control U.S. corporations is too lengthy to repeat. Among its more prominent items are: the Food and Drug Administration (FDA), the Equal Employment Opportunity Commission (EEOC), the Federal Trade Commission (FTC), the Federal Communication Commission (FCC), Federal Aviation Administration (FAA), the Securities and Exchange Commission (SEC), the Consumer Product Safety Commission (CPSC), the Environmental Protection Agency (EPA), the Federal Energy Administration (FEA), the Federal Power Commission (FPC), the Federal Reserve System (FRS), the Interstate Commerce Commission (ICC), and the Nuclear Regulatory Commission (NRC). For each of these agencies there exists accompanying congressional legislation which authorizes certain activities and sets limits on others. For example, in its present form the Environmental Protection Agency is a product of

---

[3] Marvin A. Chirelstein, "Corporate Law Reform," in *Social Responsibility and the Business Predicament,* ed. James W. McKie (Washington, D.C.: The Brookings Institution, 1974), pp. 41-77.

the Federal Clean Air Act of 1963, and its scope of operation is defined in that act and in others such as the Federal Clean Air Amendments Act of 1970 and the Federal Water Pollution Control Act Amendments of 1972. These acts define its general function, allow it to establish "standards of performance" for corporations, and provide it with enough regulatory teeth to force compliance. The EPA can issue orders of compliance and bring civil actions in federal court for violations. Other agencies have similar powers.[4]

The historical roots of regulatory control in the United States go back to the 1930's, when new laws arose in response to consumer complaints. The issues of pure food and drugs and of misleading advertising became subjects of consumer attention. Consequently, Congress passed the Sea Food Act of 1934 to allow government inspection of fish-processing plants, the Wheeler Lea Act to establish advertising standards, and the Wool Labeling Act of 1939 to stipulate rules for the accurate labeling of wool products. From these modest beginnings came the large, multilayered regulatory system now in existence.

When all three modes of controlling corporate behavior by law are taken together, what is the result? In their present form, are they adequate to ensure an acceptable level of corporate morality? Opinions differ. One corporate attorney describes the present collection of legal weaponry as "blunt and clumsy"[5] and suggests that it will never promote the level of morality the public demands. Others see law as the only answer. Whatever one's opinion, it must be admitted that a gap exists between the expectations for law and its capacity to deliver. One reason for this lies in the lack of congruence between legal threats and the interests of corporate executives. The legal machinery is often designed to punish the agent who performs the illegal act, which in this case means the *corporation*. It is the corporation which is fined, or is required to compensate, or is restricted in its business dealings, not the corporate executives who make the decisions. When the Firestone Rubber Company is sued for designing a dangerous radial tire, it is the company that pays, not its decision-makers. The upshot is that executives will often take calculated risks on behalf of the company, gambling against fines and citizens' suits, for the sake of greater profits. The interests of these individual executives are often not directly at stake—typically they are not risking personal fines or jail sentences—and thus the law may fail to correct the problem through failing to reach its source.

Although the present law is meant to encourage corporate morality, one of its assumptions is at partial odds with that goal. Present corporate law regulating the relationship between the corporation and its stockholders assumes that the primary interest of the stockholders is maximum financial return and that the obligation of the corporation is to pursue that interest with single-minded diligence. In short, the law assumes that corporate investment decisions shall be based *solely* on a presumed preference among stockholders for higher market value—regardless of

[4] See *Business and Society*, ed. Hay and Gray (Cincinnati: South Western, 1976), pp. 90-99.
[5] Chirelstein, "Corporate Law Reform," p. 46.

what moral issue is at stake.[6] This is an appropriate attitude for situations in which corporations are squandering stockholders' money or corporate executives are using company resources to make themselves rich. However, it has the ironic effect of failing to give official recognition to any corporate motive other than profit maximization. Even charitable actions by corporations are restricted within certain limits and are allowed only on the assumption that they provide indirect benefits to corporations. Here, the law has been argued to stand in the way of morality.

A further criticism of present law is directed not at the law itself but at its accompanying social institutions: in particular the habits and attitudes of lawyers who fight corporate battles. A pervasive tendency among corporations—one encouraged by their lawyers—is to meet regulatory standards at a bare minimum and to press for interpretations that restrict the law's effect. This is the spirit that prevails among corporate attorneys, and it is the spirit they are trained by law schools to adopt. Thus, no matter how morally praiseworthy, compliance with regulations is seen by corporations as a burden to be avoided.

Finally there is the problem of the law's tendency toward ethnocentrism. Because domestic law is designed to protect citizens, it often fails to consider the morality of actions affecting the citizens of other nations. In the United States the Consumer Product Safety Commission banned "Tris-treated" children's sleepwear after discovering it caused cancer. However, at the same time a manufacturer could sell the sleepwear abroad. At the time of this writing, many products banned from U.S. markets, including certain pesticides and drugs, may legally be exported. Bribery laws have since been changed, but when Lockheed Aircraft Corporation bribed the Japanese government with millions of dollars to secure its Tri-Star contract, Lockheed's president could declare that no U.S. laws were broken. In large part, the law's ethnocentrism is unavoidable, since law's formal function is to protect its own citizenry and not that of other nations.

Existing mechanisms of legal control, then, are inadequate to ensure that in every instance an acceptable level of corporate moral behavior will be reached. Mead Corporation exemplifies this point. Legal mechanisms were present throughout the struggle between Mead and the townspeople, and Mead was exposed to possible suits from citizens as well as sanctions from Michigan state regulatory agencies. Yet none of the existing legal mechanisms persuaded Mead to bargain with the citizens in good faith. Mead was able to comply with the law while using an agent of the law, the attorney-general, to strike down attempts by the community to alter its behavior.

DRAWBACKS TO LEGAL SOLUTIONS

If present laws fail to guarantee good corporate behavior, why not press for new and tougher laws? Though such a step would fall short of ensuring perfect behavior, might it not succeed in raising the standards of corporations? Unfortunately, what-

[6]Chirelstein, "Corporate Law Reform," pp. 41, 73.

ever the answer to these questions, there are deeper problems affecting the law's capacity to encourage morality and these reach to the very heart of law and morality.

No matter how legal mechanisms might be reconstructed, they would need to be—as they always have been—standardized and applied according to general rules. But because standardized formulas never fit all situations precisely, a margin of immoral but legally permissible behavior will remain. Consider the laws that confer special minority status upon blacks, American Indians, and people with Spanish surnames. In one instance, a white named Robert Earl Lee legally changed his name to "Roberto Eduardo," thus becoming eligible for minority status and, in turn, making it possible for a corporation to hire him and bolster its minority quota.[7] Laws never fit either individuals or corporations perfectly and will forever give rise to moral loopholes.

Next there is the problem of the "negative" impact of law noted by moral philosophers such as St. Thomas Aquinas and Immanuel Kant. Laws tend to tell people what they ought *not* do, using negative terms, rather than telling people what they *should* do in positive ones. The law prescribes that citizens *not* exceed 55 m.p.h., *not* commit felonies, and *not* pollute the environment. Thus it sets a standard for minimally acceptable behavior. The law does not, however (nor probably should it), tell people what they should do in case they wish to *exceed* the minimums. Because practically speaking the law is linked to its capacity to threaten punishment, it would be odd if not useless for the law to specify high levels of moral conduct without establishing penalties for failing to do so. And even if penalties were established, the tendency would be to destroy morality rather than enhance it. The moral behavior generated by such a move would be compelled behavior, but the more behavior is compelled, as we noted in Chapter 4, the less it qualifies as genuine moral behavior. The law can specify minimum standards of acceptable behavior but it can do little to encourage wholehearted morality. It can attempt to force General Motors to install safety devices in cars, to monitor in-plant pollutants, and to hire minorities, but it cannot force General Motors to develop a genuine concern for its employees and consumers.

Laws also suffer from their incapacity to anticipate the novel or unusual circumstance. They tend to be written in *response* to events rather than in *anticipation* of them. There is an inevitable time lag between the recognition of a problem and the law's capacity to control it, so the law always runs after moral problems and, like a man chasing his coattails, can never quite catch them. Consider the introduction of laws controlling the packaging of meat and canned food products. The novelist Upton Sinclair, in his book *The Jungle,* exposed the horrors of the meat-packing industry when it was published in 1906: unsanitary conditions, diseased beef carcasses, and even instances of rats ground up in canned foods. But it was years before the law established effective controls through the Pure Food and Drug Administration. The same could be said of current examples: seat belt require-

---

[7] *U.S. News and World Report,* April 17, 1979, p. 60.

ments, truth in lending regulations, and nuclear power generating controls all occurred *after* the problems were diagnosed.

Even if the law could keep pace with the development of moral problems, certain problems would elude its grasp. Laws can frequently be effective in coercing reluctant corporate executives to remedy problems they otherwise would ignore. They are capable, for example, of forcing a company like Listerine to be cautious in the claims made in television ads and of demanding even that Listerine retract claims that its mouthwash "fights colds." Yet there exists an entirely different class of corporate abuses which the law is virtually helpless to prevent—namely, the problems that corporate executives themselves would eliminate if they only could. In a surprising number of corporate moral disasters, upper management is completely unaware of the events occurring at a lower level which prompt the disaster. Often, they would condemn the actions—if they only knew about them. Such problems stem from communication failures and entanglements of organizational structure and have already been discussed under the topic of bureaucratic ills. These problems are especially recalcitrant in the face of legal pressures; if legal means are to remedy them, then the means must be of a wholly different sort from those presently in effect.

Finally, there is the age-old conflict between efficiency and regulation; many of the business community's persistent complaints about regulation are valid. People who regulate cannot hope to have the necessary intimate acquaintance with a corporation's problems to impose restraints with maximum efficiency. The following scenario is all too common: An executive, a middle manager, or a craftsman, thoroughly familiar with the corporate operation he has worked years to perfect, is confronted with an outsider, perhaps from Washington, with little or no experience, who wishes to apply standardized rules to a nonstandard situation. Even when corporate executives sympathize with the goals of regulators, they can spot the clumsy, expensive, and inefficient "extras" which the regulators demand. Also, when regulatory agencies attempt to augment the experience of their staff by hiring people from the industry they regulate, they confront the dilemma of indoctrinating people schooled in anti-regulatory attitudes with pro-regulatory attitudes. It is little wonder that corporate executives each year love to announce the billions of dollars wasted by bureaucratic red tape. They can see the problems of regulation in their own back yards.

All the difficulties of enforcing morality through law do not imply that regulation should be eliminated; however, they clearly expose significant limitations of the regulatory process. Encouraging and improving corporate moral behavior will require more than the external threats of the law. For this reason, it is tempting to examine an entirely different tack.

CHANGE FROM THE INSIDE

Instead of forcing corporations to obey rules from the outside, why not alter corporate design and structure so that they are able to promote moral behavior from the *inside?* In other words, why not establish appropriate motivations and controls inside the corporation? This suggestion is all the more appealing in light of increasing evidence that the design of organizations is a firm determinant of organizational behavior; when design is changed, organizational behavior is often changed. Herbert Simon, winner of a Nobel Prize in economics, provides ammunition for this approach: he argues that the behavior of large corporations is not determined merely by market structure and market forces, as many suppose, but also by structural design. Changes in law are not essential; structure can be altered from the inside. Even if legal pressure were necessary to begin the process, such pressure could be removed once *internal* mechanisms of self-control were developed.

Internal charge is championed by a surprising number of contemporary corporate theorists. Here are examples of such proposals:

1. Alter corporate boards of directors to include employee representatives and consumer representatives.
2. Develop employee reward systems which motivate moral behavior.
3. Establish corporate constitutions which specify moral goals.

These suggestions, along with others, will be discussed thoroughly in the next chapter. For now, we require some means of evaluating the entire class of "internal change" proposals, to estimate their effectiveness in promoting moral behavior. An appeal to past experience is out of the question, since most of the proposals have never before been implemented. Some means is needed, then, to establish the criteria for a successful proposal, to establish the standards for selecting those suggestions that should be tried. Such criteria will possess a moral and ethical flavor, since their aim is to evaluate proposals for improving corporate morality. One promising place to begin is with an analysis of the causes of corporate *immorality*, for discovering forces that prompt immorality may shed light on how to eliminate them. Let us, then, attempt to isolate these underlying forces.

SOURCES OF CORPORATE MISCONDUCT

Profit

One source of corporate misbehavior is obvious. It is the tendency to forget about moral matters in the pursuit of profits. Although the profit motive may, as indicated in Chapters 3 and 4, work to aid society in the sense of sharpening efficiency and motivation, it has often been appealed to as an excuse to fix prices, sell dangerous products, and exploit employees. We have only to look at the personal testimony of businesspeople convicted for serious crimes to discover this. In a high percentage of cases businesspeople testify that they were tempted by the lure of greater profits. Though the nature of the conflict may vary in each instance, its general form is the same: the conflict is between profit and responsibility. So, to take obvious examples: the corporation's pursuit of profit through the use of misleading television advertising may be at odds with the requirement to communicate honestly or to provide reliable information to consumers; or the corporation's pursuit of profit through an attempt to increase worker productivity may be at odds with the requirement to provide reasonable and safe working conditions. If the tendency for such conflict could be reduced or eliminated, then surely corporate morality would benefit.

Such an obvious problem, however, defies obvious solutions. To recommend to corporations that they simply stop pursuing profits is futile. Moreover, even if this feat could be accomplished, it would result in abuse of a different sort; for, as demonstrated in Chapter 5, corporations operating in a free market environment have a moral obligation to pursue profits. What, then, is to be done?

Rather than eliminate the goal of profits, a more reasonable approach seems to be to introduce *other* goals, i.e., *moral* goals, into the corporate decision-making structure. The consequences would be to balance the motive of profit against other motives in order to improve a corporation's behavior. This approach is encouraging for it recognizes that the efficient functioning of the market system requires adherence to norms other than profit. In order for the overall system of market exchanges—with its necessary mergers, sales, acquisitions, speculations, and so forth—to function efficiently, it is necessary that contracts be honored, that the flow of information be generally reliable, and that a modicum of trust exist between exchanging parties. Without this moral backdrop of reliable expectations, the market system would be like the thief who, not knowing whether to trust his fellow thieves, wasted all his time discovering their motives.

In order to maximize its benefits to society, an economic system should produce high-quality products at reasonable prices, and it is in the service of this end that Adam Smith and others believe a free market system has optimal results. But also in order to maximize benefits to society, the market system should achieve another goal recognized as having fundamental value, namely, adherence to moral norms. It is clear that the market system can benefit society most when it both satisfies society's needs *and* lives up to reasonable moral expectations. Thus, it is clear also that *one criterion for meaningful corporate reform is the capacity to introduce moral goals alongside the goal of profit.*

System-Oriented Problems

Another underlying contributor to corporate immorality can be the very structure of the corporation itself—at least when it is conceived as a goal-pursuing system. This element has already been discussed in the context of moral agency (Chapter 2) and bureaucracy (Chapter 6), but it remains to be analyzed in the context of the issue of corporate moral improvement. Those who understand the corporation in terms of the organizational theory of Herbert Simon or John Ladd will tend to view it as deliberately structured to facilitate the pursuit of specific goals. Chapter 2 showed that Ladd was wrong to categorically deny moral agency to large, profit-making corporations, since many may be able to meet the minimal conditions for moral agency. Even so, Ladd's general criticism serves to isolate a moral failing of corporations: namely, insofar as they are merely goal-pursuing mechanisms, they have difficulties adhering to moral principles. That is, they seem plagued by a logical flaw: the goal-rational behavior they specialize in is forever at loggerheads with principled action. In the same way that a person who doggedly pursues nothing but a handful of personal goals might be blinded to the need to adhere to principles of honesty and mutual respect, so a corporation's goal-oriented design may bring similar blindness.

How, concretely, might such blindness happen? Imagine a corporation formally structured to pursue goals, with the goals at a given time being W, X, Y, and Z. Suppose W, X, Y, and Z represent maximum profit, a yearly $50,000 donation to the Red Cross, 5 percent larger market share in five years, and a decrease in the debt-to-equity ratio. Imagine also that the corporation maintains a committee system which reviews and establishes goals and evaluates corporate performance solely in terms of achieving those goals. Finally, imagine that all employees in the corporation, including the managers, are evaluated and rewarded solely in terms of how well they further the corporation's goals. With such a review mechanism, the corporation may succeed in decreasing its debt to equity ratio, increasing profits and market share, and contributing $50,000 to the Red Cross, yet it may fail to adhere to principles of fairness, honesty, and respect for employees. It may suffer, in other words, from moral myopia.

This myopia may be understood through a long-standing philosophical device known as the "open question argument." The argument has been used in an attempt to show that certain moral concepts like "goodness" or "moral responsibility" can never be fully defined. Suppose that a corporation tries to equate its moral responsibility with achieving a set of specific goals—it makes no difference what the goals are. Now, the open question argument points out that no matter what the goals are, it is always "meaningful" to ask whether the achieving of those goals is equivalent to satisfying the corporation's moral responsibility. That is, it is "meaningful" in the sense that to deny the proposition at issue does not involve a self-contradiction, as would denying the proposition, "A bachelor is an unmarried man," or "Water is H_2O." Suppose a corporation, after massive structural revisions, proceeds to pursue the goal of increasing employee salaries and aggressively seeks higher wages, more overtime pay, and bigger bonuses. Here there is no logical problem in asking whether increasing employee salaries is equivalent to satisfying the corporation's moral responsibilities. Further, no matter how many goals are added to this one, the question is still meaningful. The conclusion is that a corporation's moral responsibilities cannot be *defined* as "achieving X," no matter what is understood by "X," for it is always an open question whether achieving X is equivalent to satisfying the corporation's moral responsibilities.

Thus, no matter what goals a corporation pursues, it should recognize that moral responsibility cannot be equated with the pursuit of a finite set of goals. Many philosophers would argue that in addition to pursuing goals (including moral goals), corporations must adhere to certain moral principles. If corporations merely pursue goals, they ask, then how will they fulfill their duty to adhere to principles of advertising honesty, fair pricing, and respect for employees? If corporations merely pursue goals, then how will they fulfill their obligations to observe principles of justice as specified in the social contract?

Can responsible corporate behavior even be defined as behavior that both achieves certain goals *and* adheres to certain principles? The answer is unclear. It seems that the open question argument might also challenge this definition, in the sense that one could always meaningfully ask, "Is adhering to principle x responsible corporate behavior?" On the other hand, some principles, such as "Always treat workers with respect" or "Never perpetuate injustice" seem so universally applicable that they might be construed as part of the very definition of responsible corporate behavior. Whatever the outcome of this issue, one thing is certain: the open question argument makes clear that a corporation should stop short of equating its responsibility with the achievement of a particular set of goals, even when they are praiseworthy ones.

The last point can be demonstrated concretely. There are numerous organizations which have integrated praiseworthy goals into their formal constitutions: those include religious organizations, state welfare agencies, fraternal orders, and organizations such as the Boy Scouts of America. These groups are typically chartered with moral purposes in mind: to aid the poor, to encourage moral education, and so on. Yet even these organizations can fall prey to criticism in that their respective goals may be pursued in ignorance of other human considerations. An organization structured to pursue the goal of education could in pursuit of that goal be structurally insensitive to other issues and, say, practice racial discrimination, favor upper-level economic groups, and the like (as, indeed, many universities have been criticized for doing). Let us give the tendency to err through a preoccupation with pursuing specific goals the label "goal preoccupation."

The tendency toward goal preoccupation overlaps the tendency to pursue profits at the expense of morality. Criticism of the latter identifies a conflict between one specific goal of the corporate organization, namely profit, and the need to adhere to norms; but although the former identifies a conflict between corporate goals and responsibility, it is the mere existence of organizational goals—whatever they may be—which gives rise to the conflict, and not the specific goal of profit. The tendency toward goal preoccupation applies to any profit-oriented and nonprofit organizations, including government agencies, *so long as* they are deliberately structured to facilitate the pursuit of a given set of goals.

In order to counteract the tendency toward goal preoccupation, corporations must develop decision-making procedures that take into account a wide range of moral considerations. In addition to pursuing profits, technological advance, community reform, and so on, they also need to implement principles of honesty, fairness, and respect for the dignity of employees. One way of expressing this is to say they must pursue not only specific goals, but also the indefinite goal of "acting morally," or of "adhering to the social contract." In a sense, it is not a goal at all, but rather a general concern to behave well. A corporation's general concern to behave well would be analogous to an individual's general concern to be virtuous.

Thus from this analysis of goal preoccupation, there emerges *a second criterion: that corporations should develop decision-making procedures that avoid goal preoccupation and that reflect a general concern to behave well.*

The task of investigating concrete proposals for corporate reform, again, will be undertaken in the next chapter. However, some of the specific conditions necessary to fulfill the criteria set out above can be anticipated.

FULFILLING THE TWO CRITERIA

Interpreting Moral Responsibility

Any internal corporate change that hopes to introduce a general concern for morality must specify how that concern relates to concrete issues. Merely talking about ethical concepts is inadequate. Issuing reports to stockholders saying "Our company is concerned about morality," or delivering speeches about the depth of corporate moral concern, is often worse than nothing. There must be a means of saying "Responsible corporate behavior means removing this misleading label from the aspirin bottles, beginning next month," or "Responsible corporate behavior means lowering the noise level on these stamping machines from 120 to 80 decibels."

Even the specification of corporate obligation found in the social contract is inadequate, since the social contract identifies general obligations such as the need to minimize pollution and depletion of natural resources but is incapable of specifying whether, say, the sulfide content of a recovery furnace effluence is tolerable at a level of three parts per million. Without the ability to specify, formulate, and communicate specific obligations, the general concept of moral concern is stripped of its usefulness; it is merely an abstraction in search of an application.

Closely connected to the need to apply moral concepts concretely is the need to develop evaluation systems which have a moral dimension. If lowering employee accident rates, improving product safety, and increasing the number of blacks and women *are* corporate goals, then managers must be told this and their success in reaching such goals must be evaluated. In the case of the B. F. Goodrich scandal mentioned earlier, many of the employees responsible for falsifying the safety tests on the brake assembly were rewarded shortly after with promotions. Such an evaluation of managers' success in meeting corporate goals fails to reflect a moral dimension.

Input from Employees and Consumers

Although the social contract is unable to specify a corporation's obligations precisely, it holds implications for the manner in which corporate improvement should occur. The social contract, we remember, is two-sided: one of its sides faces the consumer and requires the enhancement of consumer interests, while the other faces the employee and requires the enhancement of his or her interests. Because corporations must be concerned with satisfying both consumer and employee interests, they must develop systems to register input from both groups. Some interests from either group are self-evident to management: clearly, consumers have an interest in product safety, and employees have an interest in safe working conditions. But some are not so obvious: for example, female employees may come to prefer regular "disability" leaves to special "pregnancy" leaves. Development of systems to register the interests of consumers and employees can improve corporate decision-making. Such systems can allow decision-makers to learn, for example, whether employees desire higher fringe benefits and lower salaries, or vice versa.

Usually corporations are better equipped to register input from consumers than from employees. Registry even of consumer input is often more keenly developed where it relates to sales. The marketing department of a breakfast cereal company is well informed about consumer preferences and about the fact that consumers prefer a tall cereal box to a squat one because it appears to contain more. It also knows that mothers are interested in finding high vitamin and mineral ratings on the box. However, less is typically known about consumer interests that are unrelated to buying habits. Marketers often know little about the nutritional interests of children and about how cereals affect the growth and lifetime health of children.

Frequently unions serve to represent employee interests to management, although even here shortcomings arise. Take the following example: Until 1969 a large synthetic rubber company in the deep South maintained four main categories of jobs: lab technicians, maintenance, craftsmen, and laborers. All jobs in the first three categories were filled exclusively by whites, and jobs in the final category were filled exclusively by blacks. All categories were represented by unions, yet despite the gross racial segregation, management heard no substantial complaints from employees until 1967, and then only through an E.E.O.C. representative. The segregation had become an accepted fact of life.[8] Still another reason for not relying on unions lies in the fact that four out of five U.S. workers do not belong to a union.

Systems of Power and Control

Any internal changes made to improve corporate morality must also be connected to ongoing systems of power and control. In one sense, this is an application of the philosophical dictum that "ought implies can," or, in other words, that the limits of responsibility coincide with the limits of one's power to affect action. Although a corporate decision-making process may be capable of specifying responsibility, of assigning moral duties to individuals, and of knowing about the interests of employees and consumers, it will be impotent if it lacks power to implement those decisions. Power held by the board of directors is often crucial. A recalcitrant

[8] Lee Stokes, "Friendly Visits from E.E.O.C.," in *Business and Society,* ed. Hay and Gray (Cincinnati: South-Western, 1976), pp. 236-39.

board of directors can sidetrack the best intentions of managers and employees. Sometimes its refusal to allocate funds to needed areas will precipitate future problems.

AVOIDING THE SIDE EFFECTS OF REFORM

Inefficiency

A few caveats are now in order. Corporate moral improvement can be undesirable when it brings new problems in its wake. Although corporations may reflect a multitude of sins, they have helped create the highest standard of living in history. The economic benefits flowing from corporations ought not be seriously compromised through misguided moral reforms. Otherwise one good is purchased at the price of another evil. If changes are made in the structure of large corporations, or if managers come to have a deepened sense of social responsibility, then such changes must avoid suffocating productive efficiency. As we saw in Chapter 3, corporate productive organizations exist in large measure to satisfy consumer interest more efficiently than otherwise is possible, and maintaining and improving efficiency should always be a principal corporate goal.

Competitive Disadvantage

A corporation concerned with self-improvement can risk placing itself at a competitive disadvantage. Self-imposed improvement may require competitive sacrifices, and a company may discontinue a popular item for moral reasons, only to be beaten by a competitor with lower scruples. "If we refused cigarette accounts," advertising executives point out, "those accounts would be grabbed by competitors." "What would be accomplished?" they ask. Decisions to alter product design to improve safety, to remove suspected carcinogens from working areas, or to raise the percentage of black and female employees may result in competitive disadvantages if undertaken unilaterally.

How, then, can competitive disadvantage be avoided? One suggestion is to select reforms that actually enhance competitive strength. A surprising number of changes may fit in this category: an improved employee-management communication, production of safer products, or improved overall corporate moral performance often has a clear economic payoff. This strategy, however, only avoids the issue; it does not solve it. When potential reforms do threaten a firm's competitive position, a better strategy may be to seek industry-wide, rather than unilateral changes. If *all* members of a given industry undertake a change, none is placed at a disadvantage competitively. Such changes can be implemented from the outside, as the government has done by establishing minimum requirements, health and safety standards, employee hiring standards, and many similar stipulations. Given the inevitable problems and inadequacies of government regulation, however, a second class of remedies is appealing: industry-sponsored reform.

Industry-sponsored reform has a surprisingly successful history. Interestingly, one of the leaders in the movement toward self-regulation is the advertising industry. In 1911, *Printers Ink,* a leading advertising journal, sponsored a statute which specified the standards for misleading advertising.[9] Later the Radio and TV Code Authority of the National Association of Broadcasters (NAB) specified in even greater detail the standards it expected member broadcasters to observe. Still in effect, this code prohibits advertising of fortune-telling and certain sex-related products. It also has "special rules regarding advertising of weight reduction products, ... gambling, hard liquor, mood drugs, and acne products. It imposes conditions on advertising aimed at children. And it is interpreted by a panel of outside experts who determine whether or not an advertisement complies with legal requirements as well as with its own standards."[10] Similar codes and voluntary agencies exist for other industries.

Whether interindustry cooperation can fulfill the dreams of some in substituting for government regulation is difficult to determine. There are unexpected legal problems arising with interindustry ethical codes, for example, which will be discussed in the next chapter. Whatever the drawbacks, however, interindustry reform has the advantage of avoiding competitive disadvantage, since if one company makes a sacrifice, so will its competitors.

Rights of Stockholders

Finally, any moral change must avoid violating the rights of stockholders. The property rights of stockholders, as we noted in Chapter 5, fail to encompass the freedom to do anything at all—to trespass on the rights of consumers, employees, or other citizens, or to violate the principles of the social contract. Yet having said this, we must recognize that in a society that respects property rights, stockholders have definite prerogatives. For example, if changes are made in management structure affecting the investment value of the stock, the stockholder must be informed. He may not desire such changes, having invested in the stock exclusively for the purpose of making money, and his desires as *de facto* owner of the corporation must be considered in corporate decision-making.

This chapter has followed the issue of corporate improvement through a labyrinth of basic issues. By isolating two tendencies toward corporate immorality in the beginning of the chapter, we were able to uncover two general criteria for effective internal corporate reform: that meaningful corporate reform (1) should introduce moral goals into the corporation alongside that of profit maximization, and (2) should introduce decision-making procedures that allow for a general con-

---

[9] "Truth in Advertising—A Panel Discussion," in *Business and Society,* ed. Hay and Gray (Cincinnati: South-Western, 1976), pp. 342-57.

[10] Robert Moskin, ed., "The Case for Advertising: Highlights of the Industry Presentation to the Federal Trade Commission" (New York: American Association of Advertising, 1973), remarks made by attorney Phillip Schwartz of Davis, Gilbert, Levine & Schwartz.

cern to behave well. Furthermore, it has been argued that any internal corporate change should:

1. Establish procedures for specifying the precise character of moral responsibility in specific instances.
2. Define obligations for individual corporate personnel which will promote fulfillment of overall corporate morality.
3. Ensure that corporate decision-making procedures effectively register input from consumers and employees.
4. Ensure that decision-making procedures embody adequate power to execute moral directions.

Three caveats are:

1. Changes should avoid or minimize reduction in productive efficiency.
2. Changes should avoid or minimize the creation of unfair competitive disadvantages.
3. Changes should avoid violating the rights of stockholders.

The purpose of this chapter has been to provide the theoretical equipment necessary to confront concrete suggestions for internal corporate decision-making. The next task is to evaluate those concrete proposals.

SUGGESTED SUPPLEMENTARY READINGS

ACKERMAN, R. W., *Corporate Social Responsiveness: The Modern Dilemma.* Reston, Reston Publishing, 1976.

BAUMHART, RAYMOND S. J., *An Honest Profit.* New York: Holt, Rinehart & Winston, 1968.

CAVANAGH, GERALD, *American Business Values in Transition.* Englewood Cliffs, N.J.: Prentice-Hall, 1976.

CHAYES, ABRAHAM, "The Modern Corporation and the Rule of Law," in *The Corporation in Modern Society,* ed. Edward Mason. Cambridge, Mass.: Harvard University Press, 1960.

GOODPASTER, K., and K. SAYRE, eds., *Ethics and Problems of the 21st Century.* Notre Dame, Ind.: Notre Dame University Press, 1979.

GOTHIE, DAVID, ed., *Business Ethics and Social Responsibilities.* (Charlottesville, Va.: University of Virginia Press, 1974.

HAMPSHIRE, STUART, ed., *Public and Private Morality.* London: Cambridge University Press, 1978.

HAY, ROBERT, and EDMUND GRAY, and JAMES GATES, eds., *Business and Society: Cases and Text.* Cincinnati: South-Western Publishing Co., 1976.

MCMAHON, THOMAS, *Report on the Teaching of Socio-Ethical Issues in Collegiate Schools of Business Administration.* Charlottesville, Va.: University of Virginia Press, 1975.

POWERS, CHARLES, and DAVID VOGEL, *Ethics in the Education of Business Managers.* New York: Hastings Institute, 1980.

SOUTHARD, SAMUEL, *Ethics for Executives.* New York: Cornerstone, 1977.

STEINER, GEORGE, and JOHN STEINER, eds. *Issues in Business and Society.* New York: Random House, 1972.

VAGTS, DETLEV, "The Governance of the Corporation: The Options Available and the Power to Prescribe," *Special Issue: Business Lawyer,* 31 (1976).

WILLIAMS, OLIVER, and JOHN HOUK, *Full Value.* San Francisco: Harper & Row, Pub., 1978.

CHAPTER 9

Corporate Morality: Proposals

$\mathbf{C}$orporations are subject to metamorphosis. Like churches, families, and governments, they evolve gradually and in the process alter not only their membership, but their power and structure. In the last 200 years Western governments have reluctantly accepted restraints on their power and authority, and in an analogous way corporations have been forced to submit to increasingly legal restraints: to proscriptions, quotas, minimums, and mandated reports. Some observers aregue that future corporate metamporphosis should imitate political evolution. They argue that just as governments have found it necessary to alter their structure by instituting internal checks and balances, so large corporations must reorganize their systems of management and their relationships with stockholders. The hope is to use nuts and bolts internal changes to effect an enlightened external attitude.

This chapter will approach the issue of corporate reform in two ways. First, it will serve as a tour guide through the confusing array of current corporate reform proposals. Second, it will analyze the proposals and evaluate their merits. Mapping out, explaining, and classifying attempts at corporate reform are essential for facilitating a reasonable evaluation. Much of the evaluation, however, is left to the reader, and the chapter will be partially successful if it only provides a well-defined smorgasbord of proposals. The evaluation in this chapter draws both on standard evaluations of well-known proposals, and upon the evaluative criteria developed in the previous chapter. Despite such theoretical aids, caution is in order. Accuracy is elusive in investigations of this kind, and the issue of how well a given proposal for corporate reform will work is largely an empirical matter. Ultimately, proposals must stand the test of the real world. Theoretical speculation is not completely futile, since it frequently can isolate promising from unpromising hypotheses. Yet without proper caution, we should find ourselves like the sixteenth-century churchmen who, through abstract speculation, proved that the moon is a glasslike, perfect sphere. Galileo, being wiser, looked through his telescope.

Different people proposing corporate reforms use different sets of assumptions. Some assume that corporations are stubborn and must be subject to ongoing external regulation. We looked at objections to this approach in the previous chapter; one consequence of regulation is a reliance upon decision-making machinery *outside* the corporate environment, i.e., on the decision-making systems of the courts, or the legislators, or government agencies. Optimistic about the capacity of corporations to make financial decisions, but pessimistic about their capacity to make moral ones, this view endorses a system of "remote control." Making an opposite assumption, some theorists see corporations as fully capable of exerting moral control over themselves, though they grant that corporations have frequently fallen down in the past. This approach relies on decision-making machinery *inside* the corporation and endorses a kind of moral autonomy.

Now there is a third view which falls midway between these two. It grants that corporations are stubborn and resist change, and it believes that the chances of corporations shaping up are slim. However, it refuses to endorse the remote-control view. Instead it recommends that *external* pressures be used to create *inside* the corporation the kind of decision-making structures necessary for moral autonomy. Thus, it agrees with the autonomous view in thinking corporate moral control should come from internal decision-making structures. This third view makes restructuring compulsory but does so *in order to* promote corporate autonomy. It may be labeled "enforced autonomy." With the same irony with which Rousseau believed men sometimes need to be "forced to be free," this approach holds that corporations must sometimes be forced to establish the conditions of their own autonomy.

Only the second and third approaches will be discussed in this chapter. This is not because the first is undeserving of consideration, but rather because the first is familiar (being presently in use) and because present legal controls suffer from the kind of problems outlined in the last chapter. Present regulatory controls have no doubt helped ease a certain class of corporate threats to society—perhaps they should be strengthened despite their shortcomings—but the form of control they exert is familiar to us, and the issue of the moral impact of such control is relatively straightforward and noncontroversial.

The second and third approaches offer hope of improved corporate morality without the customary side effects of regulation. But can they deliver? Hundreds of proposals share these approaches, and since some may succeed where others fail, the next step is to sort out and evaluate them.

All the proposals lumped under the second and third approaches may be further subdivided according to the style of change they propose. These are:

1. Shifting power among individuals.

2. Establishing internal corporate legislation and procedures.

3. Altering formal organizational structure.

Each style requires separate examination.

SHIFTING POWER AMONG INDIVIDUALS

By transferring power in corporate organizations from one set of persons to another, or by shifting the relative degrees of power, it is possible to effect dramatic shifts in overt corporate behavior. Different classes of individuals have different interests and will use power differently. Stockholders, middle managers, local townspeople, technocrats, consumers, upper-level executives, inside directors, outside directors, rank and file workers—all influence the corporation; if the role of one is increased in the corporate decision-making process, the corporate motives will adjust in line with the interests of that class. Some critics fault modern corporations for systematically excluding certain groups, especially employees, consumers, or local townspeople. The answer, they argue, is systematically to *include* them. Other critics fault modern corporations for allowing managers slowly to accumulate the bulk of corporate power, and for these critics the answer is to redistribute power where it belongs, namely, in the hands of shareholders. All such proposals reveal at bottom a spirit of organizational reform similar to the ideas of the eighteenth-century philosopher Montesquieu, who stressed the need for political systems that automatically balance competing interests. Instead of making people better (a difficult task anyway), the idea is to harmonize their interests through a system of checks and balances.

Some of the most popular suggestions for balancing interests in the corporation are (1) to create "corporate democracy" with stockholders as the electorate, (2) to shift power from "inside directors" to "outside directors," (3) to place workers and consumers on boards of directors, and (4) to create a radical "corporate democracy" in which all affected individuals collectively control corporate activity. Each proposal aims at shifting the loci of power in the corporation, yet each maintains the same underlying organizational structure, i.e., it maintains an arrangement with a single board of directors, stockholders, and traditional corporate office structure. The shift is to occur not in the structure of the corporation but in the forces that lie behind the structure.

Corporate Democracy

"Corporate democracy" represents one of the most popular movements in modern corporate reform. The idea is to divest managers of some of their power and place it in the hands of shareholders, who will then be able to exercise moral control over the corporation. Because of the remarkable history of shareholder action attempts, it is reasonable to think that shareholders will do more than merely look for higher dividends. Since the late 1960's, shareholders have attempted to force hundreds of corporations to do such things as stop making napalm, put seat belts in cars, terminate sales of infant formula to underdeveloped countries, and end business relations with South Africa.

One celebrated attempt was undertaken by Ralph Nader, who with his associates arranged in January 1970 to purchase twelve shares of General Motors common stock. The impact of this tiny group was completely out of proportion to the stock it owned. It pushed for, and received, permission to include specific resolutions on the annual stockholders' report: one demanded that G.M. establish a committee on social responsibility, and another called for new, public-oriented representatives on the board of directors. In the end, the stockholders voted over-whelmingly against the Nader proposal—but not before massive public criticism had surfaced against General Motors. Despite the vote, General Motors bowed to public pressures and established a committee for social responsibility. The committee was a mere skeleton of what critics had called for, but it signaled a turn in G.M.'s attitude.[1]

Less celebrated attempts have been even more successful. In 1978 Bristol-Meyers Company settled out of court with a group of Roman Catholic nuns who claimed that Bristol-Meyers' marketing of infant formula in poor countries contri-buted to malnutrition in babies. The Sisters of the Precious Blood, who owned 1,000 shares of stock, sued the company on the grounds that it misled stockholders when it opposed a stockholders' resolution which the sisters submitted for a vote in 1977. Bristol-Meyers' marketing practices, they argued, encouraged mothers to abandon breastfeeding and to use the company's prepared formula. But because the mothers were uneducated, they often failed to realize that nearby water supplies (for mixing with the formula) had high bacteria levels; and because the mothers lived in poverty, they often lacked money to continue buying the product. Despite their proverty, after terminating breastfeeding, they were compelled to depend on the formula. The result was statistically high levels of malnutrition in formula-fed babies. In the out-of-court settlement, Bristol-Meyers agreed to work with the nuns in resolving infant formula problems in Third World countries.[2]

In more recent attempts, students have pressured universities to use their stockholder clout to alter corporate policy. Most large universities own sizeable portfolios of corporate stock, and although in the past their attitude as stockholders has been passive, students in the late 1970's clamored for action against suspected union haters, such as J. P. Stevens Company, and companies with strong ties to the government of South Africa, such as Polaroid, Inc. In 1979, for example, students marched at the University of Chicago and, exhibiting a spirit similar to the stu-

---

[1] John W. Collins, "Campaign to Make General Motors Responsible," in *Business and Society: Cases and Text,* ed. Robert Hay and Edmund Gray (Cincinnati: South-Western, 1976), pp. 51-69.

[2] *Chicago Tribune,* January 26, 1978, "Nun-Shareholders Win Infant Formula Battle."

dent radicalism of the late 1960's, demanded that the university either sell all its stock in companies doing business in South Africa, or retain the stock and use it to persuade the companies to halt business with that country. In response to those demands, the university refused to sell the stock, claiming that the investments were profitable, but it did agree to vote the stock itself instead of delegating the responsibility to a management corporation, as it had in the past.

These and hundreds of similar attempts to lobby the corporation have kindled a movement in the United States aiming for what is called "corporate democracy."[3] If corporate giants such as General Motors, J. P. Stevens, and Bristol-Meyers can be cornered by tiny groups of shareholders, then the same tactics in conjunction with a stronger legal recognition of the role of shareholders can presumably raise the humanitarian standards of every major corporation. The idea that voting shareholders should democratically control corporations assumes, of course, that a corporation can usefully be understood as a political system. But once the assumption is granted, it is a short step to concluding that corporate power, like the power of government, must be democratic.

It may seem odd to press for shareholder control, since shareholders, as the owners, may be presumed already to control the corporation. The presumption, however, is false. Shareholders own the corporation, yet typically leave its operation to professional managers; except in small, family-held corporations they have nothing to do with corporate decision-making. Their reluctance is more than a matter of disposition: the law encourages control by management. The so-called "business-judgment" rule under state law vests management with exclusive authority over the conduct of the company's affairs.[4] For shareholders to have a louder voice in corporate governance, this law, as we shall see, would need to be reinterpreted. Moreover, in the last several decades of U.S. corporate history, attempts by shareholders to overturn decisions of management even on purely economic issues have been unsuccessful. The history of the corporation reads nothing like the history of a democratic political institution.

To understand what U.S. defenders of corporate democracy dream about in the future, we must briefly turn to the history of the legal rights of stockholders and managers in the United States. The issue of rights surfaced first in the context of disputes over corporate charity, that is, conflicts between management's desire to make charitable contributions and the opposite desires of some shareholders. Early common law viewed charity as violating the rights of stockholders to maximum return on investment—unless "direct benefit" in the form of profits could be proven to follow from the gift. Within the last four or five decades, this rule has been abandoned, largely through a series of landmark legal cases. One such case, *A. P. Smith Manufacturing Company* v. *Barlow* (13 N.J. 145. 98A. 2d 581 [1953]), concerned a stockholder's complaint that a corporate gift to Princeton University

[3] David Vogel, *Lobbying the Corporation: Citizen Challenges to Business Authority* (New York: Basic Books, 1978).

[4] Marvin A. Chirelstein, "Corporate Law Reform," in *Social Responsibility and the Business Predicament,* ed. James W. McKie (Washington, D.C.: The Brookings Institution, 1974), p. 46.

unnecessarily detracted from stockholders' profits. The gift was upheld on the grounds that although not directly beneficial to the corporation, it was "indirectly beneficial to private business" through strengthening of community relations.[5]

Even so, some legal restrictions on charity remain, no matter how "indirect," and some relationship between monetary contributions and corporate self-interest must be demonstrable. As a practical guide, court decisions have established the maximum allowable contribution at 5 percent of corporate profits. (Few corporations press this limit; the average level of contributions runs about 1 percent).

Two federal acts, the Securities Exchange Act of 1933 and the Securities Exchange Act of 1934, established machinery through which stockholders can hold managers responsible to stricter moral standards, largely in the area of responsible fiscal management. These acts, which also created the Securities Exchange Commission (SEC), established guidelines for the behavior of management, using as a rationale the authority of government to protect citizens from fraudulent securities transactions. In the 1934 act, two sections, 10-b and 14a-8, carry special significance. Section 10-b establishes rules designed to prevent fraud in the sale and purchase of securities, and prohibits, for example, managers' using inside information about a corporation's performance to play the stock market and fill their own pockets. Section 14a-8 pertains to shareholders; it requires management to inform stockholders about issues that are subject to stockholder vote.

Rule 14a-8 has become the legal battleground for shareholders pushing for corporate democracy. The rule is part of the proxy machinery, i.e., machinery for stockholder voting procedures, which is regulated by the Securities Exchange Commission. It establishes a procedure through which corporate management can be compelled to include shareholders' proposals along with other proxy materials. In its present form it allows corporations to *omit* shareholder proposals under the following conditions:

1. If they are not proper subjects for action by shareholders according to state law. (Since state law excludes ordinary "business" issues as proper subjects for shareholders—assigning them instead to management—this means a proposal will be exluded if it is primarily about "business.")

2. If they are submitted primarily for the purpose of promoting general social, economic, or political causes.

The second criterion is a matter of dispute.[6] It has been, and continues to be, an explosive issue.

A landmark case, *Medical Committee for Human Rights* v. *SEC*, was the first test of the application of 14a-8 to a shareholder social-issue proposal. A group

[5] Chirelstein, "Corporate Law Reform," p. 50.

[6] Chirelstein, "Corporate Law Reform," p. 55.

of citizens, calling themselves the Medical Committee for Human Rights, purchased a few shares of stock in the Dow Chemical Corporation and proceeded to accuse Dow Chemical of aggravating human rights violations by manufacturing and selling napalm, a jellylike substance which adheres firmly to human skin and burns intensely; at that time (1968) Dow was selling napalm to the U.S. government, which used it in Vietnam to burn foliage and flush out enemy soldiers.[7] The Committee wrote a letter asking the Dow board of directors to submit to the shareholders a proposal for the board to consider adding to the corporation's charter an amendment that would prohibit the sale of napalm unless some assurance was provided that it would not be used on human beings.

Dow refused to send the proposal to stockholders. It argued that the proposal was invalid on both of the SEC criteria: it fell outside the proper business of the stockholders as conceived by state law, and it qualified as a "political cause." After investigating the problem, the Securities and Exchange Commission upheld Dow's refusal to include the proposals.

Undaunted by the SEC's decision, the Committee contested the ruling in a federal court of appeals. The court agreed with the Committee, remanding the case to the SEC for further administrative action. The court said that Dow's exclusion of the proposals contradicted the spirit of Rule 14a-8, which was to promote corporate democracy and "to assure to corporate shareholders the ability to exercise their right—some would say their duty—to control the important decisions which affect them in their capacity as stockholders and owners of the corporation."[8] The court denied that the proposals fit the meaning of 14a-8's two excluding caveats. First, although the state law (of Delaware) considered the issue of which products a corporation should manufacture to be a "business" issue and a proper concern for managers, nonetheless, the Committee had proposed to *revise the corporation's charter*. State law furthermore explicitly considered revising charters to be a proper question for shareholders. Second, although the issue of napalm was "political" in one sense, in another it was not: namely, in the sense that it concerned possible restrictions on the use of the (shareholders') property.

The court denied that Dow had provided any reason for blocking shareholders from bringing to the attention of their co-owners "the question of whether they wish to have their assets used in a manner which they believe to be more socially responsible."[9] To support further the decision to include the proposals despite their having moral and political overtones, Judge Tamm, speaking for the court, noted that Dow had itself claimed to be manufacturing napalm not for profit, but for "moral and political" reasons.[10]

The Dow decision, taken literally, suggests that nearly any proposal with a moral or political flavor is the proper subject of a shareholder's vote. It unlocks a

---

[7] "The Napalm Affair," in *Business and Society*, ed. Hay and Gray, pp. 82-83.

[8] *Medical Committee for Human Rights* v. *SEC,* 432 F. 2d, 680-81.

[9] *Medical Committee* v. *SEC,* 681.

[10] "The Napalm Affair," p. 83.

184

host of threats to management's presumed moral authority and is a crucial issue in the entire corporate democracy movement. It is, as one might expect, enormously controversial, and those criticizing it point to the fact that corporate law traditionally requires a unanimous vote of shareholders to ratify acts of "waste," which are roughly defined as "acts whose acknowledged aim is to abandon profitable opportunities or to replace existing corporate assets with tangible property of lesser worth."[11] Thus, insofar as any social or moral proposal agreed to by stockholders would expressly contemplate a reduction in the value of the company's shares, it presumably cannot—short of a unanimous vote—force management to comply.

This is clearly a blow to the cause of corporate democracy, for it implies that in cases where share value would be lowered, a majority of stockholders cannot bind a minority who prefer maximum returns on investment. As we saw in the last chapter, general corporate law tends to assume that corporate decisions shall be based solely on a presumed preference among stockholders for higher market value. Therefore profit-minded investors have the surprising security of knowing that the law will uphold the presumption of a preference for higher value—*even* in the face of a majority stockholder vote to the contrary. On this interpretation, the only justification for the Dow decision lies in the admission by the company that it had acted not for profits, but for moral reasons. Finally, on this interpretation, corporate democracy is ultimately doomed, for the law is bound to deny application of the very principle that is the heart of democratic procedure—majority rule.

Those defending the Dow decision, on the other hand, point out the apparent inconsistency in attributing property rights to stockholders—rights that traditionally are associated with some power of control—while at the same time effectively denying stockholder control. If stockholders are prevented from determining the fate of major corporate policies and even revisions of the corporate charter, then they appear to be "owners" in name only. If this is true, stockholders are little more than legal beneficiaries, possessing the right to receive financial benefits under certain well-defined circumstances, but lacking any traditional powers of control associated with property ownership. If stockholders are owners of corporate property, as they appear to be, then they should be allowed the rights of ownership. If they are not, then the myths surrounding stockholders as owners—including the idea of a fiduciary relationship between managers (agents) and stockholder-owners—should be abandoned.

Critics of the Dow decision have reason to feel threatened by the corporate democracy movement, despite the fact that not a single morally oriented shareholder proposal has ever succeeded in gaining a majority—and probably never will. Shareholder proposals even in the celebrated cases never receive more than a tiny fraction of votes. In the General Motors campaign, for example, Nader's group succeeded in attracting only 4 percent of the votes, and in the Dow campaign the Committee received only 2 percent. But why, after only a 4 percent "yes" vote, did General Motors establish a committee for social responsibility? And why, after only a 2 percent "no" vote, did Dow Chemical stop producing napalm?

[11] Chirelstein, "Corporate Law Reform," p. 60.

The answer, of course, is public pressure. Public pressure is also the reason why critics of the Dow decision have good cause to fear the corporate democracy movement. Many annual stockholders meetings, usually drab affairs, have become frantic confrontations between corporate managers and shouting activist stockholders. Since the Dow decision the meetings have become the preferred locations for ventilating ethical problems, and thus they serve to broadcast moral issues to the general public. The scene spotlights embattled corporate executives desperately defending policies never before challenged, using rationales never before required. This, of course, is precisely the scene desired by the corporate democracy movement. It aims not for victories in elections, but for victories in the arena of public opinion. As of 1977 nearly 600 public interest resolutions had been submitted to the shareholders of more than 150 corporations.[12]

Even if the corporate democracy movement escapes the trap laid by defenders of automatic "preference for higher returns," it may succumb to a barrage of theoretical objections. Professor David Vogel, who is perhaps the movement's best-known commentator, suggests that the capacity of the movement to encourage corporate morality is inherently limited by the external forces which determine corporate behavior. The reason that a corporation, unlike a democratically elected government, cannot be politically accountable, he argues, is that the most important decisions any corporation makes are determined by economic forces outside its control.[13] The only force sufficient to counter market imperatives, Vogel concludes, is that of the government.

No doubt Vogel has diagnosed a crucial debilitating factor in the movement for corporate democracy. Even in the context of responsive management structures, corporate executives, unlike government leaders, cannot chart the course of their organization with a free hand. They are restrained by the forces of competition and the ever-present realization that the very existence of the corporation requires profits. On the other hand, as Vogel himself would admit, market restraints do not *completely* straitjacket corporate morality, because certain morally motivated actions will indeed not diminish (and may even augment) profits, and also many financial sacrifices required by morality can be comfortably extracted from ordinary profit margins. Because market forces condition but do not fully determine corporate behavior, the program of developing stockholder awareness may continue to offer significant hope.

Sharing this optimism, modern defenders of stockholder responsibility, such as John Simon, Charles Powers, and Jon Gunnemann, have worked to define and establish criteria for investor behavior. They have recommended, for example, that universities that invest in the stock market should (1) separate investment decision-making from the academic enterprise per se, (2) decide investment issues in accordance with principles generally acceptable to the academic community, and (3) focus upon corporate practices that might "violate, or frustrate the enforcement of, rules of domestic or international law intended to protect individuals against

[12] Vogel, *Lobbying the Corporation,* p. 4.
[13] Vogel, *Lobbying the Corporation,* p. 225.

deprivation of health, safety, or basic freedoms."[14] The idea here is that if universities and other investors adhere to appropriate sets of moral standards, then their influence will promote improved corporate behavior—at least within the range of freedom allowed by market restraints. Thus, even in the face of Vogel's criticism, room remains for the recommendations of defenders of corporate democracy; and if it were not for other, better entrenched criticisms, the prospects for corporate democracy might indeed be bright.

Serious criticisms have been directed at the presumed analogy between stockholder control in the corporation and political control in a democracy. The differences are fairly striking. First, political democracy means one man, one vote, certainly not one share, one vote; yet in the model of corporate democracy, political egalitarianism is sacrificed to the principle that corporate power is directly proportional to the number of shares one owns. In proxy voting, one share, one vote is the established norm. Second, whereas citizens in a democratic political system may be predicted to produce decisions that maximize overall social welfare, the same hypothesis is doubtful in a corporate context. In a political democracy that allows universal suffrage, the people voting are the same people who are directly affected by their vote, or at least this is true for decisions with a domestic rather than international impact. However, in a would-be corporate democracy, the stockholders represent only a small part of the people affected by decisions. Their decisions also impact directly upon corporate employees, consumers, and (in environmental issues) the general public.

Political democracy works as well as it does partly because self-interest is coordinated with social welfare; but the coordination breaks down with corporate democracy. The decisions of stockholders can be expected to be ones benefiting stockholders, not employees, consumers, or general citizens. Can stockholders be expected to vote their consciences rather than their pocketbooks? The history of stockholder voting seems to say no; in any case, political democracy is successful *without* heavy reliance on altruism of voters, and thus it manifests a great advantage over corporate democracy. The success of shareholder action groups has stemmed not from the altruism of shareholders (the groups having been consistently rejected by a majority of shareholders) but from the generation of public pressure by a tiny minority of shareholders. This suggests a need, perhaps, for mechanisms to alert the public to corporate problems, but does not suggest a need for the democratic control of corporations by shareholders.

Are shareholders even qualified to make sophisticated managerial decisions? Many doubt they are, and Robert Dahl has remarked that". . . it cannot be argued that investors are particularly *interested* in running the firm or especially gifted with competence to do so."[15] Unlike the case in the late nineteenth and early twentieth centuries, when technology permitted a single individual to grasp the basic requirements of production and marketing, modern problems demand

---

[14] John Simon, Charles Powers, and Jon Gunnemann, *The Ethical Investor: Universities and Corporate Responsibility* (New Haven and London: Yale University Press, 1972), p. 88.

[15] Quoted in Chirelstein, "Corporate Law Reform," pp. 19-20.

specialized expertise and an intimate acquaintance with a maze of corporate systems. Even if stockholders were interested in comprehending and resolving such problems (which may be doubted), the sheer complexity and remoteness of these problems could prevent them from doing so. People who promote stockholder control, Dahl contends, rely on the "underlying and usually unexamined assumption that investors, whether individuals or firms, have some special right to govern the firms in which they invest." "I can discover," he concludes, "absolutely no moral or philosophical basis for such a right."[16]

Some contend that shareholders should not be seen as property owners possessing the rights traditionally associated with ownership, but should be viewed on the model of *consumers*. The model of property ownership is faulty because stockholders have never, even at the historical beginning of the corporation, controlled corporate activities in the same way that the owner of a boat or piece of land controls his property. Even shareholders themselves refuse to see themselves as owners. Does the purchaser of a few shares of Exxon see herself as an owner? No, she tends to view herself as a consumer, and with good reason. The corporation provides the stockholder the service of giving a return on invested capital. There is little difference between the corporate shareholder in this sense, and the municipal bond holder who invests to receive a return on investment. The bond holder is not an owner of the municipality issuing the bond, and the shareholder is not, for purposes of control, an owner of the corporation. Like the patron of a family style restaurant, the stockholder has rights he or she expects the organization to respect— in this case, rights to receive dividends, notification of stock splits, etc.–but also like the patron, the shareholder lacks the right of management.[17]

Finally, the standard mode of expressing opposition to corporate policies is to sell one's shares, not exert control. In all these senses, then, the shareholder is more easily subsumed under the rubric of "consumer" than "owner."

Such attacks have driven many defenders of corporate democracy to safer ground where they have endorsed modified versions of shareholder control. One well-known theorist, Detlev Vagts, rejects direct control but suggests the possibility of an "open proxy and open nomination process"; under this more liberal process stockholders would recommend proposals for shareholder vote, and also shareholders would be allowed to nominate members to the board of directors.[18] Shareholders, he explains, could be allowed to nominate a person as director whenever the percentage of shareholders supporting that person exceeded a certain level. Moreover, corporations would be required to conduct and finance such shareholder campaigns. Unlike the image of full shareholder control sometimes associated with corporate democracy, proposals like this aim at mild increases in shareholder power while leaving the lion's share of power in the hands of professional managers.

[16] Quoted in Chirelstein, "Corporate Law Reform," p. 67.

[17] Carl Schneider, discussion in *Special Issue: Business Lawyer*, 31 (1976), 976.

[18] Detlev Vagts, "The Governance of the Corporation: The Options Available and the Power to Prescribe," *Special Issue: Business Lawyer*, 31 (1976), 902.

The future of corporate democracy probably lies with implementing such modified plans and retaining the public pressure strategies allowable under the Dow decision. Because of the problems listed above, almost no contemporary theorist regards a shift to full-scale shareholder democracy as defensible.

The separation of ownership from control, existing in virtually all large corporations, may even be a disguised blessing. In smaller, family-held corporations, managers and majority stockholders come from the same tightly knit group, and management decisions invariably reflect family interests. In larger corporations, managers and stockholders approach problems from different points of view, and each group includes individuals who manifest a spectrum of perspectives. Perhaps the most compelling reason for separating stockholders from managers is the one advanced by Christopher Stone: ". . . when the interests of management and ownership are one . . ." Stone remarks, "all the compromises management makes with profits come out of its own pockets. . . . But it is not so in the giant, broadly held companies."[19]

The central problem with full-scale stockholder control proposals is clearly illuminated by one of the evaluative criteria developed in the preceding chapter: namely, the criterion calling for a decision-making process that receives input from the two major groups mentioned in the social contract, employees and consumers. These two groups have interests that neither are synonymous with those of shareholders nor are readily discoverable by shareholders. Shareholders can be expected to vote their own interests and to be unconcerned about, and ignorant of, those of consumers and employees (except of course in instances where *they* happen to be consumers or employees).

Shifting Power on Boards of Directors

Although shifting power from managers to stockholders is problematic, other shiftings of power appear more promising. In particular, many proposals suggest shifting power among members of the board of directors, and even extending membership to individuals previously excluded from membership. There have been suggestions for increasing the number of "outside" directors (directors who are neither managers nor stockholders of the corporation), and various suggested formulas for giving directorships to representatives of employees, government, consumers, and the general public.

Focusing on the management side of corporate structure rather than the stockholder side solves certain practical problems. The legal problem afflicting corporate democracy—the fact that a majority of stockholders endorsing a proposal that contemplates a reduction of profits are unable to compel the minority to conform—is not a problem at the level of ordinary management. The law is exceedingly liberal in allowing corporate managers free rein. Although managers are restricted in the percentage of profits that can be given to charity (that, again, being 5 percent),

---

[19] Christopher D. Stone, *Where the Law Ends* (New York: Harper & Row, Pub., 1975), p. 233.

day-to-day business calculations are, in the words of Marvin Chirelstein, "virtually untouchable by law."[20] "The weight of the existing delegation systems," Chirelstein remarks, "together with an extreme judicial reluctance to engage in complex present-value calculations, ... allows a management ... to balance the stockholders' interests against those of other affected groups without serious concern for the imposition of fiduciary liability."[21] Stockholders who sue managers for neglecting fiduciary obligations and making poor financial decisions discover that judges are stubbornly reluctant to second-guess managers. The suits invariably fail. Nor does statutory law restrict the financial freedom of managers; for example, state corporation law, after noting that corporations must be governed by their board of directors, has little more to say.[22]

One immediate problem confronting any attempt to improve corporate morality by shifting power among board members is that corporate boards of directors frequently exercise only minimal control over their respective companies. If boards do not control corporations, then changing board constituencies will fail to alter corporate behavior. Corporate boards possess enormous nominal power, as prescribed by state law and reflected in corporate organization charts. However, they seldom use it. "The lack of active discussions of major issues at typical Board meetings," one commentator remarks, "... result(s) in most Board meetings resembling the performance of traditional and well-established ... religious rituals. In most companies, it would be possible to write the minutes of a Board meeting in advance."[23]

If reconstituted boards are to affect corporate behavior, then their nominal power must become real power. The reason boards fail to exercise power lies more in the dispositions and habits of board members than in structural or organizational impediments. Boards could wield more power if they wanted to. The problem, then, is to shift power so that it is both exercised responsibly, *and* so it lies in the hands of people who wish to use it. The hope of those defending power shifts on boards is that new constituencies will have good reason to expand board control over corporate activities.

One specific proposal is to increase the ratio of "outside" directors to "inside" directors. Including more people who are not employed by the corporation they govern, it is argued, will result in fewer self-interested decision-makers. The term "outside director" connotes not only a nonemployee, but a person in some position of authority, usually from the business world and usually sympathetic to business values. In the distant past all corporate directors were outside directors and the typical corporation had on its board, members such as the local bank president, a lawyer, and a corporate executive from another company. The

[20] Chirelstein, "Corporate Law Reform," p. 52.

[21] Chirelstein, "Corporate Law Reform," p. 52.

[22] Vagts, "Governance of the Corporation," p. 931.

[23] Myles L. Mace, "The President and the Board of Directors," *Harvard Business Review* (March-April 1972), p. 42.

trend from the turn of the century until 1970 was to include more and more corporation managers, with the result that the interests of upper-level management became represented in board decisions to an unprecedented extent. Beginning in 1970, the trend was reversed, a phenomenon we shall examine more closely in a moment.

Does the answer lie in outside directors? Many think so, arguing that outside directors could influence board conduct more than could employee representatives or consumer representatives. The "control of corporate executives," writes one advocate, "is actually a task for their peers. It is really something that had best be done by the outside directors, which means we need to redefine the role of those outside directors, their duties, their responsibilities, . . . and this is a very challenging task."[24]

To call the task challenging is perhaps an understatement. Even in the past, outside directors followed the lead of corporate managers for the obvious reason that only the managers were sufficiently knowledgeable about the details of corporate activity. Issues concerned with financial accounting, employee work conditions, and organizational structure were daily realities for managers, but they were abstractions for those who held full-time employment elsewhere; thus these directors were wholly dependent on the sketches provided by managers for their views of corporate operations. Nothing promises automatically to remedy this drawback. Outside directors might be able to detect obvious, self-interested ploys of managers, but many would remain strangers to life in the corporation and would predictably take their cues from inside directors. With full-time jobs elsewhere and no independent source of corporate information, they would appear to be poor candidates for effecting pervasive moral reform. Hoping that outside directors may still prove beneficial, some reformers recommend providing them with an independent staff which could supply relevant corporate information. (This idea will be examined later in the chapter.) Even with an independent staff, however, outside directors with jobs elsewhere would be hampered by time constraints.

Why, then, not have *full-time* outside directors? A promising suggestion, to be sure, but one which would change the meaning of "outside director": rather than including active bank officials, corporate executives, and lawyers, it would refer to people who lack significant extra-corporate duties. And whom should such directors represent? Should they be "public" representatives? And from what social arena should they be recruited? These questions are crucial to evaluating proposals for additional directors, since people tend to reflect as board members their past experiences and the interests of their long-standing social affiliations. Ex-businesspeople reflect one set of values; ex-labor leaders another, and the same differences hold among ex-academics, ex-politicians, and ex-civil servants. Also, the concept of a "public representative" suffers from the vagueness of the word "public" itself: the public constituency is simply too ill-defined.

Fortunately, someone has attempted to answer these questions and to design a system for appointing new board representatives. In his book *Where the*

[24] Robert M. Estes, discussion in *Special Issue: Business Lawyer,* 31 (1976), 944.

Law Ends,[25] the legal theorist Christopher Stone spells out procedures for creating two kinds of public directorships: general public directorships and special public directorships.

General public directorships would apply to every U.S. corporation having more than $1 billion in assets; public representatives would be placed on the board of directors of these corporations. In 1973, when Stone presented his proposal, the number of companies qualifying under this formula was 262. A distinction is made between companies primarily engaged in manufacturing, retailing, or transportation and those engaged in banking, life insurance, diversified finance, and utilities. In the case of the former, the number of general public directors appointed to the board would be 10 percent of all directors for every billion dollars of assets or sales (whichever is higher). In the case of the latter, where figures run higher, the number would be 10 percent for every $3 billion in assets. General public directors would be nominated by a Federal Corporations Commission and would be subject to approval by a majority of the corporation's board. These directors would maintain an office within the corporation and would be expected to spend at least half of their time on corporate affairs. They would be paid at the level of the highest-grade civil servant.[26]

How would Stone's proposal for general directors affect U.S. corporations? Stone says:

> Most of these companies would be affected marginally, by having one or two GPDs (General Public Directors) only. It ought to be noted, however, that under the figures used, if one did not add a proviso such as, ". . . up to 50 percent of the board" or ". . . up to 90 percent of the board," thirteen American corporations would have public directors entirely (AT&T, General Motors, Ford, Exxon, Bank America Corporation, General Electric, IBM, Texaco, Sears Roebuck & Company, First National Bank, Chase Manhattan Corporation, Prudential Life Insurance Company, and Metropolitan Life Insurance Company).[27]

Although the percentage of U.S. corporations large enough to be affected by Stone's proposal would be quite small, they account for a significant percentage of U.S. economic activity. The affected manufacturing companies account for about one-third of the entire U.S. Gross National Product and employ 70 pecent of all employees engaged in manufacturing.

The functions of the general public director would be to ensure that laws were being obeyed, to gather ethically sensitive information from inside and outside the corporate ranks, to serve as a liaison between government and business, and to function as a "superego" for the corporation. The director would receive complaints from employees about ethical abuses—e.g., complaints about safety problems such as in the B. F. Goodrich brake scandal—and would air relevant

[25] Stone, *Where the Law Ends,* pp. 158-59.

[26] Stone, *Where the Law Ends,* pp. 158-59.

[27] Stone, *Where the Law Ends,* pp. 158-59.

grievances with other board members. He or she would periodically check the internal corporate system of information flow to see if it accommodated morally relevant information. The director would also evaluate and oversee the preparation of environmental impact studies, equal opportunity reports, and employee safety evaluations.

The other class of public directorships which Stone endorses is that of special public directorships (SPD's). Special public directorships would not hinge on the size of a corporation's sales or assets. Instead, they would be activated only in the cases where either (1) a corporation has a record of ethical misconduct, or (2) an entire industry has special or intractable ethical problems.[28] An example of the first is the Holland Furnace Company, which earned an unsavory reputation through its unique method of marketing home furnaces. The company's representative would enter a home, claiming to be a furnace "inspector" and offering the owner a free safety evaluation. After dismantling the furnace, the would-be inspector would refuse to reassemble it, on the grounds that he refused to be an accomplice to a murder. The frightened homeowner was then only too happy to speak to the Holland salesperson, who miraculously appeared a few minutes later at the door.[29]

The Holland Company persisted in such sales tactics for nearly twenty years, until finally Holland executives were held in contempt and the president was sentenced to six months in prison. A company which, like Holland, exhibited persistent moral delinquency would be a prime candidate for a special public director. Since delinquent companies will already be struggling with courts and regulatory agencies, the appointment of the director, Stone suggests, should be made by the court, in consultation with the company.[30]

The second class of corporation meriting an SPD is that representing an industry with special moral problems. In the 1970's, for example, shocking information came to light concerning cancer risks in the asbestos industry. Experts estimated that one out of every five deaths among asbestos workers was caused by lung cancer, and nearly half the men studied were dying of some form of asbestos disease.[31] Other industries have been plagued by equally persistent problems: safety problems in the nuclear industry, pollution problems in the pulp and paper processing industry, and disposal problems in the chemical industry. Such special problems, Stone argues, demand the appointment of special directors to the boards of involved corporations.

The functions of a special public director would parallel that of a general director. He or she would gather information, see to it laws were obeyed, and function as an embodied superego. This director, however, would be someone with

[28] Stone, *Where the Law Ends,* p. 176.

[29] Stone, *Where the Law Ends,* pp. 175-76.

[30] Stone, *Where the Law Ends,* p. 179.

[31] Paul Brandeur, "Annals of Industry," *The New Yorker,* October 29, November 5, 12, 19, and 26, 1973.

expertise in the problem area. A person with a background in chemistry or in environmental engineering, for example, would possess relevant expertise for the directorship of a chemical company. A person with marketing and engineering skills would possess expertise relevant for the Holland Stove Company. Knowledge about the relevant technical problems, coupled with an acquaintance of the history of the corporation's relevant moral problem, would aid the special director in evaluating corporate performance, seeking out relevant information, and proposing and discussing remedies with the board.

Stone presents his proposal for public directorships in admirable detail (many details have been omitted here for want of space), and they provide concrete hypotheses for discussion. The most important question, however, remains that of whether his proposal, or a modified version of it, will effectively improve corporate moral behavior. What are the strengths and weaknesses of general and special public directorships?

Two features of the public directorships have special appeal. First, by making use of existing power arrangements in the corporation, public directorships promise to be more than window dressing. Adequate power, it will be remembered from the last chapter, is a criterion for successful moral reform. The board of directors is formally vested with the responsibility for running the corporation, and if it chooses, it can exercise that power. Critics point out that one or two public representatives lack power to dominate a board. This is true; but one or two representatives can initiate discussions, introduce previously unknown information, and bend the direction of discussion at critical moments. In the same way that 10 percent of the U.S. Senate or House of Representatives can influence national policy, so 10 percent of a board can influence corporate policy.

Second, the fact that public directors are not attached to the best-represented corporate interest groups, i.e., stockholders and corporate executives, enables them to turn toward other interest groups, especially employees, consumers, and the general public. Most boards are immunized from the latter kinds of interests, unless these somehow affect profits. Automobile manufacturers exhibited complacence for years about consumer interest in safer cars—complacence which ignored relevant auto fatality and injury statistics—until those interests were thrust on them by organized stockholders and Ralph Nader. The function of public directors should be to urge relevant interests upon boards.

Despite such strengths, Stone's proposal is open to criticism. Two problems any proposal should avoid are, as we noted earlier: (1) the creation of an unfair competitive advantage, and (2) significant reduction in productive efficiency; yet both may be argued to follow from the general directorships. The formula for appointing general directors is tied to the level of a company's assets or sales, so the larger the corporation, the greater the percentage of public directors. As Stone admits, applying his formula without limits would mean that some giant corporations would have boards consisting of 100 percent public directors. Yet if public directors can be expected to be more willing than ordinary directors to sanction corporate financial sacrifices in the name of morality (surely a reasonable expectation), then large companies could be placed at a competitive disadvantage with smaller ones. Putting aside emotional tendencies to condemn giants and favor the little guy, there seems to be no reason why size per se should be penalized.

A closely related problem concerns the capacity of public directors to function as efficiently as ordinary directors in everyday business decision-making. If unwanted inefficiency is to be avoided, public directors must develop expertise in analyzing balance sheets, evaluating marketing data, and relating corporate borrowing and spending patterns to those of the overall economy. Such expertise is rare. Most corporations select executives through a long, natural evolution of individual careers in which only a handful of competitors emerge. Is there any guarantee that a Federal Corporations Commission would be sensitive to business realities as well as moral problems?

These difficulties should not be exaggerated. Stone, indeed, has left the door open to a limit on the percentage of public representatives on a corporate board, even for giant corporations, and doing so would reduce significantly the problem of unfair competitive disadvantage. And, though it is true that a Federal Corporations Commission might err in finding proper combinations of moral and financial talents, it may also be that the traditional corporate system of selection by brute competition tends to err through emphasizing financial over moral expertise. Stone's proposal, thus, might balance the overall selection system.

Another problem exists, however. Because representatives are to be selected by a Federal Corporations Commission, those representatives are in an important sense *government* representatives. Despite being called "public" directors, and despite having the formal function of representing underrepresented interest groups, they would owe their appointments to a government agency and would tend to reflect prevailing government goals. But it is the interests of employees, consumers, and the general public which Stone's proposal hopes to communicate to the corporation, not the goals of the government. Sometimes, happily, these two functions will be identical; but sometimes, as we know from experience, they will diverge considerably. One of the least savory possibilities would involve the government's using its assocation with corporate executives to reach agreements that conflict with the public interest. As one critic puts it, there is "considerable danger that the government may seek to achieve in the quiet of the conference room what it cannot achieve in the normal administrative process."[32]

If the disadvantages of Stone's proposal are acute, radical surgery may be in order. One tempting solution is to abandon Stone's procedure of drawing directors from a Federal Corporations Commission and have board representatives come directly from the various interest groups.

Germany has instituted a two-tier board system for many corporations, in which social representatives (including labor representatives) sit on one board while active, professional managers sit on another. Volkswagen Corporation, for example, includes social representatives from the federal government, the state government, labor, and public shareholders. Whatever influence flows directly

[32]Chirelstein, "Corporate Law Reform," p. 72.

from government is countered in the Volkswagen system by the influence of labor representatives, stockholder representatives, and professional managers. Surprisingly, the German system has received high marks from some for efficiency when contrasted with the American, on the basis that whereas the American system of corporate control relies on external manuevers such as class action suits and elaborate regulatory mechanisms—all of which spawn inefficiency—the German system relies on internal control and can thus afford to reduce and simplify external control apparatus. The German system is not trouble-free, as we shall see shortly, but it avoids the problems connected with having exclusively government representatives, and it is promising as a means of cutting government red tape.

Still another suggestion, advanced by Ralph Nader and Mark Green, would combine public directors with a two-tier system of stockholders. The public directors would be drawn from among the "local citizen's groups that have gained some power in the various plants of a nationwide conglomerate."[33] In the two-tier shareholder system, one class of stock would be "voting only," while the other class would be voting plus economic benefits. The former would confer only rights to vote in proxy contests and to apply political leverage upon the corporation; it would be held by employees, community residents, and consumers—in short, by anyone "clearly and immediately affected by a corporation" but lacking any say over its actions. Such holders would *not* be entitled to dividends or other economic benefits. The latter, or economic stock, would be similar to all ordinary common stock; it would confer both voting rights and the right to receive dividends, sell stock, and so on. The question of how to apportion, "voting only" stock is given a tentative answer: require by law that "whenever a firm accounts for x percent of a community's tax base, it must allow y percent of all its stock to be political stock, up to some ceiling of stock, say 10 percent."[34]

From what we have already learned about stockholder control, it is apparent that the two-tier stock system will not affect the tendency of stockholder voting to place financial reward as the first priority. With a ceiling of 10 percent on public stock, no morally inspired stockholder proposal that would contemplate a reduction in value per share would stand a chance of winning a stockholder election; stockholders, as we saw earlier, tend overwhelmingly to vote their own financial interests. The role of two-tiered stock could be only to facilitate the submission of resolutions and the airing of grievances by "voting only" stockholders. With this mitigated role it might be complementary to the installation of public directors on the board.

Still another proposal recommends bringing all interested parties into the governing process of the corporation, but instead of bringing them in as shareholders, it suggests representing them directly on the board. According to the proposal's sponsor, Abraham Chayes, each interest group "having a relation of

---

[33] Ralph Nader and Mark Green, "Owing Your Soul to the Company Store," in *Ethical Issues in Business,* ed. T. Donaldson and P. Werhane (Englewood Cliffs, N.J.: Prentice-Hall, 1979), p. 204.

[34] Nader and Green, "Owing Your Soul," p. 204.

sufficient intimacy with the corporation or subject to its power in a sufficiently specialized way" would be given membership in corporate government.[35] In addition to traditional groups such as consumers, employees, and the general public, the board presumably would include townspeople, special interest groups, corporate customers, and suppliers.

The obvious virtue of the proposal is its all-encompassing scope: no group is left out and consequently no group's interests can dominate all others. This obvious virtue is an equally obvious vice, however, insofar as multiplying the number of groups represented also multiplies the problems connected with appointing representatives. Critics have been quick to seize on this problem. If elections are used to choose representatives, then how will votes be interpreted? As one critic, Melvin Eizenberg, points out, the formula of one worker, one vote seems acceptable for labor, But how about consumers and suppliers? Should votes be apportioned by dollar volume? Similar logistical problems arise for other groups, as well as with the issue of distributing relative power among groups. Chayes himself, though defending his plan, concedes the difficulties in identifying interest constituencies and in determining which institutional apparatus best recognizes interests.[36]

If one could roll into a ball all of these proposals for shifting power in corporate government—Stone's public directorships, the German two-tier system, Nader and Green's proposal, and Chayes' all-comprising plan—how might they be appraised? Do such proposals offer salvation for the corporation? Again, such questions must be left to the reader—with a reminder that the proof of the pudding for many of the proposals will be in their actual implementation in corporations. But perhaps two remarks are in order.

First, each of the proposals appears to offer a clear moral advantage over present corporate power allocations insofar as each recognizes relevant interest groups heretofore unrecognized. The consumer who must use the corporation's product, the local citizen whose eyes must water from the corporation's pollution, and the employee who must work under the corporation's regulations all have an immediate interest in corporate behavior. In the past these legitimate interests have often failed to be formally recognized in corporate governance. Their impact, when impact has occurred, has been limited to the effects of pressure from consumer advocate groups, unions (when unions are active) and media publicity.

Second, however, all the proposals run risks of misuse and inefficiency. If, as noted earlier, a government agency may seek to achieve in the private boardroom what it cannot in public procedures, the same is true for labor, consumers, and other representatives. Nor is there any guarantee that labor or consumers will be better than the government at picking directors who have requisite managerial skills. As Eizenberg remarks, "The skills needed to be a leather merchant (or a union official) are not necessarily those needed to decide the business or structural

[35] Abraham Chayes, "The Modern Corporation and the Rule of Law," in *The Corporation in Modern Society,* ed. Edward S. Mason (Cambridge, Mass.: Harvard University Press, 1960), p. 41.
[36] Chayes, "The Modern Corporation," p. 41.

problems faced by shoe manufacturers, nor are such skills acquired with the purchase of one or more pairs of shoes."[37]

A case in point occurred in Germany during the early 1970's. Volkswagen, Inc., had a board of directors which included representatives from the federal government, the state government, employees, and consumers. After a shift in the dollar-mark relationship in 1971, it became clear that Volkswagen automobiles should also be assembled in the United States; yet it was not possible to obtain decisive action at that time because of too many diverse interests and too many allegiances to special groups that would suffer from a transfer of jobs abroad.[38] If proposals that shift power from the exclusive hands of managers into the hands of other interest groups are to be successful, then the new representatives must exercise the art of responsible management.

INTERNAL LEGISLATION

A strikingly different approach to corporate reform is found in attempts to generate internal corporate legislation, i.e., policies or rules, in order to effect improved behavior. This approach does not attempt to shift power among individuals but takes advantage of the fact that corporations generate rules, policy statements, directives, and codes and that corporate employees tend—though sometimes imperfectly—to allow such legislation to influence their behavior. Admittedly, the written documents comprising corporate legislation constitute only one part of the overall corporate ethos, which also includes unwritten rules and tacit expectations. However, in most organizations officially promulgated legislation makes a difference. The official legislation that counts most in corporate activity from a moral perspective falls into three major classes: codes of conduct, policy statements, and new procedures. We shall examine each in turn.

Codes

Often in the history of business, codes of conduct have appeared in the limelight of moral attention. In Henry Dennison's book, *Ethics and Modern Business,* written in 1932, codes are praised as "the first attempts of a great and powerful social group to gain its own self-respect and the respect of other members of society."[39] Although such glowing optimism is not shared by all, it embodies a substantial share of common sense: after all, a code of morality is seemingly analogous on the corporate level to what personal codes of ethics are on the individual level, and individual morality has traditionally been interpreted through codes such as the Ten Commandments. If a single person's conscience can be molded and informed

[37] Melvin Eizenberg, "The Legal Roles of Shareholders and Management in Modern Corporate Decision Making," *California Law Review,* 57 (January 1969), 16-21.

[38] Vagts, "Governance of the Corporation," p. 930.

[39] Henry Dennison, *Ethics and Modern Business* (Boston: Houghton Mifflin, 1932), p. 15.

through codified pronouncements, cannot the same be done for the corporate conscience?

Another reason for the traditional optimism over codes lies not so much in what they do as how they do it. Although codes share with government statutes their outward form, their enforcement is left not to the government but to corporations. The happy consequence is that codes rely on the strength and initiative of corporate participants: executives, suppliers, consumers, and workers.

But why is there a need for written codes rather than unwritten ones? Two reasons stand out, the first of which is that written codes allow undesirable conduct to be publicly communicated and specified. The expectations of corporate executives are often obscure to lower employees, and when the stakes are high, employee misestimation of executive expectations can have disastrous consequences. If we are to believe the protestations of Hooker Chemical Company's management, Hooker never intended for employees to take the actions that resulted in the chemical dumping at Love Canal. The same failure to clarify corporate expectations is evident in thousands of other cases. The second reason for the necessity of a written code is that once undesirable conduct has been publicly identified, the imposition of sanctions becomes easier. Once a corporation has specified in its codes of conduct that buyers are not to accept gifts from suppliers in excess of fifty dollars, the enterprising employee who hauls in a new fishing outfit and a set of golf clubs cannot plead naive ignorance. Even more important, his salary can be docked, or he can be demoted, for violating a well-promulgated corporate standard. Indeed, without the threat of sanctions, codes of conduct would be next to useless and would have the same place in corporate affairs as the president's annual Christmas speech.

A serious challenge to codes emerges, however, from an unexpected corner. Because of the need to restrict competitive disadvantage, the tendency of a single corporation is to refuse implementing codes that raise moral conduct but lower profitability. This tendency finds a natural solution in the promotion of interindustry codes, codes that will share the burden of moral improvement equally among all competitors in a given industry. Many companies have thus developed interindustry codes, especially since the 1950's. So far so good. A problem emerges, however, when one is reminded that interindustry cooperation, especially when it concerns the sale of products, can lead to violations of the Sherman Antitrust Act.

The problem is significant. Hundreds of attempts to specify interindustry practices have been found to violate the Sherman Antitrust Act, from attempts to specify product quality to attempts to enforce "higher" ethical standards in marketing. The Sherman Antitrust Law, enacted in 1890, specifies that "every contract, combination, or consipracy in restraint of trade or commerce among the several states is illegal."[40] A crucial feature of this wording is the emphasis on *every* agreement in restraint of trade, and this means agreements whose principal purpose may be something other than to restrain trade. Thus, in codes of interindustry

---

[40] Earl Kintner and Robert W. Green, "Opportunities for Self-Enforcement of Codes of Conduct: A Consideration of Legal Limitations," in *Ethics, Free Enterprise, and Public Policy,* ed. R. De George and J. Pichler (New York: Oxford, 1978), pp. 248-63.

ethics, any attempt to specify standards of commercial practice that results in a restraint of trade—no matter how nobly motivated—may be struck down in court.

When the Association of Sanitary Enameled Ware Manufacturers purchased the dominant patent for the prevailing enamel production process and then licensed all members on the condition that they adhere to price schedules and refuse to market "seconds," its act was ruled in violation of the Sherman Act. When the Sugar Institute required that its members sell only in accordance with publicly announced prices, it got the same treatment. And when the Fashion Originators' Guild of America, Inc., organized a boycott to eliminate so-called "style pirates" (companies that merely copied the styles created by other companies), it too was ruled in restraint of trade. Not only product-oriented associations, but service-oriented ones have succumbed to the Sherman Act. The American Medical Association's attempt to prohibit its members from working with prepaid medical plans—presumably a consequence of ethical motives—was ruled illegal. So was the American Bar Association's attempt to establish minimum fee schedules for participating lawyers.[41]

If attempts to specify terms of sale, product quality, and market location can be ruled in restraint of trade, what is left to be proclaimed by ethical codes of conduct? The answer is, "not much"; but what remains may still have ethical worth. A code can prescribe honesty and "fair" dealing for its intended members without legal risk, although any further attempt to identify commercial practices of competitiors can raise problems. A code can prohibit certain forms of advertising, as when the broadcast industry banned cigarette commercials. A code can also rule out practices already prohibited by law and can even establish adherence to legal standards as a condition for membership. (Thus, the American Bar Association can expel members who are convicted of serious crimes.) A code's capacity to imitate legal rules is more significant than may appear at first glance.

Because the government finds it difficult or impossible to police many classes of corporate behavior, the industry may be in a better position to exercise a watchful eye than the government. When the Justice Department and the Federal Trade Commission decide to attack corporate corruption, they proceed on a case-by-case basis, taking only one company at a time. Such methods are not only slow and erratic, they are highly expensive. Corporations resist government pressure every step of the way. Were corporations to abandon hostility toward government pressure and direct that same energy toward self-enforcement, then all parties might benefit. Thus, industry self-policing is preferable to external control for reasons of form and efficiency. Moral suasion appears preferable to legal coercion.

Examples of successful interindustry codes are numerous. The National Beer Wholesalers Association of America (NBWA) drafted a Code of Fair Practices which includes pledges such as:

> I shall refrain from selling malt beverages to any retail outlet which chronically engages in unlawful actions or undesirable practices offensive to members of my community.

[41] Kintner and Green, "Opportunities for Self-Enforcement," pp. 248-63.

I shall neither personally, nor through any other agency, attempt to procure special favors or privileges from a government official.

I shall never divulge any information obtained legitimately from a wholesaler in confidence to an unauthorized third party.

I shall not engage in illegal bar spending and will take appropriate measures to minimize this practice in my market.

I shall not solicit the franchise of another beer wholesaler without notice to the wholesaler.

When taken seriously, such publicized principles can improve the atmosphere in which an industry operates.

The drawbacks of codes, however, are equally striking. Codes gain their power from the willingness of participating corporations to obey, and from the sympathy that participants manifest for moral behavior. When these are lacking, codes are powerless. Even worse, in such circumstances they can give misleading window dressing to the low moral standards actually prevailing in an industry, with the result that the industry escapes deserved criticism it would have received in the absence of a code. Once we know the National Beer Wholesalers Association professes ethical standards, we may be more reluctant to pursue our suspicions about industry practices, yet if the Association has hoisted its code merely to deflect attention, that is precisely when we *should* be looking further. Codes have a sound and fury, yet for all that, they may frequently signify nothing.

Even codes with long and venerable histories are open to charges of ineffectiveness and inadequacy. Consider the dramatic accusations leveled at the U.S. Association of Professional Accountants. The Association publicizes two specific codes for accountants: the Generally Accepted Accounting Principles (GAAP) and the Generally Accepted Auditing Standards (GAAS). The former provides a theoretical and conceptual infrastructure for accounting practices, and the latter provides specific standards to ensure reliable, professional audits. The enforcement of both codes rests in the hands of an organization of professional accountants (COPE), which is to examine evidence, determine whether infractions have occurred, and when necessary, assign penalties. Despite such an elaborate scheme, with two codes and an enforcing organization, critics claim the scheme is ineffectual. "The trilogy," Abraham Briloff remarks, "has not produced much sweetness and light."[42]

Whatever absence of sweetness and light exists probably owes itself to many factors. Although GAAP is meant to inform accountants about the limits of acceptable behavior, critics charge that there exists no effective organization to interpret its application to specific cases save COPE, and that COPE is motivated largely by political pressure which forces it to retreat in the face of large interest

---

[42] Abraham J. Briloff, "Codes of Conduct: Their Sound and Their Fury," in *Ethics, Free Enterprise, and Public Policy*, ed. R. De George and J. Pichler (New York: Oxford, 1978), pp. 264-87.

groups. For instance, critics such as Briloff claim that during the middle and late 1970's the Financial Accounting Standards Board, which was created at the time for interpreting codes, backed down to bank pressure that sought to prevent the exposure of deteriorated bank assets (e.g., loans which, while uncollectable, were still listed as bank assets). The GAAS receives few complaints about the principles it espouses, but many about the way they are applied. Can GAAS really be effective, critics ask, when it is intended to ensure responsible audits yet it failed to prevent, especially in the 1970's, numerous slush funds, kickbacks, and bribes? When the Securities Exchange Commission granted U.S. corporations a special amnesty period in which foreign bribes could be revealed at no risk of legal action, literally hundreds of corporations stepped forward to reveal their secret activities. Yet presumably all these companies had undergone audits by professional accountants during the very periods bribes were occurring. How, it may be asked, were the auditors accounting for the bribes? And where was GAAP?[43]

In the period from 1970 to 1977, COPE took 121 actions against professional accountants yet did not take actions against many firms suspected of doing cover-up work for large corporations. Even Maurice Stans, Chairman of the Campaign to Re-elect the President, was cleared by COPE for his role in the Nixon mess. In order to make COPE and the two codes it enforces more effective, many urge that the power held by a small number of accounting firms (nicknamed the "big eight") be broken, especially insofar as they influence the principal professional organizations and their various organs. For COPE to be more effective it must have freer rein, be able to take stronger action, to authorize more public proceedings, and to disclose the names of firms it censures. It must, critics urge, not await the outcome of litigation against accountants in court, as it has in the past, but press forward with censure using its own investigative process.

In fairness to COPE and the accounting profession, it should be said that many problems are not consequences of bad faith, but intractable features of codes and interindustry organizations. A professional organization is not a court of law. It is not provided with investigatory services, the power to subpoena, or any of the other powers in the legal arsenal held by official courts. Yet its threats, especially censure and expulsion from membership, can ruin the career of an individual and damage his reputation as surely as a jail sentence or court-imposed fine. Accountants stress the need to be cautious in taking punitive action, to be slow to condemn without adequate evidence, and to prefer that an unethical accountant slip through the net rather than that an ethical one erroneously be ruined.

Interindustry codes and organizations are limited through the simple fact that they owe their existence to the industry they must regulate. A code created by an industry will fail to manifest the dispassionate objectivity many desire, even when it is the result of sincere efforts. Beer manufacturers will lean toward the interests of those who make beer, even in their moments of pristine soul-searching, if only because they have constructed their world view largely through intercourse with their colleagues.

[43] Briloff, "Codes of Conduct," pp. 264-87.

Another inherent limitation of interindustry codes is their relative weakness when confronting issues that affect overall industry profits. We remember that the touted strength of interindustry codes (in contrast to single corporation codes) is that they do not create competitive disadvantages. (For example, if a single accounting firm refused to cater to the desires of a giant corporate client, it would suffer while rival firms picked up the business.) Now obviously such an advantage carries weight only in instances where overall industry welfare is maintained. But certain morally praiseworthy actions may affect overall welfare, as when the beer industry must consider whether to use environmentally objectionable disposable cans and bottles rather than environmentally desirable, but less convenient, returnable bottles. Here the beer industry must contemplate the consequences of switching to returnable bottles, such as a possible reduction in the general consumption of beer. (Inconvenience may lead consumers either to lower their consumption of malt beverages or to switch to other beverages such as wine.) This unevenness in the capacity of interindustry codes to combat certain ethical problems is clearly a drawback.

Thus, we should remind ourselves that codes reveal a mixture of strengths and weaknesses. Both company codes and interindustry codes can give precision to the moral expectations of management and provide a solid basis for imposing sanctions. In this, they are clearly valuable. Both, furthermore, are able to rely upon business initiative and internal control instead of government coercion. Yet both also suffer the pains of subjectivity, which inevitably follow from the fact that their origins lie in the organizations they must control. A special irony is apparent in the fact that the special strength of codes—their internal origin—is at the same time their special weakness. As we have seen, the special drawback for *interindustry* codes is the threat of their accidentally stepping into the domain of antitrust legislation, a threat which is no less real for those who frame codes with good intentions. No doubt there is a crucial role for codes to play in business ethics, a role currently unrecognized by many corporate executives; but the spiritual exuberance of Henry Dennison in 1930 must give way to the mild, though informed cynicism of the present era. The role that codes play in the moral evolution of the corporation is a supporting rather than a starring one.

Policy Statements

A different class of internal corporate legislation is corporate policy statements. Usually delivered at stockholders' or board of directors' meetings, and frequently included in the stockholders' annual report, such statements, if they are not merely intended as window dressing, can set the moral tone for companies' activities. In contrast to codes, policy statements tend to be vague rather than precise and are meant to establish a corporate image or ethos rather than enforce specific principles. Although the vagueness of such statements can occasion ambiguity in interpretation, and at worst, neglect, the statements themselves can significantly affect corporate conduct. When a corporation claims to pride itself on its standards of quality and fairness, and broadcasts this image to its employees and consumers, then its claims, as if in self-fulfilling prophecy, will eventually filter into employees' daily decisions. Policy statements may not play a decisive role in every instance, but they will influence corporate life.

Since the early 1970's, policy statements embracing moral norms have become more common. A good example is the statement from Ruben Mettler, president of TRW Inc. It included the following:

> A meaningful definition [of TRW's social role] requires looking at the three levels at which TRW should have a positive impact on society.
>
> The first concerns the basic performance of the company as an economic unit. How many jobs does it provide? Is its productivity increasing? Is it profitable enough to pay employees and shareholders fairly? What is the quality of its goods and services? Does it provide stability and growth in employment? What is its contribution to the economy of the countries in which it operates? . . .
>
> The next level concerns the quality of the conduct of our internal affairs. For example, are we ensuring equal employment and advancement opportunity for all? Is there job satisfaction? Do we provide proper health protection and safety devices. . . ?
>
> The third level concerns the additional things we do in relating to our external environment. This includes charitable and cultural contributions programs, youth projects, urban action programs, assistance to educational institutions, employees' participation in community affairs and our good government program.[44]

Such a statement performs the task of defining the standards of self-evaluation, in this case, through questions which specify areas of performance. Although it is easy to be cynical about the ultimate effect such standards have, many companies touting them have good moral track records. An unusual alternative to the standard policy statement is utilized by Weyerhaeuser Corporation, which not only prepares a standard policy statement, but also commissions a well-respected person outside the corporation to prepare a formal criticism of Weyerhaeuser's social policies, which is then printed in the company's annual report. The technique has been successful in raising Weyerhaeuser's awareness of problems and elevating its reputation (though some company executives have expressed surprise that the company pays for its own criticism).

One important policy statement is the written information contained in the corporation's constitution or articles of incorporation. Such documents shy away from articulating moral goals, even in the vaguest of terms, but the possibility of doing so exists. If nothing else, corporate constitutions might refer to what is conceived as the corporation's underlying social mission and proceed to specify the

---

[44] From *Business and Society: Cases and Text,* ed. Robert D. Hay, Edmund R. Gray, and James E. Gates (Cincinnati: South-Western Publishing Co., 1976), p. 49. Reprinted by permission of John E. Mertes, University of Arkansas at Little Rock.

functions, both moral and nonmoral, of the board of directors. As many observers have noticed, the moral stance of corporate directors is frequently compromised by the simple fact that there is no ready means for directors to know precisely *how* they should function.

The problem of policy statements is similar to that of codes. Like codes, policy statements are effective only when acted upon; when they are opposed by forces demanding greater profitability, security, and market share, and when they are left without help from existing mechanisms of corporate governance, they become merely items in the public relations portfolio. Like codes, they promise to supply moral direction to corporate conduct but can do so only in conjunction with the right mix of surrounding forces.

Implementing New Procedures

In addition to drafting codes and policy statements, corporations can implement new procedures designed to promote ethical behavior. Four procedures deserve special attention: (1) regularized disclosure policies, (2) social audit policies, (3) new reporting policies, and (4) reward systems for moral excellence.

The government already mandates certain disclosure practices. Most corporations must be audited periodically and pass specific information along to shareholders, to the SEC, and sometimes to government regulatory agencies. Yet these requirements are designed primarily for the benefit of the shareholders, to protect their investments from fraud and mismanagement, and not for the benefit of consumers, employees, or the general public. Many believe that if corporations were to take upon themselves, or be required to take on, the task of disclosing information relevant to these other interest groups, then corporate morality would be enhanced. If corporations were required to disclose information about their actions affecting these interest groups, then pressure would mount to justify those acts; and justifying one's acts, most ethicists would grant, is the first step toward improving one's behavior.

Of course, disclosing information requires that one have means to collect the information in the first place, and although corporations regularly gather financial data for accounting reports, they typically lack the means to gather socially relevant data. Here is where the so-called "social audit" becomes important. It is designed on analogy with ordinary financial audits in that the social audit reports on corporate performance by listing relevant corporate actions and trans-actions for a given time period. However, unlike the financial audit, the social audit is designed to pinpoint relevant moral and social behavior.

Social audits became increasingly popular in the late 1970's and are now available in a variety of forms. Some take an "inventory" approach, in which the corporation carefully itemizes its socially responsible activities. Some adopt a "cost" approach, in which the corporation both discloses its socially responsible activities and indicates the amount spent on each activity. Others divide their evaluations according to the social goals designated at the beginning of a reporting period, and then indicate how successfully the goals were achieved. Still others first disclose which socially responsible activities the corporation undertook, along with the cost of those activities, and then proceed to estimate the overall *value* the activities have to the company.

Social audits can use either quantitative or qualitative methods. Abt Associates, a Cambridge consulting firm, showed how to represent monetary costs and benefits that relate to corporate social impact along with a company's traditional financial statements. Abt assumes that social benefits created by corporations can be quantified in dollar amounts, so that any given benefit, such as improved health, security, equality, or environment, can be expressed in terms of money, using as a guide the amounts traditionally expended to achieve such benefits or to avoid equivalent costs.[45] Nonquantitative social audits are also possible. Raymond Bauer and Terry McAdam are known for advocating a qualitative focus, which uses numbers only when quantitative performance measures are well-accpeted and which conveys the remaining information through qualitative analyses of areas of social concern, e.g., working conditions, consumer relations, investor relations, community welfare, and employee welfare.[46]

Even without a thorough look at the various forms of social audit, certain strengths and weaknesses are apparent. The obvious strength of the social audit is its affinity to traditional corporate procedures. Like everyone else, businesspeople are creatures of habit and accept change less grudgingly when it is packaged in familiar colors. If corporations accept *financial* audits, then why not *social* audits? Also, the explicit purpose of the social audit—to specify areas of corporate responsibility and evaluate corporate success in those areas—fulfills one of the criteria for moral improvement identified in the last chapter: that procedures must exist for specifying the precise character of responsibility in a given instance.

The weakness of the social audit probably lies in the failure of the analogy between financial and social audits. Social audits are not, after all, financial audits, and instead of working with easily quantifiable sums of money, they work with difficult to quantify areas of human conduct, of human well-being, happiness, self-respect, and obligation. It is little wonder that Jeremy Bentham's nineteenth-century attempt to quantify ethical reasoning through the "utilitarian calculus" remains today as only an odd, nearly forgotten museum piece in the history of philosophy. People intuitively rejected the concept of using mathematics to discover moral answers, and they tend to do the same today.

Even when stripped of its quantitative packaging, the social audit has problems. It or any other form of social audit is only as powerful as the tendency of corporate executives to take it seriously and act on its conclusions, and to date, social audits have been treated primarily as public relations efforts (though some believe the trend is changing).

---

[45] Joanne Giunta, *Introduction to Corporate Social Responsibility Management* (Philadelphia: Human Resources Network, 1977), p. 64.

[46] See Raymond A. Bauer and Dan Fenn, Jr., "What *Is* a Corporate Social Audit?" *Harvard Business Review,* January-February 1973.

Two more procedural changes worth mentioning involve changing organizational habits. The first is to implement reporting procedures which require subordinates regularly to inform superiors about relevant activities in their sphere of operations. For example, department heads might be required to have monthly conferences with superiors, at which facts that might have remained buried could be revealed. At such conferences, superiors could ask questions and assure themselves that no dangerous holes exist in the corporate information net. Such procedures might avoid the syndrome appearing in B. F. Goodrich and other corporations, where moral disasters ferment and explode before top management can discover what is happening.

The second procedural change involves implementing reward procedures which utilize moral considerations. Employees are normally rewarded for increased productivity, reliability, longevity, and ability to cooperate with other workers, and they are penalized for failures in these areas. But should not raises, promotions, bonuses, and vacations also be tied to responsible behavior? Many argue that the employee who is caught accepting a bribe—even when corporate profits are not affected—should be treated differently from one who refuses. If morality is omitted as a factor in a company's reward systems, then it may be wondered whether employees will trust the company's sincerity about prizing responsible behavior.

ALTERING MANAGEMENT STRUCTURE

The third and final group of proposals attempts to alter corporate behavior by altering corporate structure. These proposals are seen by many as the most promising of all, since clear successes with structural change have been achieved already, and since business executives appear receptive to structural innovation. The proposals are similar to the earlier ones recommending shifting power among individuals, in that the emphasis is upon the process of corporate decision-making. But the two groups are also distinct. Whereas the first advocates shifting power in the context of essentially the same decision-making structures, this group advocates changing the structures themselves. For example, proposals in the first group recommend shifting power inside the board of directors by introducing, for example, outside directors, public representatives, and employees' representatives, but it leaves the structure of the board the same. Proposals in this third group, however, recommend dividing the board, or creating new committees, or creating new corporate offices. With new corporate structures, it is believed many corporations might turn over a new moral leaf.

Some of these proposals appear relatively painless. One is simply to establish new offices which would fill recognized moral needs. A company working with asbestos in its manufacturing process, or with dangerous chemicals, or with nuclear radiation, might create—if it has not already done so—a formal office of safety, staffed by someone with appropriate expertise. A company with a poor record of communicating and gathering ethically relevant information might establish an office to facilitate the flow of information. As we learned in cases such as B.F. Goodrich, vital information about corporate activity, such as about test problems with brakes, may exist somewhere in a company yet not be communicated. A corporate information office could undertake information searches, become familiar with information-gathering techniques, and thus aid other corporate offices in receiving relevant information.

Another obvious proposal in the same vein is simply to create an office of social responsibility. By appointing a well-qualified person to head such an office, at an appropriate level, a corporation is assured of having at least one principal executive whose formal job description includes reference to social responsibility. Already, successes have been achieved this way. Cummins Engine Company has made headway through establishing a Vice-President for Corporate Responsibility, and the same is true of scores of other corporations. Creating such an office is more than printing a name on a door. Support services must be provided, and the corporation must respond to the office-holder's initiative.

One of the most frequently heard proposals is to restructure the power center of the corporation: its board of directors. Nominally the corporation's controlling committee, but often merely its figurehead, the board of directors could become a revitalized force for moral improvement, some contend, if working committees could be split off from the main board and given significant power. An outsider-dominated, financial audit committee could be split off and given investigative and reportive powers; or an outsider-dominated, nominating committee could be split off and given power to search for and nominate future board members; or an outsider-dominated, social responsibility committee could be split off and given investigative and reportive powers. Or all three could be done.

There are encouraging signs for such proposals. Outside directors, whose presence on U.S. boards dwindled steadily from the turn of the century, have since 1970 multiplied rapidly. By 1979, 70 percent of the 1,000 largest corporations in the United States had boards composed of a majority of outside directors.[47] Thus, there is a ready supply of outside directors for the proposed working committees. Boards of directors, moreover, are becoming more assertive; that is, they are less willing to accept what management tells them and more willing to push for moral and economic reform. This more assertive stance is spurred in part by the requirement made by the New York Stock Exchange in 1978 for all its members to form audit committees of outside directors. Its action marked the first time the Stock Exchange had made structural reform a prerequisite for membership. The result was that by 1979, 97 percent of the largest 1,000 U.S. corporations had audit committees composed largely of outside directors. The new stance is also prompted by the Securities Exchange Commission, which beginning in 1977 stepped up its investigation into director misconduct and, in certain cases, even demanded that boards add outside directors.

Many factors conspired to persuade people that reform in the board of

[47] *Business Week,* September 10, 1979, p. 72.

directors was due, not the least of which was the spectacular collapse of the Penn Central Transportation Company in the early 1970's. When the Penn Central filed for reorganization under the Bankruptcy Act, the members of the board seemed as surprised as the general public. Their surprise testified to the fact that they had been merely a rubber-stamp board, routinely approving the financial shenanigans of management while being blind to impending disaster. Penn Centrral stockholders sued the company, charging the directors with negligence; although the shareholder suits were never adjudicated, the financial world was made painfully aware of the need for sweeping board reforms.

So far the reforms have extended only to the creation of financial audit committees, the function of which is to appoint professional auditors and to investigate financial strategies and accounting practices, and then to report findings and recommendations to the board. In a number of instances, however, such committees have revealed moral problems, as in the case of a Grumman Corporation subsidiary where illegal payments were uncovered.

The capacity of outside directors to influence corporate events depends on the willingness of such directors on occasion to rock the corporate boat. As we saw earlier, the long-standing tendency of outsiders has been routinely to approve the actions of management. Thus the mere addition of outside directors to boards may fail to generate sweeping changes. Yet in the face of new external pressures on directors from agencies like the SEC and from new working committees, outside directors may come to life. In a handful of important cases in the 1970's outside directors took uncommonly aggressive stances. For example, in 1979 outside directors for General Automation reacted with outrage when Lawrence Goshorn, the company's founder, president, and largest shareholder, announced that company headquarters were being moved to one of the posh areas of San Diego. Goshorn also proposed that the company purchase a nearby ranch for $3.5 million which he, Goshorn, would use as his residence. After a long and bitter struggle, the outside directors emerged victorious, ejecting Goshorn and naming a new president.

In 1978 outside directors for Itel, Inc. showed equal aggressiveness when they began to suspect managerial trouble after Itel incurred its first quarterly loss in years. Their attention was turned immediately to the president's office, where the president himself lacked financial expertise. Within a matter of months the outsider-dominated board (nine outsiders, three insiders) totally overhauled the executive office, assigned new executives to key posts, and relieved the president of his duties.[48]

Having concluded our investigation of concrete proposals for corporate change, the obvious question, of course, is: Will they work? Will they bring corporations closer to adherence to the social contract? Or will they frustrate initiative, proliferate the already numerous corporate bureaucratic mechanisms, and leave

---

[48] See entire article, "End of the Directors' Rubber Stamp," *Business Week,* September 10, 1979.

behavior as it is? The answers, as suggested earlier, are in part empirical ones, for even the best of theories can be broken on the rocks of practice. Despite Plato's glowing endorsement of monarchs, experience has taught us that power corrupts. Experience also must be a teacher here. Despite the inherent attractiveness of forming social responsibility committees, or nominating committees, or public representatives on boards, or any combination of the proposals we have examined, it is impossible to prove their viability short of actual experiment.

The primary goal is relatively clear: it is to improve corporate responsibility. Yet all of the proposals examined in this chapter also assume the subsidiary goal of achieving such improvements by designing morality *into* the corporations rather than employing a system of ongoing, external regulation. Every proposal considered lends itself to being monitored by management. In short, we have considered only proposals recommending what we earlier called "autonomy" or "enforced autonomy."

Perhaps the chapter has erred in omitting discussions of proposals for external control. Intriguing new proposals for direct control have been made; among them are (1) to stiffen legal penalties for directors' misconduct, (2) to introduce legal penalties for failures by technocrats, e.g., engineers, accountants, chemists, and safety inspectors, (3) to increase on-site government inspections, especially in troubled industries such as asbestos or nuclear power utilities, (4) to establish a requirement for renewable, federal charters (in addition to the unlimited state charters now required) which would force corporations to adhere to government standards in order to have their charters renewed. If proposals of the voluntary kind fail, then the obvious recourse appears to be direct controls such as these.

There is no doubt that businesspeople, especially corporate executives, will be reluctant to endorse changes favoring corporate autonomy. They will ask the same hard questions which were asked in Chapter 8. Will this or that proposal avoid unfair competition? Will it avoid or minimize reductions in productive efficiency? Will it avoid violating shareholder rights? Certainly, some proposals pose problems in these areas. Yet businesspeople may eventually lose sight of such questions, and even embrace strategic changes, when they consider that the alternative to corporate moral autonomy is direct government control.

SUGGESTED SUPPLEMENTARY READINGS

BRILOFF, ABRAHAM J., "Codes of Conduct: Their Sound and Their Fury," in *Ethics, Free Enterprise, and Public Policy,* ed. Richard De George and Joseph Pichler. New York: Oxford University Press, 1978.

CARNOY, MARTIN, and DEREK SHEARER, *Economic Democracy: The Challenge of the 1980s.* White Plains, N.Y.: M.E. Sharpe, 1980.

CHIRELSTEIN, MARVIN A., "Corporate Law Reform," in *Social Responsibility and the Business Predicament,* ed. James McKie. Washington, D.C.: The Brookings Institution, 1974.

GIUNTA, JOANNE, *Introduction to Corporate Social Responsibility Management.* Philadelphia: Human Resources Network, 1977.

HETHERINGTON, J., "Fact and Legal Theory: Shareholers, Managers, and Corporate Social Responsibility," *Stanford Law Review,* January 1969.

HOFFMAN, MICHAEL, ed., *Proceedings of the First National Conference on Business Ethics.* Waltham, Mass.: Bentley College, 1978.

―――, *Proceedings of the Second National Conference on Business Ethics,* Washington, D.C.: University Press of America, 1979.

JONES, DON, *Business Ethics Bibliography: 1971-75.* Charlottesville, Va.: University of Virginia Press, 1977.

POWERS, CHARLES, *Social Responsibility and Investment.* Nashville: Abingdon, 1971.

PURCELL, T., and G. CAVANAUGH, *Blacks in the Industrial World.* New York: Free Press, 1972.

SIMON, JOHN and CHARLES POWERS, and JON GUNNEMANN, *The Ethical Investor: Universities and Corporate Responsibility.* New Haven, Conn.: Yale University Press, 1972.

STONE, CHRISTOPHER, *Where the Law Ends.* New York: Harper & Row, Pub., 1975.

Index

Abt Associates, 205
Accountability, of individuals, 110-12, 118-21
Advertising, 161, 172, 174
Agent-principal duties, law of, 133
Alienation of employees (*see* Employees, alienation of)
American Airlines, 154-55
American Bar Associaion, 199
American Chemical Society, 149
American Civil Liberties Union, 151-52
American Medical Association, 199
Aquinas, Thomas, 14, 165
Aristotle, 30, 116, 124
Association, right of, 5-6, 43, 72, 79
Association of Professional Accountants, 200
Association of Sanitary Enameled Ware Manufacturers, 199
Autonomy:
　corporate, 178, 209
　enforced, 178, 209
Avco Steel Corporation, 147

Bait and switch, 161
Basic needs, 140
Bauer, Raymond, 205
Becker, Lawrence, 55
Blackstone, William, 139
Blades, Lawrence, 131
Blood, market in, 102-103
Blood Plasma International, 97
Board of directors, 45, 56, 123, 166, 172-73, 179, 188-97, 207-208 (*see also* Outside directors)
Bolivar, Tennessee, 154
Boulding, Kenneth, 94
Brake scandal (*see* B. F. Goodrich)
Briloff, Abraham, 200-201
Bristol-Myers, 33, 180
Buckley Amendment, 150
Burkey, Lee, 150
Business judgment rule, 181

Capitalism and Freedom, 68
Capitalistic states, 104-106
Carnegie, Andrew, 98
Carr, E. H., 103
Catallaxy, 69-70
Certainty, in economic propositions, 105
Charitable contributions, by corporations, 181-82
Charters, of corporations (*see* Corporations, charters of)
Chaudhuri, Joyotpaul, 84-85
Chayes, Abraham, 195-96
Chirelstein, Marvin, 189
Chisso, case, 1-2, 36-37
Christian Church, 61, 75
Cicero, 14
Civil rights, 134
Claims, valid, 134
Clark, John, 73
Clayton Anti-Trust Act, 74, 161
Clean Air Amendments Act of 1970, 163
Coal Mine Safety Act, 133
Codes of conduct, 174, 197-202

Committee decisions, 111, 115, 126
Communism, 78
Communist states, 105
Competition, 73-74, 95-96, 173-74
Competitive disadvantage, 173-74
Complexity, aggravated in bureaucracies, 114-15
Connecticut Mutual Life Insurance Company, 154
Consumer freedom, 72, 79
Consumer perceptions, 97
Consumer Product Safety Commission, 164
Consumer sovereignty, 72
Contradictions, in markets, 92-93
Cooperative management, 153-54
Cooperative rules, 100
Corporate democracy, 179-88
Corporate responsibility, model of, 124-27
Corporations:
　board of directors (*see* Board of directors)
　charters of, 4-6, 183, 209
　conditions of moral agency, 30-31
　considered as artifact, 19
　decision-making in, 21-22, 29-31, 46-47, 110, 114-15, 124-27
　definition of, 2-3, 6
　goals of, 168-70
　goodwill of, 84
　hierarchy in, 110-12
　information office, 123, 206-207
　intelligence of, 125
　intentions of, 21-22, 125
　Organizational Process Model, 27-28
　policy statements of, 202-204
　Political Egoism Model, 28
　productive and nonproductive, 2-3 (*see also* Productive organizations)
　punishment of, 6, 15, 26, 163
　Rational Agent Model, 27-28
　responsibility, bureaucratic model of, 124-27
　rights of, 18-22, 38, 43, 55-56, 69, 80-90, 136
Crozier, Michael, 113
Cummins Engine Company, 10, 207

Dahl, Robert, 186-87
Dalton, George, 105
Daniels, Norman, 87
Declaration of Independence, 88, 134
Dehumanizing work, 51, 52, 132, 136-37
Demand, in markets, 99
Dennison, Henry, 197, 202
Deontological argument, 71-73, 79-90
Depression, Great, 95, 103
Discrimination, racial and sexual, 85, 138-40, 172
Dishonesty, as problem in markets, 91-92
Distributive justice, 98-100
Donagan, Alan, 80, 89
Dow Chemical Corporation, 182-85
Drucker, Peter, 112-14
Due process (*see* Employee rights: to due process)
Du Pont Corporation, 130, 182-85